Conversation

Conversation

A History of a Declining Art

STEPHEN MILLER

Yale University Press   New Haven and London

Published with assistance from the Annie Burr Lewis Fund.

Set in Minion type by Integrated Publishing Solutions, Grand Rapids, Michigan.
Printed in the United States of America by Vail-Ballou Press, Binghamton, New York.

Library of Congress Cataloging-in-Publication Data
Miller, Stephen.
Conversation : a history of a declining art / Stephen Miller.
        p.   cm.
Includes bibliographical references (p.   ) and index.
ISBN-13: 978-0-300-11030-2 (hardcover: alk. paper)
ISBN-10: 0-300-11030-8 (hardcover: alk. paper)
1. Conversation analysis. I. Title.
P95.45.M54 2006
302.3'46—dc22
2005026860

A catalogue record for this book is available from the British Library.

10 9 8 7 6 5 4 3 2 1

In memory of Larry Day and Bill Murphy, whose conversation was a great pleasure

We establish the *rules of good-breeding,* in order to prevent the opposition of men's pride, and render conversation agreeable and inoffensive.
—David Hume, *A Treatise of Human Nature*

If you don't stop the little things, the little things become big.
—Bonnie Tryon, Principal of Golding Elementary School, Cobleskill, New York

Contents

Preface

"Conversation," the modern British philosopher Michael Oakeshott says, "distinguishes the human being from the animal and the civilized man from the barbarian." Oakeshott himself was a good conversationalist. John Casey notes that when Oakeshott was in his late eighties he regularly attended a dining society, now named after him, where he stayed half the night "enchanting undergraduates with his conversation."

By conversation Oakeshott means face-to-face conversation—not phone conversation. Oakeshott died in 1990, before virtual conversation—conversation by e-mail or Instant Messaging—became commonplace.

I became interested in the art of what might be called "real" conversation after reading Oakeshott about two decades ago. (Oakeshott, a reviewer in the *Times Literary Supplement* says, "has reasonable claims to be regarded as the pre-eminent political philosopher in the British political tradition" of the twentieth century.) My interest in conversation increased about a decade ago, when I was writing a book about eighteenth-century British thought. I noticed that many eighteenth-century writers wrote about the pleasures (and pains) of conversation. They include Jonathan Swift, Joseph Addison, Richard Steele,

Daniel Defoe, the Earl of Shaftesbury, David Hume, Henry
Fielding, and Samuel Johnson. There was also a great deal of
interest in the quality of someone's conversation. When Johnson interviewed a friend of Alexander Pope, the first question
he asked was: "What kind of man was Mr. Pope in his conversation?"

Women were also interested in the art of conversation. In
her letters, which were unpublished during her lifetime, Lady
Mary Wortley Montagu talks frequently about conversation.
Hester Thrale, Johnson's friend, often evaluated the conversation of her friends and acquaintances. The novelist Frances
(Fanny) Burney said of Hester Thrale's conversation: "It is so
entertaining, so gay, so enlivening, when she is in spirits, and
so intelligent and instructive when she is otherwise, that I almost as much wish to record all she says, as all Dr. Johnson says."
Burney's friendship with Thrale collapsed when Thrale married Gabriel Piozzi, yet three decades later Burney and Thrale
met again and enjoyed each other's conversation. As Burney,
now Madame D'Arblay, says in a letter to Thrale's daughter:
"We talked, both of us, in Dr. Johnson's phrase, 'our *best*,' but
entirely as two strangers, who had no sort of knowledge or
care for each other, but were willing, each to fling & to accept
the Gauntlet, *pour faire la belle conversation.*"

In the twentieth century the possibility of conversation
has been questioned by many novelists and thinkers (from
psychologists to postmodernists), who say that we are all solipsists and that what we say is shaped mainly by subconscious
passions or by ideas that enter our psyche subliminally. "There
is no such thing as conversation," the novelist and essayist Rebecca West argues. "It is an illusion. There are intersecting
monologues, that is all." Writing about the novelist and play-

wright Michael Frayn, a contemporary critic refers to "the hit-or-miss uncertainty, the artificiality, the baffling complexity of conversation."

Though the eighteenth-century writers on conversation said that good conversationalists were hard to find, they thought conversation was not only possible, it was also beneficial. Conversation, they said, promotes psychological health and intellectual development. And conversation is one of the great pleasures of life. Several eighteenth-century writers also argued that there is a correlation between political stability and the extent of what Hume calls the "convisible world." Like Hume, Addison and Johnson thought that if Britain's educated classes neglected the art of conversation, Britain could become embroiled in violent civil discord.

If many eighteenth-century Britons, especially during the first half of the century, cultivated the art of conversation, most contemporary Americans have little or no interest in this art. There are far more books on improving one's sex life than on improving one's "conversation life." (In the past month the *New York Times Book Review* has run a full-page review of seven books on sex.) The number of books published on a subject is not necessarily an index of the subject's importance, but it is safe to say that most Americans are not preoccupied with the quality of their conversation.

In an essay that appeared in the *Wall Street Journal* (18 August 2000) I argued that "America's professional class . . . does not take the art of conversation seriously."

In making this point, I was not going out on a limb, for a number of recent books and articles have claimed that, owing mainly to anger, conversation is in bad shape in contemporary America. In *The Argument Culture: Moving from Debate to Di-*

alogue (1998) Deborah Tannen says: "Our spirits are corroded by living in an atmosphere of unrelenting contention—an argument culture." In *The Changing Conversation in America* (2002), William F. Eadie and Paul E. Nelson note: "Everyone seems to be angry at something—and more than willing to express that anger." In the *Washington Post* (13 February 2004) Peter Carlson claims: "This is the age of the screed, the rant, the tirade, the jeremiad, the diatribe, the venom-fueled, white-hot harangue!" I made roughly the same point as these observers in an article titled "Anger Mismanagement" (*Wall Street Journal*, 19 March 2004).

Expressing anger is understandable and even appropriate on occasion, but writers on conversation have always warned that anger undermines conversation. Two thousand years ago Plutarch spoke of acquaintances whose anger "made them incapable of preserving their . . . pleasant conversation and persuasiveness . . . in company." Anger, Plutarch says, "is worse than undiluted wine at producing undisciplined and disagreeable results: wine's results are blended with laughter, jokes and singing, while anger's results are blended with bitter gall." Plutarch quotes Sappho: "When anger takes over your heart, guard your babbling tongue."

In *Restraining Rage: The Ideology of Anger Control in Classical Antiquity* (2001), William Harris stresses that many classical thinkers, including Aristotle, worried about the political effects of anger. Political anger, of course, is not a new thing in the United States. Election campaigns have often been acrimonious. What is new is an ideology of anger that arose in the 1960s. Championing authenticity, theorists of the counterculture often implied that civility is a repressive force. Express yourself, they said—especially if you are angry. In so doing, you will be acting authentically. You will also feel better for it.

In the summer of 2004 a surprising person invoked the counterculture's argument: Vice-President Dick Cheney. He did so to defend his use of vulgar language on the Senate floor. Angered by Senator Patrick J. Leahy's charges of cronyism in the awarding of contracts in Iraq—many contracts were awarded to Halliburton, a firm that Cheney headed before he became vice-president—Cheney told Leahy, who had come up to greet him, to go "fuck yourself." The next day Cheney defended his remark: "I expressed myself rather forcefully, [and] felt better after I had done it." He also added: "Ordinarily I don't express myself in strong terms, but I thought it was appropriate here."

Defending Cheney's foul language, the columnist Charles Krauthammer raised the banner of authenticity—praising "Cheney's demonstration of earthy authenticity in a chamber in which authenticity of any kind is to be valued." Krauthammer's main concern, though, was what he regarded as a double standard on the part of the media. Cheney, he said, had been taken to task for his angry comment to Leahy, but Al Gore had not been criticized for his intemperate remarks about Bush. "The former vice president of the United States," Krauthammer said, "compared the current president to both Hitler and Stalin in the same speech—a first not just in hyperbole but in calumny—and nary a complaint is heard about a breach of civility."

Whatever one thinks of Cheney's and Gore's outbursts, many Americans praise authenticity and think of conversation mainly as a venting of opinions. According to Judith Martin, who writes under the name Miss Manners, "Intellectual stimulation, to most, means hearing themselves deliver lectures on matters they have already figured out to their own satisfaction." In a recent cartoon in the *New Yorker* a wife says to her husband: "I converse. You declaim." The future of conversation in America (and elsewhere as well) is also likely to be affected—mainly in a negative way—by the proliferation of what I call conversation avoidance mechanisms.

At first I thought it would be useful to look at contemporary American conversation from the vantage point of eighteenth-century Britain. But the eighteenth-century British writers on conversation often refer to ancient writers on conversation, so I decided to widen my horizons and include a discussion of conversation in the ancient world.

This work, then, is an extended essay on conversation in Western civilization. I stress the word *essay*—an informal attempt to clarify a subject, one that includes personal anecdotes. I've written this book for the general reader, but I make extensive use of recent scholarship on the history of conversation.

This work differs from most contemporary books on conversation, which are concerned with the present or the immediate past and mainly focus on public discourse—how we converse about public affairs. In *Public Discourse in America: Conversation and Communication in the Twenty-first Century* (2003), Judith Rodin speaks of the need "to start a conversation—among scholars, practitioners, and the general public—about the centrality and effectiveness of public discourse in American society." I am more interested in the informal conversations that take place in private settings.

In short, this book is about everyday conversation—including what we call light conversation or small talk. In Chapter One I explain what I mean by conversation. In Chapter Two I discuss conversation in the ancient world, focusing on two works: the book of Job and Plato's *Symposium*. In Chapter Three I look at three questions that writers on conversation have debated. What effect does religion have on conversation? What effect does commercial expansion have on conversation? Should women be included in the conversible world? In Chapters Four, Five, and Six I look at conversation in the Enlightenment—focusing on conversation in eighteenth-century Britain. Chapters Seven, Eight, and Nine are devoted to conversation in America—from colonial times to the present. In the concluding chapter I discuss the future of conversation.

Acknowledgments

I would like to thank all the friends who discussed this project with me over the years, especially Jeff Field, with whom I had numerous enjoyable and valuable conversations about the art of conversation. Many people also supplied me with useful information and suggestions, including George Core and Erich Eichman.

I greatly appreciate the enthusiasm and advice of Lara Heimert, who read the first draft of the manuscript when she was at Yale University Press. John Kulka's suggestions improved the manuscript, and Jeff Schier's copyediting was invaluable. I also want to thank Mary Traester and Molly Egland for their help. I am indebted to the two anonymous reviewers of the first draft, whose comments were very helpful.

A special thanks to my daughters, Katherine Miller and Elizabeth Miller, for listening to my ideas about conversation and providing useful insights—especially about contemporary culture. Finally, this book could not have been written without the support, encouragement, and conversation of my wife, Eva Barczay.

Conversation

I

Conversation and Its Discontents

Michel de Montaigne, the sixteenth-century French essayist, loved conversation. "To my taste," he says, "the most fruitful and natural exercise of our mind is conversation. I find the practice of it the most delightful activity in our lives."

According to Montaigne, "studying books has a languid feeble motion, whereas conversation provides teaching and exercise all at once." Montaigne thinks of conversation as an intellectual sporting event that will improve his mind. "If I am sparring with a strong and solid opponent he will attack me on the flanks, stick his lance in me right and left; his ideas send mine soaring. Rivalry, competitiveness and glory will drive me and raise me above my own level. . . . Our mind is strengthened by contact with vigorous and well-ordered minds."

Montaigne wants people to attack his ideas. Agreement is boring and intellectually deadening. Yet few people, he says, are worthy opponents. One man "counts every word and believes they are as weighty as reasons. . . . Another is armed with pure insults. . . . Lastly, there is the man who cannot see reason but holds you under siege within a hedge of dialectical conclusions and logical formulae."

Montaigne especially dislikes pretentious conversationalists who parade their learning. He says of such a man: "Let him remove his academic hood, his gown and his Latin; let him stop battering our ears with raw chunks of pure Aristotle; why, you would take him for one of us—or worse." In other words, a man who parades his learning may be hiding his lack of intelligence.

Joseph Epstein says that the academic world—where of course there are learned people in abundance—is not a place where conversation flourishes. "In academic life, in my experience, there is no real conversation; just various people awaiting their own turn to hold forth." My own experience—having taught for a decade at three colleges—is that academics tend to be more dogmatic than other professional people, perhaps because they spend so much of their time lecturing to students.

According to Montaigne, the conversation of many people is bad for one's mind. "Just as our mind is strengthened with vigorous and well-ordered minds, so it is impossible to overstate how much it loses and deteriorates by the continuous commerce and contact we have with mean or ailing ones." I have met many intellectuals whose conversation was bad for my mind: Marxists, existentialists, postmodernists. A Marxist colleague at the *National Enquirer,* where I worked for several months in the mid-1960s, never stopped ranting about the evils of "the System." (He had a Ph.D. in history.) A colleague at a Washington think tank, where I worked in the mid-1970s, talked continually about the negative effects of modernity. (He had a Ph.D. in philosophy.) If I hear someone say modernity or dialectical or existential or psychoanalytical, I can no longer pay attention, for I am thinking—perhaps unfairly—that this person is going to bore me to death.

Montaigne says the main reason conversations are unsatisfying is that many people get defensive when their views are questioned. "Most people, when their arguments fail, change voice and expression, and instead of retrieving themselves betray their weaknesses and susceptibilities by an unmannerly anger." Once, at a dinner party, I disagreed with an eminent sociologist. He disliked Flannery O'Connor. I said she was one of the best American writers of the postwar period. He looked at me, gave me an odd grin, and turned to talk to the person on his left. He never said another word to me for the remainder of the evening.

Most people who make their views known on t-shirts and bumper stickers do not want to be questioned about their opinions. I once was accosted by a young woman who was raising funds for some organization. I could not pay attention to what she was saying because I was interested in what her t-shirt said: "War is not the answer."

I asked her what the remark on her t-shirt meant. She found my question annoying. "Warmonger!" she yelled at me, and strode away.

Recently I saw a man wearing a t-shirt that said: "You Can Either Agree With Me or Be Wrong." Would this man be a good conversationalist? Maybe he would, since he seems to take a good-humored view of his own opinionated-ness.

One cannot be a good conversationalist if one lacks a sense of humor. Equally important is being a good listener. The seventeenth-century French aphorist La Rochefoucauld says that most people are poor listeners. "One of the reasons why so few people are to be found who seem sensible and pleasant in conversation is that almost everybody is thinking about what he wants to say himself rather than about answering clearly what is being said to him. The more clever and polite think it enough simply to put on an attentive expression while all the time you can see in their eyes and train of thought that they are far removed from what you are saying and anxious to get back to what they want to say."

La Rochefoucauld's remarks cut close to the bone. I have often nodded while someone else is talking—waiting for my chance to say what I wanted to say.

Swift—like Montaigne and La Rochefoucauld—also thought good conversationalists were hard to find. In "Hints Towards an Essay on Conversation," which was not published in his lifetime, Swift says he "was prompted to write my Thoughts upon this Subject by mere Indignation, to reflect that so useful and innocent a Pleasure, so fitted for every Period and Condition of Life, and so much in all Men's Power, should be so much neglected and abused." He laments about "how little Advantage we make of that which might be the greatest, the most lasting, and the most innocent, as well as useful Pleasure of Life."

Swift argues that conversation can be reformed. "The truest Way to understand Conversation, is to know the Faults and Errors to which it is subject, and from thence, every Man to form Maxims to himself whereby it may be regulated." Yet he also implies that few people are capable of improving their conversation. Some people will always talk too much about themselves and their medical problems. "Some, without any Ceremony, will run over the History of their Lives; will relate the Annals of their Disease, with the several Symptoms and Circumstances of them." Others will attempt to be witty all the time. "It is A Torment to the Hearers, as much as to themselves, to see them upon the Rack for Invention, and in perpetual Constraint, with so little Success."

Swift lists two common faults in conversation that are difficult to remedy: talking about one's own profession, which Swift calls pedantry, and "impatience to interrupt others, and the Uneasiness of being interrupted ourselves." There are also those who suffer from "the Itch of Dispute and Contradiction, [and the] telling of Lies." And there are people "who are troubled with the Disease called the Wandering of the Thoughts that they are never present in Mind at what passeth in Discourse." According to Swift, "Whosoever labours under any of these Possessions, is as unfit for Conversation as a Mad-man in Bedlam."

Conversation, Swift also says, suffers from a decline in raillery—good-humored, intelligent wit and banter. Raillery, which Swift calls "the finest part of Conversation," has been adulterated; it has become "what is generally called Repartee, or being smart." Repartee, he says, is vulgar raillery, where the main concern is coming up with a clever put-down. "It now passeth for Raillery to run a Man down in Discourse, to put him out of Countenance, and make him ridiculous, sometimes to expose the Defects of his Person, or Understanding."

In stressing the importance of raillery, Swift was following many seventeenth-century French writers on conversation, including La Rochefoucauld, whose work he admired. Raillery, La Rochefoucauld says, "is an agreeable gaiety of spirit, which makes conversation cheerful, and which binds the company when it is good-natured but which disturbs it when it is not." Raillery, both La Rochefoucauld and Swift imply, can go off the rails if the good humor turns sour. (In contemporary America there is organized vulgar raillery that goes under the name of "celebrity roast.")

Many people, Swift says, claim they enjoy the pleasures of conversation but really prefer a more passive form of amusement. At many gatherings a "Player, Mimick, or Buffoon" has been hired "to divert the Company. . . . You go there as to a Farce, or a Puppet-Show; your Business is only to laugh in Season, either out of Inclination or Civility, while this merry Companion is acting his Part." Swift says he too enjoys such entertainment, but he is irritated when he is invited to a gathering where he expects to engage in conversation only to find that he has been misled. "I only quarrel, when in select and private Meetings, where Men of Wit and Learning are invited to pass an Evening, this Jester should be admitted to run over his Circle of Tricks, and make the whole Company unfit for any other Conversation." Imagine going to a dinner party and upon arrival learning that you will be entertained by a stand-up comic.

Swift has a simple recommendation for improving conversation: include women. He praises the conversation at the court of Charles I: "The Methods then used for raising and cultivating Conversation, were altogether different from ours" because "both Sexes . . . met to pass the Evenings in discoursing upon whatever agreeable Subjects were occasionally started." The presence of women—even the display of gallantry and the possibility of romance—raises the level of conversation. "If there were no other use in the Conversation of Ladies, it is sufficient that it would lay a Restraint upon those odious Topicks of Immodesty and Indecencies, into which the Rudeness of our Northern Genius is also apt to fall."

Swift's point is that men become more refined in the presence of women—more likely to engage in witty raillery than in vulgar repartee. He condemned the habit of having women withdraw from the company of men after dinner, "as if it were an established Maxim, that Women are incapable of all Conversation."

In the remainder of the essay Swift seems gloomy about the prospects for reform. "Good conversation," he says, "is not to be expected in much company, because few listen, and there is continual interruption." Most people, he says, rattle on— relating "Facts of no Consequence." Swift concludes by saying that long-winded speakers will cause conversation to "flag, unless it be often renewed by one among them, who can start new Subjects." In other words, a bore can easily cast a deadening spell on conversation.

In two other unpublished essays—"Hints on Good Manners," and "On Good-Manners and Good-Breeding"—Swift addresses a question that continues to preoccupy writers on conversation: Is there a tension between pleasing people and having a good conversation? One can please people by flattering them, but flattery is not conversation. According to Swift, "nothing is so great an instance of ill manners as flattery. If you flatter all the company you please none; if you flatter only one or two, you affront the rest. Flattery is the worst, and falsest way of shewing our esteem." Swift is contemptuous of conversationalists who show a mindless eagerness to please—"those men and women whose face is ever in a smile, talk ever with a smile, condole with a smile, *etc.*"

Swift also disapproves of argument. "Argument, as usually managed, is the worst sort of conversation." Yet he doesn't say where raillery ends and argument begins. He acknowledges that foolish people often take offense for no reason: "I have often known the most innocent raillery, and even of that kind which was meant for praise, to be mistaken for abuse and reflection [that is, censure or reproof]." Those who take offense at innocent raillery are fools, but Swift acknowledges that not

all raillery is innocent. "To speak in such as manner as may
possibly offend any reasonable person in company, is the highest instance of ill manners." Swift implies that it is easy to distinguish between raillery that is innocent and raillery that is
nasty (or what he calls repartee). Is he right? I know that I have
occasionally offended people whom I didn't mean to offend,
owing to my raillery.

Swift had many hours of good conversation in the house
of Esther Johnson, a close friend who was the Stella of Swift's
Journal to Stella. Fourteen years younger than Swift, Esther
Johnson lived in Dublin—supported by an annual allowance
from Swift as well as by a small legacy from Sir William Temple,
a leading statesman and essayist for whom Swift had worked
(1689–1699). In "On the Death of Mrs. Johnson," written in
1728 but published posthumously, Swift discusses her conversation—first making the general point that "people of all sorts
were never more easy than in her company." (Mrs. Johnson
never married. In the eighteenth century the term *Mrs.* signified a woman of a certain age.)

According to Swift, Esther Johnson was an unusual woman.
"Never was any of her sex born with better gifts of the mind,
or more improved them by reading and conversation." Her
conversation was very rewarding. "All of us who had the happiness of her friendship, agreed unanimously, that, in an afternoon or evening's conversation, she never failed before we
departed of delivering the best thing that was said in the
company."

Esther Johnson was well educated. She had read philosophy and also "had good insight into physic, and knew somewhat of anatomy." She also was a good listener: "She listened to
all that was said, and had never the least distraction or absence
of thought." Though she knew how to please in conversation,

she could be caustic in her assessment of people. "Among a few friends, in private conversation, she made little ceremony in discovering her contempt of a coxcomb, and describing all his follies to the life."

She also could show her disapproval if someone was vulgar in conversation. When a "coxcomb . . . in his flippant way began to deliver some double meanings" to her and several lady friends, she said to him: "Sir, all these ladies and I understand your meaning very well, having, in spite of our care, too often met with those of your sex who wanted [lacked] manners and good sense. But believe me, neither virtuous nor even vicious women love such kind of conversation." She did not give the man a second chance; she told him that from now on she would always avoid his company.

Swift praises her position. "I believe the practice of it [women avoiding the company of vulgar men] would soon put an end to that corrupt conversation, the worst effect of dullness, ignorance, impudence, and vulgarity, and the highest affront to the modesty and understanding of the female sex." By "corrupt conversation" he means conversation that relies heavily on sexual innuendo. Corrupt conversation, he says, is dull as well as an affront to modesty. If men engage in corrupt conversation, the women should leave.

Esther Johnson also disliked dogmatic conversationalists. "She was never positive [dogmatic] in arguing, and she usually treated those who were so, in a manner which well enough gratified that unhappy disposition; yet in such a sort as made it very contemptible, and at the same time did some hurt to the owners." The sentence is puzzling. How did she gratify them—in other words, make them feel that it was all right to be dogmatic—yet at the same time make them feel contemptible? Did she make a distinction between dogmatic people whose opinions she agreed with and dogmatic people whose opinions she thought were wrong? Swift says she preferred to avoid arguing with dogmatic people whose opinions she thought were wrong. "When she saw any of the company very warm in a wrong opinion, she was more inclined to confirm them in it than oppose them. The excuse she commonly gave when her friends asked the reason, was that it prevented noise and saved time."

Though Esther Johnson thought it was best to humor dogmatic people, she disliked it when other people acted the way she did. "Yet I have known her very angry with some whom she much esteemed for sometimes falling into that infirmity." Swift calls her view an "infirmity." He thinks one should not confirm "wrong opinion."

There are limits, Swift says, to the art of pleasing in conversation. One should not worry about trying to please fools. One should only be concerned about pleasing reasonable people. He offers a maxim that was a commonplace of eighteenth-century British thought. "Good Manners is the art of making every reasonable person in the company easy, and to be easy ourselves." But opinions about someone's reasonableness often differ, and Swift thought many Whigs were unreasonable. In contemporary America many liberals think conservatives are unreasonable—indeed that they are fools. And many conservatives have the same view of liberals.

What Is Conversation?

In their discussion of conversation Montaigne and Swift touch on a number of questions that remain with us today. Can conversation be reformed? Do men and women have different ways of conversing? How can we make people feel "easy" yet

avoid flattery? How can we enjoy raillery yet not offend someone? Are there people we cannot have a conversation with because they are unreasonable? But first we need to ask a question whose answer is not as obvious as it may first seem: What
is conversation?

In eighteenth-century Britain conversation mainly signified what it means now: "the informal interchange of information, ideas, etc., by spoken words; ability or proficiency in
this," which is the *Oxford English Dictionary*'s fifth definition
of the word. Conversation also meant social interaction in
general: "the action of consorting or having dealings with others," as the *O.E.D.* says. In *Henry IV, Part II* Lancaster says: "but
all are banished till their conversations / Appear more wise
and modest to the world."

Conversation also meant sexual intercourse. In Britain
there was a law against "criminal conversation"—adultery.
In the *Dictionary* Johnson compiled, he defines a whore as "a
woman who converses unlawfully with men." *Gonosologium
Novum* (1709), a "libertine" work, claims to be a medical treatise for those who suffer from "infirmities and diseases hinder-
ing Conjugal Conversation." Often the word has both meanings. When the Earl of Halifax died and left his widely admired
mistress Catherine Barton a bequest of twenty thousand
pounds, a political enemy wrote that Halifax appreciated
Barton's "excellent conversation." In John Gay's *The Beggar's
Opera* (1728), when Polly says of Macheath "But then he flies,
absents himself, and I bar myself from his dear, dear conversation," the word means sexual intercourse as well as ordinary
conversation.

In Defoe's *Moll Flanders* (1722) there are several examples
of conversation's different meanings. Describing a night Moll
spent with a new husband after learning that he was not rich,

she says: "We had a great deal of close Conversation that Night." Here the word means all forms of intimacy, from talk to sex. When one of Moll's many husbands learns that he is her brother, he assures Moll that he now regards her as a sister and then says: "We shall have all the honest part of Conversation." He means that he will continue to be intimate with her but refrain from having sex.

In the eighteenth century conversation also referred to a semi-formal social gathering where the discussion focused on art, literature, science, and the human condition. Johnson writes Hester Thrale: "I have been invited twice to Mrs. Vesey's conversation." Boswell says: "I was at a conversation at Langton's"; he also notes that he is going to "Sir Joseph Banks's Conversation." The Italian cognate *conversazione* was often used to describe such a gathering. In 1781 Hester Thrale writes Fanny Burney: "Yesterday I had a conversazione. Mrs. Montagu was brilliant in diamonds, solid in judgment, critical in talk. . . . Johnson was good-humoured, Lord John Clinton attentive, Dr. Bowdler lame, and my master [her husband] not asleep."

Finally, the term *conversation-piece* (or sometimes simply *conversation*) refers to an informal group portrait of people, usually a family. In his early years Thomas Gainsborough did many "conversation" portraits. In a recent study of Gainsborough there is a chapter entitled "Conversations."

Is there a difference between talk and conversation? For most observers there is no difference. Conversation Analysis is an academic subdiscipline in the field of sociology; it focuses on basic social interaction—on all types of talk. The writers in this field use talk and conversation interchangeably. So does Diane McWhorter in an essay entitled "Talk." She says "talking is what binds us into a people." A few lines later, she says: "I am speaking of conversation."

Johnson usually made no distinction between talk and conversation, though Boswell notes that on one occasion he did. "Though his [Johnson's] usual phrase for conversation was *talk*, yet he made a distinction; for when he once told me that he dined the day before at a friend's house, with 'a very pretty company;' and I asked him if there was good conversation, he answered, 'No, Sir; we had *talk* enough, but no *conversation*; there was nothing *discussed*.'"

There was no conversation, Johnson implies, because there was no exchange of ideas, but Johnson often suggests that one can have a conversation without having an exchange of ideas. He usually spoke of intellectual conversation as "solid conversation." Like Montaigne, he liked solid conversation in which he often "talked for victory," but he also praised light conversation, where no one is "eager of victory." He said he loved "conversation without effort." Johnson's favorite conversationalist was a man named Hawkins Browne: "Of all conversers . . . the late Hawkins Browne was the most delightful with whom I ever was in company: his talk was at once so elegant, so apparently artless, so pure, and so pleasing, it seemed a perpetual stream of sentiment, enlivened by gaiety, and sparkling with images."

Though there is no clear distinction between talk and conversation, most writers on conversation argue that conversation is not instrumental. It is not a means toward an end, such as pleasing a boss or getting some information. In *Miss Manners' Guide to Excruciatingly Correct Behavior* (1983), Judith Martin says: "From the direct sales pitch to a play for the goodwill of influential people, the rule is that if it is designed to advance your career, it isn't conversation." In *The Age of Conversation* (2005), a study of conversation in seventeenth- and eighteenth-century France, Benedetta Craveri says that salon conversation's aim was "none other than the pleasure of conversation for its own sake."

Oakeshott also says that conversation is purposeless. It "has no determined course, we do not ask what it is 'for.'" Conversation, he argues, "is an unrehearsed intellectual adventure. It is with conversation as with gambling; its significance lies neither in winning nor in losing, but in wagering."

An interview is not a conversation. Two decades ago, I interviewed Sir Isaiah Berlin. I was writing a book on the National Endowment for the Humanities (NEH), and he was head of the British Academy, which is roughly the equivalent of NEH. It was a memorable hour, for Sir Isaiah dazzled me with witty and eloquent replies to my questions, but it was not a conversation. I was there for a purpose. I wanted information, and he provided it.

We enjoy good conversationalists, Hume says, because of the pleasure they give, not the information they provide. "All the merit a man may derive from his conversation (which, no doubt, may be very considerable) arises from nothing but the pleasure it conveys to those who are present." Good conversationalists, he says, are "immediately agreeable." A conversation may be purposeful in the sense that those present are trying to clarify an idea. In this sense all "solid conversations" have a purpose. I belong to a monthly discussion group that has a purpose insofar as we discuss public policy questions, but the members do not attend in order to advance their careers.

To my mind, then, talk is generally purposeful whereas conversation is not. To be sure, conversation often metamorphoses into talk. At a dinner party we may ask someone's advice about choosing a doctor or buying a car. Or we may learn that one of the guests may be able to help our career in some way. But we don't usually go to a dinner party to get advice or advance our career; we go because we think we will enjoy the pleasures of conversation.

Friendships are mainly based on the pleasure we derive from a person's conversation. Friends who are always asking for something are called "needy," or "high maintenance." In general, one tends to resent such people rather than enjoy their company. Writing about the late Philip Hamburger, who was her husband and—after they got divorced—her best friend, Edith Iglauer says: "We began a conversation that lasted sixty-five years." The conversation of two friends may often turn into talk—one friend may seek advice from the other—but a friendship is likely to collapse if one friend always thinks of the other in purposeful terms (as a source of advice or a path to success).

Johnson tells the story of a good conversationalist who lost his conversational skills when asked to be witty for a purpose. A wealthy landowner who enjoyed the man's conversational skills told him that he had invited "all the gentlemen in the neighborhood" to dinner because he wanted to show them how witty his guest was. The gentleman, the conversationalist says, "did not forget to hint how much my presence was expected to heighten the pleasure of the feast." In order to prepare for this dinner the conversationalist "passed the night in planning out . . . the conversation of the coming day." Despite the extensive preparation, the conversationalist failed miserably; he could not be witty on demand. The same thing happened to a friend of mine whom I shall call Larry. He was introduced to someone with the remark: "I want you to meet Larry. He's incredibly witty." Of course Larry couldn't think of a single witty thing to say.

In "Essay on Conversation" (1743), Henry Fielding takes a view of conversation that is similar to Johnson's. He defines conversation as "that reciprocal Interchange of Ideas, by which

Truth is examined, Things are, in a manner, turned around, and sifted, and all our Knowledge communicated to each other." Fielding does not limit conversation to intellectual topics. He criticizes someone for "constantly advancing learned Subjects in common Conversation," and he praises a man who "can submit to discourse on the most trivial Matters. . . . He can talk of Fashions and Diversions among the Ladies; nay, can even condescend to Horses and Dogs with Country Gentlemen." Fielding admires people who are flexible conversationalists— who can move from an interchange of ideas to small talk. "This man is very learned and is equal to dispute on the highest and abstrusest Points," he says, but he can "likewise talk on a Fan, or a Horse-Race."

Defending those who enjoy "small talk," Joseph Epstein shrewdly points out that people who say they have no small talk are probably bragging. "What they are really saying is, of course, I have no patience with triviality; I am too deep, too penetrating, to engage in the mere chit-chat of small talk."

What I mean by conversation may be further clarified by a remark the essayist Jonathan Raban made in a recent interview. Raban said that he misses what he used to enjoy in London: "the mocking talk of six people sitting across from each other at dinner." By "mocking talk" Raban means good-humored disagreement, or what Swift calls raillery. According to Raban, mocking talk is in short supply in Seattle, where he now lives. "So much social life consists . . . of dreary fundraisers for good causes, like saving the salmon."

To engage in "mocking talk" one needs to be a good listener as well as a good talker. Hester Thrale apparently was a good listener. One acquaintance says that "she excelled in the delicate art of exciting and encouraging others to talk." Some people thought Johnson was not a good listener, but a con-

temporary said that Johnson knew how to get "people to talk
on their favourite subjects, and on what they knew best. . . .
They gave him their best conversation, and he generally made
them pleased with themselves, for endeavouring to please
him." Robert Brustein says Jonathan Miller "may be the most
brilliant talker in the Western world," but is Miller a good listener? An acquaintance of President Clinton said: "He just
talks. You don't really have a conversation with him."

Goethe said of his meeting with Madame de Staël: "It was
an interesting hour. I was unable to get a word in; she talks
well, but at length, at great length." Goethe was considered to
be a good listener. Describing an evening at Weimar when
Goethe was present, one observer says: "The conversation was
general, lively, and never came to a halt. Goethe led it in mas-
terly fashion, but without ever restricting anyone else." Another observer says of Goethe: "He was all the more charming
when he felt sociable and carried on a light-hearted discussion
in some small circle, where everyone in turn contributed his
mite. He was usually not ostentatiously witty or overflowing
with ideas; indeed he even eschewed them, preferring for the
most part a tone of good-humored irony."

Is there such a thing as being too good a listener? Gilbert
Ryle said of the late Sir Bernard Williams, a British philosopher: Williams "understands what you're going to say better
than you understand it yourself, and sees all the possible objections to it, all the possible answers to all the possible objections, before you've got to the end of the sentence."

Undoubtedly, at many eighteenth-century social gatherings—particularly when men were drinking a lot—there was
not much listening. In Fielding's *Joseph Andrews* (1741) a gentleman deplores the conversation of a group of dissolute men.
"Their best Conversation was nothing but Noise: Singing, Hol-

lowing, Wrangling, Drinking, Toasting, Sp-wing [uttering obscene oaths]." In *Modern Midnight Conversation* (1733), one of William Hogarth's most popular prints, a number of men, including a parson, are drunk and clearly incapable of having a conversation. (There are twenty-three empty wine bottles in the room.)

In some British clubs there was heavy drinking, yet in many others there was some drinking but also good conversation. In 1772 Boswell writes in his journal that he expects to have many good conversations during his stay in London: "My views in coming to London this spring were: to refresh my mind by the variety and spirit of the metropolis, [and by] the conversation of my revered friend Mr. Samuel Johnson and that of other men of genius and learning."

Finally, all the eighteenth-century writers on conversation agreed that conversation can take place only among equals. The essayist Richard Steele says that "equality is the Life of Conversation; and he is as much out who assumes to himself any Part above another, as he who considers himself below the rest of the Society." Between a benefactor and a dependant, Johnson says, there can be no "general conversation" because the dependant is not disinterested.

One of Johnson's essays takes the form of a letter from a writer who has wasted his inheritance and now must flatter a patron. "I was obliged," the writer says, "to comply with a thousand caprices, to concur in a thousand follies, and to countenance a thousand errors. I endured innumerable mortifications, if not from cruelty, at least from negligence, which will creep in upon the kindest and most delicate minds when *they converse without the mutual awe of equal condition* [emphasis mine]. I found the spirit and vigour of liberty every moment

sinking in me, and a servile fear of displeasing, stealing by degrees upon all my behaviour."

When I was the director of a grants program at the National Endowment for the Humanities, I experienced the unsettling effects of inequality in conversation. I was a minor
government official in charge of a program that dispensed $3.5
million in grants. In effect, I was a patron of sorts. Consequently, distinguished academics and deans would flatter me
when they came to Washington. Any offhand remark I made
about a book or a movie would often be greeted with an enthusiastic: "I agree!" I remember the Dean of Arts and Sciences
of Harvard responding to a commonplace observation that I
made about a contemporary writer: "Yes, absolutely!"

Do We Need Conversation?

Like Montaigne, the eighteenth-century writers on conversation often spoke of the intellectual benefits of conversation. In
his journal Boswell quotes the remark of his actor-friend, West
Digges, that "conversation is the traffic of the mind; for by ex-
changing ideas, we enrich one another."

In *Tom Jones* (1749) the narrator says: "A true knowledge
of the world is gained only by conversation." Conversation, he
suggests, teaches us about human nature, so scholars who spend
more time reading than talking to people do not know much
about the world. "There is another sort of knowledge beyond
the power of learning to bestow, and this is to be had by con
versation. So necessary is this to understanding the characters
of men, that none are more ignorant of them than those
learned pedants, whose lives have been entirely consumed in
colleges, and among books."

The Newcastle Literary and Philosophical Society associated intellectual progress with "free conversation." A pamphlet put out by the society argued that "the free conversations of associated friends . . . [have] served as hints for the most important discoveries." Hume agreed. In his view, men who did not engage in conversation would stagnate intellectually or would propound bizarre views. "What can be expected from Men who never consulted Experience in any of their Reasonings, or who never search'd for that Experience, where alone it is to be found, in common Life and Conversation?"

Modern writers on conversation tend to dwell on the emotional rewards that come from conversation. They argue that conversation is good for the psyche (or soul) or that conversation strengthens our ties with friends. According to Tannen, "In conversation we form the interpersonal ties that bind individuals together in personal relationships." McWhorter quotes the Jesuit intellectual Walter Ong to suggest that in conversation "persons commune with persons, reaching one another's interiors." Charlie Rose, the host of a highly regarded television talk show about books, says that "I believe that there is a place in the spectrum of television for really good conversation, if it is informed, spirited, soulful."

Communing with persons or having a conversation that is soulful was not what the eighteenth-century writers had in mind by conversation. (The word *soulful* did not exist in the eighteenth century.) Intimate talk about a "relationship" or about the nature of one's psyche would not in their view qualify as conversation. The eighteenth-century writers did not question the need for talk—Johnson certainly talked to Hester Thrale, confessing many of his deepest anxieties to her—but they argued that conversation also has psychological benefits. According to Swift, Hume, and Johnson, spending time in the conversible world is likely to make people more sociable—more able to control their dark passions. According to Adam Smith, "Society and conversation . . . are the most powerful remedies for restoring the mind to its tranquility, if, at any time, it has unfortunately lost it."

Swift says that if we lack the "useful Pleasure" of conversation, "we are forced to take up either poor Amusements of Dress and Visiting, or the more pernicious ones of Play [gambling], Drink and Vicious Amours." In *Gulliver's Travels* (1726) the Struldbruggs are immortal but their lives are miserable because they cannot converse with most people, since they do not understand the language of people who were born generations after them. "The language of this Country being always upon the Flux, the Struldbruggs of one Age do not understand those of another; neither are they able after two Hundred Years to hold any Conversation (farther than by a few general Words) with their Neighbours, the Mortals; and thus they lye under the Disadvantage of living like Foreigners in their own Country."

Johnson speaks of the benefits of what he calls "honest conversation," by which he means conversation that does not promote immoral conduct. "It is scarcely possible to pass an hour in honest conversation, without being able when we rise from it, to please ourselves with having given or received some advantages." At the very least honest conversation prevents the mind from being "empty and unoccupied." He once told Boswell: "If you come to settle here, we will have one day in the week on which we will meet by ourselves. That is the happiest conversation when there is no competition, no vanity, but a calm interchange of sentiments."

Johnson says that "there are not many minds furnished for great variety of conversation." Yet he implies that most conversations are likely to prove beneficial in some way. "He that amuses himself among well chosen companions, can scarcely fail to receive, from the most careless . . . merriment which virtue can allow, some useful hints; nor can converse on the most familiar topicks, without some casual information. The loose sparkles of thoughtless wit may give new light to the mind, and the gay contention for paradoxical positions [may] rectify the opinions."

Echoing what Swift and Johnson say about the benefits of conversation, Samuel Taylor Coleridge says that conversation helped him control his dark passions—specifically his despair over his drug habit. "The stimulus of Conversation suspends the terror that haunts my mind; but when I am alone, the horrors I have suffered from Laudanum, the degeneration, the blighted Utility, almost overwhelm me."

The *New York Times* reports that Finland, a country where "silence is a sign of wisdom and good manners," and where people rarely have conversations during meals, has one of the world's highest rates of suicide, depression, and alcoholism. Yet it is probably misguided to make a correlation between the silence of the Finns and their high suicide rate. Hungary has a higher suicide rate than Finland yet Hungarians are not known for being silent. (I have met many Hungarians—having married a Hungarian émigré—but I've never encountered a taciturn one.)

Whatever the effects of conversation, the eighteenth-century writers on conversation enjoyed it immensely—and they disliked doing without it. In *Journal of a Voyage to Lisbon,* which was posthumously published in 1755, Fielding talks about how miserable he was because he was "shut up within the circumference of a few yards, with a score of human creatures, with not one of whom it was possible to converse." (Fielding was sailing to Lisbon in a desperate attempt to restore his failing health.) Fielding, who was a great conversationalist, says the captain was "the only person . . . in whose conversation I might indulge myself; but unluckily, besides a total ignorance of every thing in the world but a ship, he had the misfortune of being so deaf" that the weak Fielding had to use his wife as an intermediary in order to carry on a conversation with him.

When Fielding arrived in Lisbon, he was still suffering from not being able to find a good conversationalist. He wrote his brother John, asking him to send a "conversible Man to be my companion in an Evening, with as much of the Qualifications of Learning, Sense and Good humour as you can find." Fielding died two months later—presumably without having his wish fulfilled.

One may get a sense of how important conversation is by reading about people who lived under regimes where a conversible world did not exist—or was extremely small. In *I Will Bear Witness* (2001), a diary of his life under Nazi rule, Victor Klemperer, a Jew married to a non-Jew, writes (in May 1943): "Thus the arrests are attributed to 'politically suspect conversation,' which have somehow been overheard, denounced, perhaps inadvertently betrayed. One man is interrogated, pulls down the others with him—out of weakness, out of stupidity, unintentionally. What is a politically suspect conversation? Everything and anything."

Despite the risk of being arrested, Klemperer continued to have conversations. Nadezhda Mandelstam did not take such risks. In *Hope Against Hope* (1976), which is about her life under Stalin, Mandelstam says she was afraid to have an honest conversation with anyone. "I certainly would not have survived in our terrible times without lying. I have lied all my life—to my students, my colleagues, and even the good friends I didn't quite trust (this was true of most of them). In the same way, nobody trusted me. . . . It sometimes seemed as though the whole country was suffering from persecution mania." The effect of this fear of conversation was a feeling of isolation and mental suffocation. Her husband, the poet Osip Mandelstam, said the aim of Stalin "was to destroy not only people, but the intellect itself." Johnson would have understood Mandelstam's point, for he argues that "the mind stagnates without external ventilation."

In contemporary North Korea the conversible world is nonexistent. Nicholas Kristof points out that "entire families sometimes [are] executed if one member gets drunk and slights the Dear Leader." Moreover, even if one wants to risk having a conversation in the privacy of one's apartment, it is almost impossible to do so. "Nearly every home [is] equipped with a speaker that issues propaganda from morning to night."

Though conversation is good for the mind and good for the psyche, the skeptic might well ask: "Why worry about the state of conversation in America when there are far more important things to think about: terrorism, global warming, poverty, AIDS?"

Hume and other eighteenth-century thinkers would argue that it is difficult to discuss political questions if we lack the art of conversation—and terrorism, global warming, etc., are political questions because they are about the allocation of resources in a democratic society. Freedom is necessary for conversation, but conversation will not flourish simply because there is freedom. Without a "polite" citizenry, conversation will suffer.

Judith Martin says we cannot discuss any question of importance unless we follow etiquette, by which she means what the eighteenth-century writers meant by the art of conversation. "Far from squelching substantive discussion and debate, etiquette is what makes them possible. . . . Without such rules, there are no exchanges of ideas, only exchanges of set positions and insults. People who disagree rapidly move from talking over one another to shouting one another down, and from expressing their opinions on the matter at hand to expressing their opinions on the intelligence and morality of those who disagree with them."

Many colonial Americans took the art of conversation as seriously as Johnson and Hume did. When Benjamin Franklin was twenty-four he wrote the essay "How to Please in Conversation." At the age of fourteen George Washington wrote *Rules of Civility & Decent Behavior in Company and Conversation,* which is based on a seventeenth-century French book on conversation. Washington says to himself: "Let your Conversation be without Malice or Envy, for 'tis a Sign of a Tractable and Commendable Nature." He also tells himself: "Be not tedious in Discourse, make not many Digressions, nor repeat often the Same manner of Discourse."

Jaida Sandra and Jon Spayde, the authors of *Salons: The Joy of Conversation* (2001), also talk about the importance of conversation, but they imply that conversation has a purpose: to turn people into political activists. "Passionate conversation often led to passionate action, to lives risked, and sometimes sacrificed in efforts to achieve social and political change." The eighteenth-century writers on conversation would disagree. They wanted Britons to be less passionate about politics, not more. Worried about overheated passions, Addison tells the readers of the *Spectator* to amuse themselves "with such Writings as tend to the wearing out [the reduction] of Ignorance, Passion, and Prejudice." Passion undermines politeness, and therefore it is the enemy of conversation.

In the eighteenth century politeness was a stronger term than it is now. Politeness signified a way of thinking as well as acting, a dislike of extremes in thought. As the anonymous author of *The Polite Companion* (1760) puts it: "A man must be Master of himself, his Words, his Gesture, and Passions; . . . nothing must escape him, to give others a just occasion to complain of his Demeanour." Lawrence Klein, the leading historian of politeness, says: "Though the term politeness had many uses in this period, it referred most directly to the protocols of good conversation."

Politeness was a term of French origin—from the French verb *polir* (to polish). In Britain a man skilled at the art of conversation was often called "polished" (or refined). In mid-seventeenth-century France there was an extensive debate about "*la politesse*"—a debate that continued into the eighteenth century. In the *Encyclopedia*, edited by the philosophe Denis Diderot, the article on *politesse* says: "*La civilité* is good, but it is also more common and less excellent than *la politesse*." Craveri speaks of "the enormous importance of *politesse*. . . . It occupied the minds of the greatest eighteenth-century thinkers."

Politesse is a hard word to translate into English. Leonard Tancock translates La Rochefoucauld's "*la politesse de l'esprit*" as "courtesy of the mind," while Louis Kronenberger translates it as "well-bred thinking." These translations sound stuffy to me; I would prefer "agreeability of the mind"—a mental disposition to please others.

There was some disagreement about who could be polite, but most writers did not think politeness was an attribute of class, though one had to be educated in order to be polite. Defoe was a tradesman for several years, yet he regarded himself as a member of the polite world. He was incensed when he was accused of not being polite. In response to the "Impotent Slanders," he asks: Can these attackers "charge my Conversation with the least Vice or Immorality, with Indecency, Immodesty, Passion, Prophaneness or any thing else that deserves Reproach?"

At first glance it would seem that contemporary society in the West suffers mainly from a lack of politeness. In popular culture rude people are celebrated as authentic, and those skilled at the art of conversation are often depicted as superficial or effeminate or dishonest (or all three). On television opinion-mongers announce their views as if they are issuing a challenge. "That's my opinion," they imply. "Do you have a problem with that?" It seems as if many people aspire to be confrontational. Reviewing a contemporary memoir, a critic in an English newspaper said: "Frey [the author] can really write. Brilliantly. And if you don't think so, f*** you."

Yet if conversation suffers from a lack of politeness, it also suffers from an excess of politeness. Watching daytime television talk shows, I heard the word *judgmental* uttered at least five times over a period of a week. In his autobiography, *Ringmaster!* (1998), Jerry Springer says: "We're not a judgmental show; so our motto is, and has always been, 'Come as you are.'" To question someone's views is to risk being labeled judgmental or rude or arrogant (or worse).

The notion that one is entitled to one's opinion now means (in some circles) that all opinions are equally valid. But many people who don't believe that all opinions are valid often say that they are going to share their thoughts. Sharing is not a neutral word. It implies a generous act—as if one were giving someone food. Just as it would be rude to criticize the food someone "shared" with you, it would be rude to criticize thoughts that are shared. Sharing puts a dampener on conversation. Instead of conversation we have confession. If sharing increases, raillery will decline, and conversation will languish because of suffocating politeness.

In 1959 Oakeshott spoke of the need to rescue conversation, but he said that he had no philosophical program for doing so. "To rescue the conversation [of mankind] from the bog into which it has fallen and to restore to it some of its lost freedom of movement would require a philosophy more profound than anything I have to offer."

Rescuing conversation may be an impossible task in a culture that admires both angry self-expression and nonjudgmental "supportive" assent. Yet perhaps some people may be persuaded to pay more attention to their "conversation life" if they come to realize that they will get more pleasure out of life if they do so. Johnson says (and Addison, Hume, Swift, and Fielding would agree) that "there is in this world no real delight (excepting those of sensuality), but exchange of ideas in conversation."

II

Ancient Conversation: From the Book of Job to Plato's *Symposium*

When did conversation begin? To raise this question is to ask: When did the faculty of language develop? Many observers argue that humankind acquired language roughly fifty thousand years ago, and that this development led to what anthropologist Richard Klein has called the dawn of human culture. According to Klein, "Elaborate graves with unequivocal ideological or religious implications show up only after 50,000 years ago, and they are an important part of what we mean when we talk about the dawn of human culture." Since the advent of language coincided with the construction of elaborate graves, there probably were conversations about how to commemorate the dead—and about why one should commemorate the dead.

Paleolithic hunter/gatherers probably did not spend much time in conversation, since they continually had to search for food. In an agricultural society there is more leisure time—at least for some people. The rise of agriculture twelve thousand years ago on the eastern shores of the Mediterranean led to the birth of cities and eventually to the rise of Sumer. The Sume-

rians, Karen Nemet-Nejat says, "turned an agricultural community into the first urban civilization in the world."

If Hume is right that urbanization promotes conversation, it is likely that in Sumer, where there were many city-
states, the conversible world greatly expanded. According to
scholars, by the end of the third millennium the vast majority
of Sumerians lived in cities. Moreover, the Sumerians invented
writing, and the availability of texts probably stimulated conversation. Sumerian literature includes conversation poems where
two protagonists pair seasons, animals, plants, metals, and im-
plements and discuss which is more useful for humankind. In
the literature of the Sumerians and their successors—the
Akkadians, Babylonians, and Assyrians—there are also conversation poems about the unfairness of life.

The *Babylonian Theodicy* is a conversation poem about
why bad things happen to good people. One speaker complains that even though he has led a pious existence, he is poor.

> A cripple rises above me, a fool is ahead of me,
> Rogues are in the ascendant, I am demoted.

The friend replies:

> You blaspheme in the anguish of your thoughts,
> Divine purpose is as remote as innermost heaven,
> It is too difficult to understand, people cannot
>   understand it.

In arguing that the ways of God (or the gods) are mysterious,
the poem anticipates the book of Job.

In "Dialogue of Pessimism" a master and servant discuss
what the master should do. The servant at first agrees with what-

ever the master proposes, but toward the end of the poem the servant mocks the master. In response to the master's question "What, then, is good?" the servant replies: "To break my neck and your neck and throw (us) in the river is good. Who is so tall as to reach to heaven? Who is so broad as to encompass the netherworld?" Angry, the master says: "No, servant, I will kill you and let you go first." In his reply, the servant implies that the master will do no such thing because the master is dependant upon him: "Then my master will certainly not outlive me even three days!" The poem is about the impossibility of conversation between unequals. When the servant acts as if he were the equal of the master, the master is offended.

In the civilizations of Mesopotamia and ancient Greece people were more interested in prophecy and divination than in conversation. Prophets communicated messages from the gods that came in the form of visions, voices, or dreams. The oracle of Apollo at Delphi was consulted by innumerable Greeks, including Xenophon and Socrates. When the plague came to Athens during the Peloponnesian War, many Athenians blamed Pericles—a skeptic who paid no attention to the oracles. The Spartans took divination very seriously. "Military divination," Paul Cartledge says, "was for the Spartans no less a part of the technique of warfare than the more obvious physical and mental preparations and exertions."

Divination has nothing in common with conversation. The supplicant wants information about the future, which can be derived from a number of methods. They include consulting an oracle, "reading" a sacrificed animal's entrails (extispicy), and practicing augury, which the *Oxford Classical Dictionary* defines as "the observation and interpretation of the number, species, flight, cries, eating, and other symbolic acts of birds." Xenophon, J. K. Anderson says, "repeatedly represents himself

as sacrificing before military operations, in order to determine, from the entrails of the victims, whether a projected op-
eration would succeed or fail."

In the Hebrew Bible divination is frowned upon as the
work of idolaters and false prophets. "Then the Lord said unto
me [Jeremiah], The prophets prophesy lies in my name: I sent
them not, neither have I commanded them, neither spake unto
them; they prophesy unto you a false vision and divination,
and a thing of nought, and the deceit of their heart." What
about the good prophets—Amos, Isaiah, Jeremiah? Though
they at times predict the future, their main concern is to warn
the Israelites that the Lord is angry because they have not been
righteous. Jeremiah says: "Woe unto him that buildeth his
house by unrighteousness."

God and the prophets command, lecture, scold, and
threaten the Jewish people; they do not converse with them.
As Amos says: "The Lord will roar from Zion, / And utter his
voice from Jerusalem." In the Hebrew Bible God is the mysterious other who must be obeyed. In his commentary on his
translation of *The Five Books of Moses* (2004), Robert Alter
says: "God's holiness, whatever else it may involve and however
ultimately unfathomable the idea may be, implies an ontolog-
ical division or chasm between the Creator and the created
world." Elijah warns the children of Israel: "How long halt ye between two opinions? If the Lord be God, follow him: but if Baal,
then follow him. And the people answered him not a word."

The only extended conversation in the Hebrew Bible is in
the book of Job. Job and his friends are equals, and God is off-
stage except at the beginning and the end of the narrative. The
conversation is purposeful only in the sense that Job is in search
of understanding. He is not trying to make a decision. To be
sure, at the beginning of the narrative Job must decide whether

to heed the advice of his wife, who tells him to "curse God, and die," but he immediately rejects her counsel.

The book of Job, Raymond Scheindlin says, "contains more obscure words, phrases, and passages of disputed meaning than any other book of the Bible." In addition, the many translations available in English are based on different ancient texts. Scheindlin's translation includes lengthy remarks by Elihu—a figure who does not appear in a translation by Stephen Mitchell. Scheindlin acknowledges that "Elihu's speeches may be hard to justify within the dramatic structure of the book, and they may indeed have been added by a later editor."

Although there are many difficulties with the text of the book of Job, it is easy to say what it is about. It is an extended conversation between Job and his friends about the meaning of Job's suffering. But it is a failed conversation—not because it lacks raillery, which of course would be inappropriate for a conversation about suffering. It is a failed conversation because the friends do not listen to what Job has to say. They are certain that Job's suffering can be explained. It is because Job has sinned. They have come to this conclusion in order to comfort themselves with the thought that what happened to Job could never happen to them. Throughout the conversation Job insists that he has done no wrong. We know Job is innocent because we are told so at the beginning of the narrative.

The book of Job often sounds like an interrogation, for the friends want Job to confess his guilt. Eliphaz, the first friend to speak, is the soft cop. He offers reassurance: all will be well if Job agrees with him that there is a reason for his suffering. "You are lucky that God has scolded you," he says. Job resents his friend's assumption that he deserved his suffering. Though angry, Job is still half-willing to have a conversation with his friends, for he says to Eliphaz (and by implication to all three):

"Teach me, and I will be silent / Show me where I have been wrong." (The citations are from Mitchell's translation.)

Bildad, the next speaker, is the hard cop. He bluntly says that the sons of Job sinned, which is why God punished them. He also accuses Job of talking nonsense. Job rages against Bildad. He also says he wants to talk to God. Though Job wants an explanation from God, he seems to feel that he will never get one. Filled with despair, he laments his existence. "Why did you let me be born?"

Zophar, the third friend, is even nastier than Bildad. He tells Job that he is a liar. Job angrily replies: "You, it seems, know everything; / perfect wisdom is yours." Job wants his friends to shut up.

> For *you* smear my words with ignorance
> And patch my body with lies.
> Don't you have sense?
> Will you never shut your mouths?

Job cannot make up his mind how to deal with the obtuseness of his friends. He feels almost desperate because he cannot get them to take his argument seriously.

The friends do not change their views. If at first they thought Job might have forgotten that he had sinned, now they are certain he is lying. In the second round of conversation, Eliphaz ridicules Job:

> Does the wise man spout such nonsense
> And fill his belly with gas?
> Does he blurt out useless arguments,
> Words that can do no good?

Job again tells his friends to shut up.

> Enough—I have heard enough!
> I am sick of your consolations!
> How long will you treat me with insults?
> Will your malice never relent?

Job's anger eventually turns to despair. At first he pleads for pity, but then he becomes composed and even hopeful. He implies that in the future he will be exonerated.

But the friends remain angry with Job. Zophar begins his second speech by saying: "My mind is seething with anger." Zophar paints a dark picture of what happens to those who persist in their sinful ways. Once again Job responds by urging his friends to listen to what he has to say, but this time his remarks are tinged with sarcasm, as if he knows that his friends will never accept his protestations of innocence.

> Listen now to my words;
> let that be the comfort you give me.
> Bear with me; let me speak;
> when I finish, then you can laugh.

Finally, Job takes a new approach. Instead of protesting his innocence, he questions the assumption that righteousness is always rewarded. "Why do the wicked prosper / And live to a ripe old age?" He elaborates upon this theme—ending on a note of contempt for his friends: "Your answers are empty lies."

Does Job's argument carry any weight with his friends? Not in the least. In his third speech Eliphaz says he doesn't agree with Job's argument.

> Would he [God] sentence you for your piety
> Or punish you for your faith?
> Your guilt must be great indeed;
> Your crimes must be inconceivable.

Job does not respond to Eliphaz's remarks. Instead, he wearily wishes he could talk to God.

> If only I knew where to meet him
> And could find my way to his court.
> I would argue my case before him . . .
> For he knows that I am innocent.

When Bildad implies that it is absurd for man—"that vile, stinking maggot"—to think he can argue his case before God, Job offers a sarcastic reply to all three friends.

> How kind you all have been to me!
> How considerate of my pain!

He no longer asks them to have pity on him or to listen to what he has to say. He says with dignity:

> I will never let you convict me;
> I will never give up my claim.
> I will hold tight to my innocence;
> My mind will never submit.

Job gets the last word against his friends, but "The Unnamable" [Scheindlin uses "Yahweh"] answers Job from "within the Whirlwind," making it clear that it is presumptuous for Job to want to talk to him. The Unnamable's lengthy speech, in which there are frequent references to the wonders of nature, persuades Job that he must accept the mystery of suffering. As Job says: "I have spoken of the unspeakable / and tried to grasp the infinite."

The book of Job is a sympathetic portrait of a man in torment—a man who cries out in anger and despair. It is also a scathing portrait of self-righteous grief counselors. Job wins our sympathy because we know that he was wrongly accused of having sinned. Moreover, we see him struggling to maintain his composure and dignity as his irritating friends grill him. It is altogether appropriate for the book of Job to end with God saying to Eliphaz: "I am very angry at you and your two friends, because you have not spoken the truth about me, as my servant Job has."

The book of Job has great resonance in the present. Modern society is filled with smug explainers who talk down to people. Such people don't engage you in conversation; they lecture to you. If you are sick, they point out that you eat the wrong foods or have too much stress in your life. More pernicious than such explainers are those who resort to theodicy—explaining evil and suffering by saying that they are part of God's plan. After the attacks of 9/11, several American ministers made the repulsive charge that the murder of almost three thousand persons was a sign of God's displeasure with a decadent America. After the tsunami of 26 December 2004, several Christian, Moslem, and Jewish clerics made a similar charge. Sounding like Job's comforters, an Israeli Sephardic rabbi called the disaster "an expression of God's wrath with the world. The world is being punished for wrongdoing—be it people's needless hatred of each other, lack of charity, moral turpitude."

The essayist Leon Wieseltier recounts a friend's poignant attempt at theodicy. When Wieseltier offered condolences for the murder of his friend's son at the World Trade Center, the friend "assured me of his trust in the Lord of the Universe. Such a spectacular death, he explained, must have been an element in a divine plan." One can understand the father's desperate need for meaning and consolation, yet I prefer Wieseltier's response when he watched a replay of the attack: "Watching the towers burn again and fall again, I found myself without wisdom again." Montaigne would agree. Decrying those who try to understand the ways of God, he quotes Solomon: "For what man can know the counsel of God: or who shall conceive what the Lord willeth?"

The devout Samuel Johnson disliked writers who explained away suffering by complacently saying that it is part of God's plan. In a review of Soame Jenyns's *A Free Inquiry into the Nature and Origin of Evil* (1757), a book that purports to explain human suffering, Johnson says that Jenyns "decides too easily upon questions out of the reach of human determination." The same can be said of Job's friends.

The book of Job describes a failed conversation, but it is also about the limits of conversation. When we are grief-stricken, we don't want advice, however well-intentioned, and we don't want to have a conversation about the meaning of suffering. Historians rightly discuss the causes of the Holocaust and theologians rightly discuss the meaning of the Holocaust, but the appropriate initial response to the Holocaust—or to suffering of any kind—is silence or condolences. And for many people—even irreligious people—there also is a desire for prayer. When the Austrian novelist Ingeborg Bachmann visited Auschwitz, she said: "I cannot talk about this because . . . there is nothing to talk about. Before I would have been able to say something about it but since I have seen 'it,' I think I cannot any more."

There are times when conversation is inappropriate.

Conversation in Plato's *Symposium*

Scholars think the book of Job was written between 600 and 400 BC. If it was written around 400 BC it was roughly contemporaneous with Plato's *Symposium*, which was written between 384 and 379 BC. *The Symposium*, as every educated person knows, is one of many dialogues that Plato wrote. The dialogue form was popular in classical Athens. Robin Waterfield points out that, at the time, writing Socratic dialogues constituted a minor industry and a sub-genre of Greek prose literature.

Nowadays, the word *dialogue* is often used as a verb—implying an exchange of views on the part of those with different ethnic backgrounds, religious affiliations, or political persuasions. I use the word *dialogue* simply to mean "a literary work in conversational form," which is the *O.E.D.*'s first definition of the word.

Perhaps the dialogue was a popular literary form in fifth-century BC Athens because Athens was known throughout Greece for its lively conversation. (Plato was born in Athens in 427 BC.) The Athenian city-state (*polis*), which was what we would call a participatory or direct democracy, placed a high value on debate and discussion in the Assembly (*ekklesia*) as well as in the Council (*boule*) of five hundred citizens who prepared the agenda for the Assembly. Athenian citizens spent very little time at home. Athenians deliberated at the Pnyx hill near the Acropolis, which was where the Assembly met, and they congregated in the Agora, which served as a marketplace and meeting place. The Agora, Robert Garland says, was a place for Athenians "to engage in their favorite pastime—lively and animated discussion."

Athenian citizens had a high rate of literacy. More than half the male population could read and write. Athenian citi-

zens, however, numbered no more than 15 percent of the population, and they depended on metics (foreign-born workers),
women, and slaves to do the work that enabled them to have
the leisure required for conversation. Yet some of the metics,
women, and slaves were literate as well.

Historians have pointed out the many shortcomings of
Athenian democracy, and they have noted that Athens was an
imperial power that harshly treated many of the Aegean islands under its dominion. Whatever the flaws of Athenian democracy, the conversational freedom found in Athens made it
a magnet for intellectual and artistic Greeks from other cities.
Plato has Socrates say (in the *Gorgias*) that of all the Greek
cities Athens has the most freedom of speech. There is a consensus among scholars that Athens was the most democratic
and most culturally influential Greek city-state.

Athenian citizens continued their conversations in the
evening at symposia that aristocratic Athenians held in their
homes. Symposium has been translated as "drinking together"
or "drinks-party." At some symposia the drinking got out of
hand, but at many it did not. The guests were supposed to follow strict rules that were enforced by a symposiarch—the master of the evening. The wine served at symposia was weak—
mixed with water in proportions usually of two or three of
water to one of wine.

In Plato's *Symposium* the drinking gets out of hand after
a large group of revelers disturbs the party. "There was noise
everywhere, and all order was abandoned; everyone was forced
to drink vast amounts of wine." Nevertheless, three of the principle figures continue to engage in conversation. They are Agathon, a tragic playwright at whose house that symposium takes
place; Aristophanes, a comic playwright; and Socrates. Eventually Agathon and Aristophanes fall asleep. Only Socrates stays

awake, and in the morning he goes off to spend "the rest of the day as he did at other times." A night spent conversing and drinking apparently had no effect on him, which suggests that Socrates was an extraordinary man.

Symposium, which is based on an actual symposium that took place in 416 BC, is a complex work that is not easy to interpret. It is difficult to know what to make of the ideas put forth by the principal conversationalists. It is also impossible to know whether the ideas advanced by Socrates are ideas the historical Socrates held or are ideas that Plato held, though most scholars argue that in Plato's early dialogues (*Symposium* is one of them) Socrates advances his own views, not Plato's.

One thing about *Symposium* is clear: it is a celebration of Socrates. It begins with a conversation that took place long after the actual symposium was held. The conversation is between two men. Glaucon is eager "to get the full story of the party at Agathon's," especially what Socrates said. Glaucon approaches Apollodorus because he assumes Apollodorus was at the symposium. Apollodorus, who reveres Socrates and makes it his job to "find out what he says and does every day," replies that he was not present at the symposium, which took place "a long time ago." He heard about it from Aristodemus, who did attend.

Thus in the opening pages of *Symposium* we learn that the "drinks-party" at Agathon's has achieved near legendary status among the admirers of Socrates. We also learn that on the way to the symposium Socrates suddenly became lost in thought. "This is one of his habits," Aristodemus says to Agathon. "Sometimes he goes off and stands still wherever he happens to be."

Much later in *Symposium,* after the attendees have offered their views on the God of Love (*Eros*), Alcibiades—a famous Athenian politician and general—makes the same point even more strongly. "One morning he [Socrates] started thinking about a problem, and stood there considering it, and when he didn't make progress with it he didn't give up but kept standing there examining it. When it got to midday, people noticed him and said to each other in amazement that Socrates had been standing there thinking about something since dawn." Socrates stood there all night. "He stood there till it was dawn and the sun came up; then he greeted the sun with a prayer and went away."

Alcibiades is a good-looking and politically powerful man who possesses what we would call charisma, yet he acknowledges that the ugly and politically powerless Socrates is his superior. "He is like no other human being, either of the past or the present. . . . This person is so peculiar and so is the way he talks, that however hard you'll look you'll never find anyone close to him, past or present."

How seriously should we take Alcibiades' remarks about Socrates, since he admits that he is very drunk? (Alcibiades was not one of the original attendees of the symposium. He crashed the party soon after Socrates finished talking.) Perhaps Alcibiades' drunkenness allows him to be more frank in his views than he intended to be, for he has mixed feelings about Socrates. "He's the only person in whose company I've had an experience you might think me incapable of—feeling shame with someone; I only feel shame in his company."

Roughly the last quarter of *Symposium* is devoted to Alcibiades' attempt to explain the erotic power of Socrates. *Eros* means desire. Many Athenians desire to hear what Socrates said—desire even to be questioned by him. Alcibiades says: "Whenever anyone hears you speak or hears your words reported by someone else . . . whoever we are—woman, man or boy—we're overwhelmed and spellbound." Alcibiades also regards Socrates as an erotic figure in the conventional sense; he is physically attracted to Socrates but he admits that Socrates has spurned his sexual advances. We should not think of *eros* in a one-dimensional way. According to Gregory Vlastos, Socratic *eros* "is even-keeled, light-hearted, jocular, cheerfully and obstinately sane." By contrast, Platonic *eros* "generates an emotion that has torrential force." Platonic *eros* is a kind of madness.

The Socrates we see in Plato's dialogues is a man who stirs up *eros* in his listeners, but is he a great conversationalist? He possesses one trait that great conversationalists have. He is a good listener who treats his fellow conversationalists with respect. He does not tell them what to think. He wants them to examine their ideas because, as he says in the *Apology,* "the unexamined life is not worth living by a human being." He is the opposite of Job's friends insofar as he does not claim to have knowledge. Yet Socrates is a disturbing conversationalist because he usually subjects his fellow conversationalists to "scrutiny" (*elenchus*). According to R. M. Hare, "Socrates' method of 'scrutiny' consists in eliciting from his victims answers to his questions, and then demolishing them by showing them to be inconsistent with other opinions which the victims are not willing to give up."

Victims? The word seems excessive, since many Athenians did not object to Socrates' "scrutiny." Indeed, they welcomed it. In *Symposium* Agathon implies that Socrates has benefited him. "It looks, Socrates, as though I didn't know what I was talking about then." Yet in the *Euthyphro,* Euthyphro becomes annoyed by Socrates' "scrutiny." In response to yet another question from Socrates, Euthyphro says he has had enough. "Some other time, then, Socrates. For now I am in a hurry to go somewhere, and it is time for me to go away." Some Athenians were under Socrates' spell, but many were not—probably because they disliked being told they were not wise. Socrates says in the *Apology:* "And then I tried to show him [a prominent politician] that he supposed he was wise, but was not. So from this I became hateful both to him and to many of those present."

It might be objected that *Symposium* is not a conversation, as I have defined conversation, since the attendees are not equal: Socrates is by far the dominant figure. But by equality I mean only that no one at the symposium is beholden to another person. Socrates is not anyone's master or boss. All those who attend are of equal status, though all look up to Socrates because of his analytical powers.

The Socrates we see in Aristophanes' play *The Clouds* is different from the Socrates we see in *Symposium.* He is not a conversationalist who uses "scrutiny." He is an educator who undermines Athens's civic and family values. He turns a young man, Pheidippides, into someone—the Chorus says—who is "clever / at speaking notions opposed / to the just things." Pheidippides is smugly satisfied with his new view of things: "How pleasant it is to consort with novel and shrewd matters/and to be able to look down on the established laws!"

According to Thomas West, the resemblances between Aristophanes' and Plato's Socrates are "numerous and inescapable." Most scholars would disagree with this view. In their view the Socrates depicted in *The Clouds* has little in common with the historical Socrates, who was like the Socrates in Plato's early dialogues. In Aristophanes' play Socrates is a teacher, whereas in Plato's dialogues Socrates teaches nothing; he only raises questions about what his fellow conversationalists say. Socrates is an unsettling conversationalist. Though he is calm, good-humored, and humble, he wants to jar people from their mental complacency. Alcibiades describes his mixed feelings about Socrates: "Often I've felt I'd be glad to see him removed from the human race; but if this did happen, I know well I'd be much more upset. I just don't know how to deal with this person."

The major writers on conversation admired Socrates. Montaigne refers to him innumerable times. "Socrates," he says, "always laughingly welcomed contradictions made to his arguments." Johnson refers to him favorably, and Addison mentions him in the *Spectator:* "It was said of *Socrates* that he brought Philosophy down from Heaven, to inhabit among Men; and I shall be ambitious to have it said of me, that I have brought Philosophy out of Closets and Libraries, Schools and Colleges, to dwell in Clubs and Assemblies." Hume asks: "Who admires not Socrates; his perpetual serenity and contentment, amidst the greatest poverty and domestic vexation; his resolute contempt of riches, and his magnanimous care of preserving liberty, while he refused all assistance from his friends and disciples, and avoided even the dependence of an obligation?"

Cicero, the Roman politician and essayist, also admired Socrates. In *On Oratory* (55 BC), he recommends Socrates as a guide to conversation. In *On Duties,* written eleven years later, he praises the Socratics—the followers of Socrates. "Conversation, in which the Socratics particularly excel, ought . . . to be gentle and without a trace of intransigence; it should also be witty."

Written as an extended letter to his son, *On Duties* is a guidebook for the Roman governing class. Cicero argues that the Romans have neglected the art of conversation, which "should be found in social groups, in philosophical discussions and among gatherings of friends—and may it also attend dinners!" Many guidebooks, he says, exist for oratory, but none for conversation: "no one is devoted to learning about conversation."

Cicero offers suggestions on topics for conversation, but he is flexible about what constitutes an appropriate topic. "Conversations are for the most part about domestic business or public affairs or else the study and teaching of the arts. We should, then, even if the discussion begins to drift to other matters, make an effort to call it back to the subject; but we should do so according to the company: for we do not at all times enjoy the same subjects in the same way."

Cicero says we should avoid personal abuse in conversation. "We must take particular care to be seen to respect and have affection for those with whom we share conversations." If we do need to reprove someone, it should be done in an even-tempered manner. "One ought for the most part to resort only to mild criticism, though combined with a certain seriousness so as to show severity while avoiding abusiveness." He also warns against anger. "Anger itself should be far from us, for nothing can be done rightly or thoughtfully when done in anger." Even when we are provoked we should refrain from anger: "even in disputes that arise with our greatest enemies, and even if we hear unworthy things said against us, [we should] . . . maintain our seriousness and . . . dispel our anger."

Cicero implies that if the educated classes follow his prescriptions, Rome will have the kind of leadership it needs if the republic is restored. Yet he was not sure the republic would be restored. Writing *On Duties* during a time of political turmoil that followed the assassination of Julius Caesar, Cicero at times sounds hopeful: "Freedom will bite back more fiercely when *suspended* than when she remains undisturbed." Yet in other passages he is gloomy about Rome's prospects. One year after *On Duties* was completed, Cicero was proscribed—declared an enemy of the state—by the new triumvirate of Antony, Lepidus, and Octavian (Cicero had frequently attacked Antony). Eight months later Cicero was murdered by government soldiers.

Cicero is a central figure in the history of conversation. In *The Art of Conversation* (1993), Peter Burke says of the manuals on conversation that appeared in Italy, France, and Britain in the sixteenth, seventeenth, and eighteenth centuries: "It would not be very much of an exaggeration" to call them "a series of footnotes to Cicero." In the *Enquiry Concerning Human Understanding* (1748), Hume says that "the fame of Cicero flourishes at present, but that of Aristotle is utterly decayed."

Cicero was the first writer to make the case that liberty might lead to violent civil discord if the educated classes lacked the art of conversation. Hume, whom Paul Langford calls "a renowned campaigner for the value of conversation," praised *Of Duties*. "Upon the whole, I desire to take my catalogue of Virtues from Cicero's *Offices* [Duties], not from the *Whole Duty of Man*." (*The Whole Duty of Man,* published in 1658, was the most popular religious self-help book in eighteenth-century Britain.) Hume goes on to say: "I had, indeed, the former Book in my Eye in all my Reasonings."

Sparta: The Anti-Conversation City-State

When we talk about conversation in ancient Greece, we think mainly of Athens. If Athenians were known for their conversation, Spartans were known for being laconic. The word *laconic* is derived from Laconia, the region surrounding Sparta that was controlled by the Spartans. The ancient Greeks even had a verb that meant to imitate the Spartan way of talking: *lakonizein*. Spartan education, Cartledge says, "included a rich variety of imaginatively nasty punishments . . . for failing to answer a question sufficiently 'laconically' (i.e. snappily and wittily)." One punishment was having one's thumb bitten by the teacher.

In the early years of the fifth century, Sparta was in league with the Athenians against Persia, but for most of the second half of the century Sparta and its allies were at war with Athens. In 404 the Spartan alliance defeated Athens, and the Athenians lost their empire, but in 371 the Spartan army was defeated by Thebes, and Sparta began a long decline.

Trained to be laconic, the Spartans thought men who talked a lot were not likely to be men endowed with military spirit. The Spartans, Anton Powell says, "appear to have prided themselves on avoiding, even on [an] inability to understand, lengthy and complex argument." The Spartans considered the Athenians to be a disorderly and decadent people. A Spartan in Plato's *Laws* says that in the cities controlled by Sparta there are no symposia and no one gets away with drunkenness. The extent of literacy among Spartans is unknown, mainly because the Spartans did not write books—only a few inscriptions.

An oligarchy with a dual kingship, Sparta enforced a rigorous uniformity in its citizenry by taking male children away from their parents at the age of seven and requiring them to live in common quarters until age thirty. For twenty-three years they had to undergo the *Agoge* (Raising/Upbringing), which included not only intense military training but also what has been called "ritualized pederasty." After age twelve, Spartan boys were required to have a young adult warrior as their lover. Sparta, Cartledge says, made "a concerted and determined effort to minimize the importance of the family—or, to be more accurate, family life—and to emphasize rather the cardinal and overriding significance of communal ties." Spartan men ate in a communal mess and served in the military until age sixty.

Athens or Sparta: which had the better prescription for a successful city-state? The ancient Greeks debated this question. So did the Romans. Thucydides was not an admirer of Sparta. Sparta, he said, was an "archaic" city-state. Plato, who worried about the dangers of free conversation, admired Sparta for its political stability, as did many ancient writers, including Herodotus and Xenophon. According to Jasper Griffin, "the influential conservative tradition of Plato and others, hating democracy and inclining to paranoia about the dangers of free discussion and the arts, idolized Sparta as far preferable to the volatile and unreliable democracy of Athens." In a dialogue Xenophon has Socrates praise the Spartans for their self-discipline and leadership. Given Cicero's interest in the art of conversation, it is not surprising that he found Sparta repellent.

The Athens-Sparta debate, which simmered for fifteen hundred years and boiled over in the eighteenth century, is in part a debate about the role of conversation in maintaining political stability. Thinkers who admire Sparta usually have the same distrust of conversation the Spartans had, though—oddly enough—Montaigne, who loved the pleasures of conversation, often praises Sparta, calling it "a venerable, great, awe-inspiring form of government, where letters were not taught or practised but where virtue and happiness long flourished."

Jean-Jacques Rousseau, who thought the conversational world of eighteenth-century Paris reeked of hypocrisy, often praised Sparta. "Sparta, which I have never cited often enough as the example we ought to follow, cultivated its citizens with modest games and simple festivals." He thought Athens declined in part because of its love of the dramatic arts.

Rousseau did acknowledge that the Spartans were able to devote themselves to military affairs because the helots—a servant class composed mainly of prisoners of war—provided

them with life's necessities. "In some unfortunate circumstances one can preserve one's own freedom only at the expense of someone else's. . . . Such was the situation of Sparta."

Like Rousseau, the Scotsman Adam Ferguson, who spent
nine years in the military, wanted to promote Spartan values.
In *Essay on the History of Civil Society* (1767), which had a wide
readership, Ferguson often praises Sparta. He speaks of the
Spartan "who feared nothing but a failure in his duty, who
loved nothing but his friend and the state." The Spartans, he
says, "confined their studies to one question, How to improve
and to preserve courage and the disinterested affections of the
human heart?"

Though Ferguson enjoyed conversation in the clubs of
Edinburgh, he thought politeness—the trait most associated
with the art of conversation—was overrated. Ferguson asks:
"What persuasion can turn the grimace of politeness into real
sentiments of humanity and candour?" The polite man, he also
says, is not likely to have the courage necessary to defend the nation from external attack. "Mankind generally flatter their own
imbecility under the name of *politeness.*" Worried that Britons
are in danger of becoming "a supine or an abject people," Ferguson argues that Britain needs "institutions that fortify the
mind, inspire courage, and promote national felicity."

If Rousseau and Ferguson were in the Spartan camp,
Hume and the chemist Joseph Priestley were in the Athenian
camp. Though Hume was a friend of Ferguson's, he did not
admire Ferguson's *Civil Society.* Hume argues that a society
that devotes itself to inculcating its citizens with a devotion to
the state is bound to fail in the long run because such a project
goes against human nature. According to Hume, "Sovereigns
must take mankind as they find them, and cannot pretend to
introduce any violent change in their principles and ways of

thinking. . . . The less natural any set of principles are, which support a particular society, the more difficulty will a legislator meet with in raising and cultivating them." In Hume's view those who want to transform citizens into people who only think of the common good are not taking into account "the common bent of mankind."

Priestley, who in addition to his scientific work was a prolific essayist on religion and politics, had a very low opinion of Sparta. "What advantage did Sparta (the constitution of whose government was so much admired by the ancients, and many moderns) reap from those institutions which contributed to its longevity, but the longer continuance of, what I should not scruple to call, the worst government we read of in the world?" Sparta, he continues, had a government "which a man who had a taste for life would least of all choose to be a member." Sparta "produced no one poet, orator, historian, or artist of any kind." He concludes by saying that "the convulsions of Athens, where life was in some measure enjoyed, and the faculties of body and mind had their proper exercise and gratification, were, in my opinion, far preferable to the savage uniformity of Sparta."

The debate about Sparta continues. As Cartledge puts it, "Sparta, to put it laconically, lives." A reviewer of Cartledge's *The Spartans* (2002) on Amazon.com says (somewhat unfairly, to my mind): "Cartledge's obvious admiration for the society of Sparta is . . . curious. Sparta built a society based on gender separation, eugenics, forced homosexuality, forced child sexual abuse, constant war, enslavement of neighboring societies, and opposition to democracy."

In the twentieth century the Nazis admired the Spartans, but the desire to control thought and inculcate civic virtue—the desire, that is, to destroy the conversible world—has often been the aim of Marxist revolutionaries: Leninists, Maoists, and Castroites. Sparta is akin to modern totalitarian societies because it had a secret police that, as Griffin says, "prowled about at night to detect unrest among the subjugated Helots and to make away with those suspected of it." Yet Sparta differs from modern tyrannies because it never had a leadership cult.

In the mid-twentieth century many writers—among them Jean-Paul Sartre and Mary McCarthy—praised neo-Spartan regimes (China and North Vietnam) but preferred to live in neo-Athenian regimes. They were like the many ancient writers who praised Sparta but did not choose to live there. Xenophon was an exception. He was an Athenian who admired Sparta, which is perhaps why he was formally exiled from Athens around the turn of the century. From 399 to 394 he fought for Sparta, and for the next thirty years he lived the life of a country gentleman under Spartan protection. The last years of Xenophon's life are obscure, but one historian speculates that after the decree exiling him from Athens was repealed in 368 Xenophon may have moved back to Athens—living there from 365 until his death in 354. If Xenophon did in fact return to Athens, perhaps he did so because he missed the conversations (and drinking) that took place at Athenian symposia.

III

Three Factors Affecting Conversation: Religion, Commerce, Women

Cicero's *Of Duties,* which Hume and Johnson admired, did not become an important text until the Renaissance. Did conversation suffer during the Middle Ages? It is impossible to answer this question, though Peter Burke points out that no equivalent existed at the time to classical or modern discussions of ordinary conversation. Dante's *Commedia* is a series of intense conversations, but they are conversations with a purpose; the pilgrim Dante wants to know why a certain person is where he is in the afterworld. Or the souls in the afterworld want to know who Dante is and why he is journeying through the afterworld.

In the Renaissance Christian thinkers such as Erasmus, Montaigne, and Bacon, who wanted to promote the art of conversation in order to reduce the likelihood of violent civil discord, advocated what might be called polite Christianity. A polite Christian avoids zealotry and does not dwell on abstruse theological questions. A polite Christian has a sense of humor. In *The Praise of Folly* (1511), Erasmus ridicules the fanaticism of monks and the pomposity of theologians. He also makes fun of learned men who like to lecture others. "Bring a wiseman to a party: he will disrupt it either by his gloomy silence or his tedious cavils. . . . Drag him along to a public festival: his face alone will be enough to put a damper on people's gaiety. . . . If he joins a conversation, everyone suddenly 'clams up.'" Erasmus was telling Christians, in effect, to lighten up.

Erasmus also wrote dialogues. He was influenced by Lucian, a Hellenistic Greek who lived in the second century AD. Erasmus and Thomas More translated several of Lucian's dialogues into Latin. (Lucian was said to be Hume's favorite classical writer. Adam Smith reported that when Hume was on his deathbed he was reading Lucian.) It would be wrong, though, to assume that those who wrote dialogues favored religious toleration. In *Dialogue Concerning Heresies* (1529), More argues that it is lawful and beneficial to burn heretics.

Two influential Renaissance works that discuss the art of conversation and advocate a polite Christianity are Baldesar Castiglione's *The Courtier* (1528), which is in the form of a dialogue, and Giovanni Della Casa's *Galateo* (1558). Both authors pay homage to Cicero's *Of Duties,* and both imply that good conversationalists are hard to find. Della Casa sounds as if he were writing about contemporary American conversation when he says: "Most people are so infatuated with themselves that they overlook other people's pleasures; and, in order to show themselves to be subtle, intuitive, and wise, they will advise, and correct, and argue, and contradict vigorously, not agreeing with anything except their own opinions."

Della Casa offers many suggestions for improving one's conversation: do not sound like a public speaker ("In speaking, a man should avoid . . . the pomposity of a public speaker. Otherwise, he will be unpleasant and tedious to hear"); be an attentive listener ("You should pay attention to someone who is speaking so that you will not have to say, again and again: 'Eh?' or 'What?' Many people have this fault"); do not speak too much but do not be silent ("To keep quiet when others are engaged in conversation seems to show an unwillingness to pay one's share of the bill").

Castiglione's and Della Casa's books were influential not only in Italy but throughout Western Europe. In praising them two centuries later Samuel Johnson wrote: "*To regulate the practice of daily conversation*, to correct those depravities which are rather ridiculous than criminal, and remove those grievances which, if they produce no lasting calamities, impress hourly vexation, was first attempted by Casa in his book of *Manners*, and Castiglione in his *Courtier;* two books yet celebrated in Italy for purity and elegance, and which, if they are now less read, are neglected only because they have effected that reformation which their authors intended, and their precepts now are no longer wanted. Their usefulness to the age in which they were written, is sufficiently attested by the translations which almost all the nations of Europe were in haste to obtain" (emphasis mine).

Though Castiglione was writing mainly for courtiers, Johnson thought many of the recommendations Castiglione made were useful for anyone interested in conversation. He told Boswell that the *Courtier* was "the best book that ever was written upon good breeding"—by good breeding he means politeness—and he urged Boswell to read it.

Johnson also advocated polite Christianity. A polite Christian, he said, should avoid enthusiasm, which he defines as "a vain belief of private revelation; a vain confidence of divine favour or communication." All the eighteenth-century writers on conversation, regardless of their religious beliefs, had a negative view of enthusiasm. Enthusiasts, Addison says, are terrible conversationalists because they frequently quote from Scripture and arrogantly assume that they alone know how to interpret the word of God. "An Enthusiast in Religion," he says, "is like an obstinate Clown."

Both Johnson, a devout Anglican, and Hume, a religious skeptic, argue that enthusiasm is a destructive political force. They often use the words *enthusiasm* and *fanaticism* interchangeably. Deploring the devastation wrought by Presbyterian zealots in seventeenth-century Scotland, Johnson says: "the change of religion in Scotland . . . raised an epidemical enthusiasm, composed of sullen scrupulousness and warlike ferocity." Writing about Scotland at the time of Mary Queen of Scots, Hume says that the people were "unacquainted with the pleasures of conversation, ignorant of arts and civility, and corrupted beyond their usual rusticity, by a dismal fanaticism, which rendered them incapable of all humanity or improvement."

In *History of England* Hume talks about the terrible effect that Puritan enthusiasm had on conversation. On the eve of English civil war, he says, "All orders of men had drunk deep of the intoxicating poison [of religious enthusiasm]. In every discourse or conversation, this mode of religion entered; in all business, it had a share; every elegant pleasure or amusement, it utterly annihilated; many vices or corruptions of mind, it promoted. . . . Learning itself, which tends so much to enlarge the mind, and humanize the temper, rather served on this occasion to exalt that epidemical frenzy which prevailed." He adds that "noise and fury, cant and hypocrisy, formed the sole rhetoric, which, during this tumult of various prejudices and passions, could be heard or attended to." Johnson agreed with Hume's characterization of Puritan conversation. "Enthusiasts of all kinds," Johnson says, "have been inclined to disguise their particular tenets with pompous appellations, and to imagine themselves the great instruments of salvation."

According to Hume, in the long run Puritan enthusiasm had the unintended effect of promoting liberty and toleration, but in the short run it destroyed conversation. Speaking of the "parliamentary party" (the Puritans or Roundheads), Hume says: "Gaiety and wit were proscribed: Human learning despised: Freedom of enquiry detested: Cant and hypocrisy alone encouraged." Describing Cromwell's "elocution," Hume says it was "always confused, embarrassed, and unintelligible"; it had "no glimmering of common sense or reason."

Hume praises the conversation of Charles I and Charles II. Though he is somewhat critical of Charles I, he says his conversation was that of a reasonable man. "The good sense, which he [Charles] displayed in his discourse and conversation, *seemed* to warrant his success in every reasonable undertaking." Hume is also somewhat critical of Charles II, but he says that "the easiest manners, the most unaffected politeness, the most engaging gaiety accompanied his conversation and address." Hume pays him a very strong compliment—saying that Charles II "improved the politeness of the nation." For Hume, the more polite a nation is, the more politically stable it is likely to be.

Hume and Johnson agreed that religious enthusiasts were enemies of conversation, but they disagreed on the extent to which eighteenth-century Britain was plagued by enthusiasm. Johnson thought it was a minor problem, while Hume thought it was potentially a major problem, since he believed that most Christians were zealots. Writing to Adam Smith, Hume describes a dinner party at which he made a weak joke about wanting to become a bishop. His joke angered a real bishop who was present. "The Right Reverend without any further Provocation, burst out into the most furious, and indecent, and orthodox Rage, that ever was seen." Hume was not surprised "because I had on other Occasions observed the most orthodox Zeal swell within him, and it was often difficult for him to converse with Temper [meaning converse without getting angry] when I was present."

Hume, though, had many Christian friends. One was Hugh Blair, the leading Scottish clergyman. Hume enjoyed his conversations with Blair—except when the topic was religion. Hume writes Blair that he likes talking about many subjects, "but when the conversation was diverted by you from this channel towards the subject of your profession . . . I own I never received the same satisfaction. . . . I would therefore wish for the future . . . that these topics should be forborne between us."

The British writer who is closest to Hume on the question of Christianity and conversation is the Earl of Shaftesbury—nominally an Anglican but closer to deism than to orthodox Christianity. In *Characteristics of Men, Manners, Opinions, Times* (1711), Shaftesbury says that zealotry is the main threat to conversation as well as to political stability. Speaking of zealots, he says: "To them, freedom of mind, a mastery of sense and a liberty in thought and action imply debauch, corruption and depravity." All zealots, Shaftesbury says, are intolerant, and if they become a significant force liberty will suffer.

Shaftesbury, like Hume, often implies that being devout is the equivalent of being a zealot. He often uses the two words in the same sentence. He speaks of the "devout and zealous reader," and he refers to "a certain narrowness of spirit, which . . . is peculiarly observable in the devout persons and zealots of almost every religious persuasion." Addison, Swift, Fielding, and Johnson would disagree that there is a correlation between devoutness and zealotry.

All the British writers on conversation were also opposed to superstition, which refers to a religion that relies heavily on rites and ceremonies. Johnson's second definition of superstition is "observance of unnecessary and uncommanded rites or practices." Superstition usually was a code word for Catholicism, and many Britons associated superstition with despotism and servile politeness. According to Addison, "a Superstitious Man [is] like an insipid Courtier."

Addison implies that the Reformation not only reformed Christianity, it also led to reforms in conversation. "Conversation, like the *Romish* Religion, was so encumbered with Show and Ceremony, that it stood in need of a Reformation to retrench its Superfluities, and restore it to its natural good sense and Beauty." Hume, however, thought many Britons exaggerated the negative effect that Catholicism had on conversation.

What would Addison, Johnson, and Hume say about Christianity and conversation in contemporary America? Hume, of course, would disapprove of any attempt to promote Christianity; he wished Christian belief would fade away. Addison and Johnson thought Christian belief generally helped people control their antisocial passions, so they would probably approve of Bible study sessions and probably would support faith-based initiatives. But they would disapprove of enthusiastic Christians who quoted Scripture continually. Johnson disliked religious people who were guided by the notion of an "inward light." He told an acquaintance that "if a man . . . pretends to a principle of actions of which I can know nothing . . . how can I tell what that person may be prompted to do?" Addison and Johnson would certainly condemn those who pore over obscure phrases in the book of Revelation in the hope of divining the future.

Several years ago the wife of a friend of mine became a religious enthusiast. According to her husband, who is irreligious, she started mentioning God all the time and began watching television evangelists for several hours a day. On weekends she often went to Christian retreats with other women. Before becoming infected with enthusiasm, she visited us and we enjoyed her company. After she became an enthusiast she no longer visited us even though her husband remains a close friend. Perhaps she now wants to associate only with churchgoing Christians. Perhaps there are other reasons. But it is clear that after she became an enthusiast she dropped out of the conversible world.

Commerce and Conversation

What does commerce have to do with conversation? According to Hume and Johnson, there is a correlation between the extent of a society's commerce and the size of its conversible world. In the *History of England* Hume contrasts rude (or unrefined or unpolished) societies with refined societies. By the former he means predominantly agricultural societies where there are few cities and the level of literacy is low. Hume's *History* is in large part the story of how the expansion of commerce—or what he calls the growth of luxury—transformed England from a rude society into a polished society, one where conversation flourishes. Luxury roughly means commercial activity that goes beyond meeting basic needs.

Hume generally thought history was the story of progress. Roughly a decade before he began writing the *History* he wrote: "In reality, what more agreeable entertainment to the mind than . . . to see the policy of government and the civility of conversation refining by degrees." But Hume never suggests that progress is inevitable. Given "that inconstancy, to which all human affairs are subject," there will always be setbacks to progress. He describes mid-seventeenth-century England in the following way: "No people could undergo a change more sudden and entire in their manners than did the English nation during this period. From tranquility, concord, submission, sobriety, they passed in an instant to a state of faction, fanaticism, rebellion, and almost frenzy."

Yet if Hume acknowledges that there are setbacks to progress, he implies that Britain has progressed from a rude society to a polished society. The people in Anglo-Saxon England "were in general . . . rude, uncultivated . . . ignorant of letters, unskilled in the mechanical arts, untamed to submission under law and government, [and] addicted to intemperance, riot, and disorder." In the Middle Ages England remained a rude society marked by continual disorder. During Henry II's reign the cities, which are "always the first seat of law and liberty," were neither "numerous nor populous." Summing up medieval England, he says: "The languishing state of commerce kept the inhabitants poor and contemptible. . . . Every profession was held in contempt but that of arms."

England changed, owing to the growth of luxury. In sixteenth-century England the nobility "acquired by degrees a more civilized species of emulation, and endeavoured to excel in the splendour and elegance of their equipage, houses, and tables." As a result "the common people, [who were] no longer maintained in vicious idleness by their superiors, were obliged to learn some calling or industry." The growth of luxury made the nobles less warlike and the common people less idle.

In "Of refinement in the Arts," which was originally called "On Luxury," Hume argues that the growth of luxury also promotes sociability. "The more these refined arts advance, the

more sociable men become; nor is it possible, that, when en-
riched with science, and possessed of a fund of conversation,
they should be contented to remain in solitude, or live with their
fellow-citizens in that distant manner, which is peculiar to ignorant and barbarous nations." In refined ages people "flock into
cities." As a result, "particular clubs and societies are every where
formed. Both sexes meet in an easy and sociable manner; and
the tempers of men, as well as their behaviour, refine apace."

Hume stresses the positive effect of increased conversation. "So that, beside the improvements which they [men and
women] receive from knowledge and the liberal arts, it is impossible but they must feel an increase of humanity, *from the
very habit of conversing together* and contributing to each other's
pleasure and entertainment" (emphasis mine). An expanded
conversible world increases the stock of benevolent passions in
a country and thus reduces the likelihood of violent political
discord. Writing about seventeenth-century Dutch burghers,
the historian Simon Schama similarly points out that burghers
led lives of Christian civility. The burgher was "indifferent or
hostile" to the feudal preoccupations of war, land, and honor.

Many Britons, including Swift and Shaftesbury, disagreed with Hume's positive view of luxury. Many thought
luxury bred moral decay. Hume thought the critics of luxury
had an idealized view of the past. "To declaim against present
times, and magnify the virtue of remote ancestors, is a propensity almost inherent in human nature. And as the sentiments
and opinions of civilized ages alone are transmitted to poster-
ity, hence it is that we meet with so many severe judgments
pronounced against luxury."

Johnson's view of luxury—including its effect on conversation—is the same as Hume's. In *Journey to the Western Islands* (1775), which is Johnson's account of the trip he made to

Scotland with Boswell in 1773, Johnson speaks of "primitive" societies. A primitive society, he says, is conversationally underdeveloped as well as economically underdeveloped. In the Scottish Highlands there is talk, but not much conversation. "The Highlander gives to every question an answer so prompt and peremptory, that skepticism itself is scared into silence." In primitive societies people tell tall tales and expect their listeners not to question them. "The traditions of an ignorant and savage people have been for ages negligently heard and unskillfully related." Owing to "the laxity of Highland conversation . . . the inquirer . . . knows less as he hears more."

Because people in primitive societies spend more time in solitude than people in refined societies, they are more likely to brood about things and therefore are more likely to be infected with religious fanaticism. In primitive societies people have a limited circle of acquaintances. They converse "only with each other," so if they are infected with fanaticism there is no "gradual influx of new opinions" to dilute their zealotry.

According to Johnson, in the Highlands—as in all primitive societies—the talk is limited in scope. The tall tales one hears are often about either the brave deeds of one's forefathers or the evil deeds of outsiders. "Thus every Highlander can talk of his ancestors, and recount the outrages which they suffered from the wicked inhabitants of the next valley. Such are the effects of habitation among mountains, and such were the qualities of the Highlanders, while their rocks secluded them from the rest of mankind." The endless talk about grievances promotes violence, not benevolence.

Johnson gives another reason for the Highlanders' "laxity of conversation." There is a correlation between literacy and conversation. The Highlanders are "an illiterate people whose whole time is a series of distress; where every morning is labouring with expedients for the evening; and where all mental pains or pleasure arose from the dread of winter, the expectation of spring, the caprices of their Chiefs, and the motions of the neighbouring clans, where there was neither shame from ignorance, nor pride in knowledge; neither curiosity to inquire, nor vanity to communicate."

Johnson did not think that everyone who lived in the Highlands or the Western Islands of Scotland lacked the art of conversation. He made a detour to visit Lord Monboddo, a distinguished Scottish jurist and philosopher, because of "the magnetism of his conversation." When Johnson went to the island of Inch Kenneth, he was surprised by the conversation of its chief inhabitants: Sir Allan Maclean and his two daughters. "Romance does not often exhibit a scene that strikes the imagination more than this little desert in the depths of western obscurity, occupied not by a gross herdsman, or amphibious fisherman, but by a gentleman and two ladies, of high birth, polished manners, and elegant conversation."

The Macleans are the exception. Johnson commends the conversation of very few people he met in the Highlands or the Western Islands. The best he can say about the conversation of the Islanders, which he appears to rate more highly than that of the Highlanders, is that it is "decent and inoffensive." In Edinburgh and Glasgow, which are not primitive societies, Johnson implies that conversation is flourishing. In Edinburgh he "passed some days with men of learning . . . [and] women of elegance."

In Johnson's view the growth of luxury improves conversation in three ways. First, it reduces the unsociable passion of religious fanaticism. In the Western Islands, he says, "the ancient rigour of puritanism is now very much relaxed, though all are not yet equally enlightened." Secondly, it increases the number of people who have time to read and converse. "Without intelligence," he says, "man is not social, he is only gregarious; and little intelligence will there be, where all are constrained to daily labour, and every mind must wait upon the hand." Finally, it brings more people together, so that there are more opportunities for conversation. The Highlanders, he says, are "now losing their distinction [distinctiveness] and hastening to mingle with the general community."

Hume disliked Johnson's book. According to Boswell, "he spoke of Mr. Johnson's *Journey* in terms so slighting that it could have no effect but to show his resentment." Yet what Hume says about the Highlanders in the *History* is roughly the same as what Johnson says about the Highlanders in the *Journey*. "The highlanders," Hume says, "were the people the most disorderly and the least civilized." Though Hume and Johnson held each other in low regard—Hume thought Johnson was a religious zealot—both argued that the expansion of commerce promoted moderate passions, as well as an interest in the pleasures of conversation.

Women and Conversation

Should women belong to the conversible world? Addison, Swift, Hume, and Johnson thought they should, even though they belonged to clubs that did not allow women to become members. Shaftesbury disagreed. He thought the presence of women made it more likely that men would be "effeminate" in their thinking—that is, deficient in logic and boldness. "It is no compliment to them [women] to affect their manners and be effeminate. Our sense, language, and style, as well as our voice and person, should have something of that male feature and natural roughness by which our sex is distinguished." Shaftesbury says the modern practice of letting women participate in polite conversation is a mistake. "Our modern conversations . . . lose those masculine helps of learning and sound reason." His point is that men will not think logically or boldly if women are present.

Swift, as we have seen, thought the presence of women improved conversation, and he also thought women were capable of holding their own in conversation with men. Swift agrees with a speaker in Castiglione's *Courtier,* who says: "I say that everything men can understand, women can too; and where a man's intellect can penetrate, so along with it can a woman's." The speaker also says: "If you study ancient and modern history . . . you will find that women as well as men have constantly given proof of their worth, and also that there have been some women who have waged wars and won glorious victories, governed kingdoms with the greatest prudence and justice, and done all that men have done. As for learning, cannot you recall reading of many women who knew philosophy, of others who have been consummate poets?" Another speaker strongly disagrees with him, but the speaker who defends the intellect and abilities of women gets the better of the argument. In any case, women are included in the world of the *Courtier.* They participate in the conversation, though men dominate it.

Johnson agreed with Swift that, in conversation, women could hold their own with men. Among his friends were several women writers, including Elizabeth Carter, a classical scholar and translator—she knew at least seven languages—who contributed several essays to Johnson's periodical the *Rambler.* In 1739 Johnson urged her to translate Boethius's *Consolation of Philosophy* (Boethius was a late Roman Christian thinker), but she declined because she thought the work was not likely to find an audience. Johnson remained friends with Carter for the rest of his life.

In May 1784, six months before Johnson died, he told Boswell that the previous day he had dined with Carter and two other women writers he admired: Fanny Burney and the essayist Hannah More. Johnson also admired the literary critic Elizabeth Montagu, even though their relations were occasionally stormy, owing to differences of opinion about several contemporary writers. "Mrs. Montagu," he told Boswell, "is a very extraordinary woman; she has a constant stream of conversation, and it is always impregnated; it has always meaning." Mrs. Montagu, he told Hester Thrale, "diffuses more knowledge in her conversation than any woman I know, or, indeed, almost any man."

In several essays Johnson attacks the prevailing view that men and women should be educated differently. He thought it was scandalous that women were mainly taught to learn domestic skills. In his *Life of Milton* he criticizes Milton for his "Turkish contempt of females as subordinate and inferior beings," as shown in the "mean and penurious education" Milton gave his daughters.

Hume also thought women should belong to the conversible world. Though Hume praises classical civilization for its religious tolerance, he criticizes the ancient Greeks for excluding women from conversation. "Among the ancients, the character of the fair-sex was considered as altogether domestic; nor were they regarded as part of the polite world or of good company." As a result, "the arts of conversation were not brought so near to perfection among them [the ancient republics] as the arts of writing and composition."

(Hume's generalization about the position of women in ancient Greece needs to be qualified. Though Athenian women generally were not given an education, Spartan women usually were. Many could read and write, and many participated in athletic events. Spartan women, Cartledge says, "ran races . . . threw the javelin and discus, wrestled . . . and performed gymnastics, all completely naked and in full public view, to the consternation of Greek visitors from other cities." Spartan women did not have to do housework because that was the job of Helot women and men. Aristotle thought Spartan women had far too much power. In the *Politics* he says the men of Sparta are "ruled by their women," but most historians think Aristotle exaggerates their power. The main function of Spartan women was producing healthy male offspring, for the Spartans continually worried about their military manpower.)

Hume argues that the presence of women stimulates gallantry, which promotes good manners, thereby making conversation more pleasurable. Hume does not think gallantry makes conversation trivial. Gallantry, he says, "is not less consistent with *wisdom* and *prudence*, than with *nature* and *generosity*." What kind of conversation is likely if women are not present? Hume offers a bleak picture: "Mixt companies [men from different stations and professions] without the fair-sex, are the most insipid entertainment in the world, and destitute of gaiety and politeness, as much as of sense and reason. Nothing can keep them from excessive dullness but hard drinking; a remedy worse than the disease."

Conversation flourishes in Catholic France, Hume argues, for two reasons: women and men converse together, and the monarchy promotes politeness. "Politeness of manners . . . arises most naturally in monarchies and courts." Hume realizes that there is no equality in court circles, so an honest conversation is unlikely, but he thinks the inclination to please one's superiors leads to an inclination to please others in general. "Among the arts of conversation, no one pleases more than mutual deference or civility, which leads us to resign our own inclinations to those of our companion, and to curb and conceal that presumption and arrogance, so natural to the human mind." Hume, like Addison and Johnson, frequently argues that it is not natural to be polite. "Thus, as we are commonly proud and selfish, and apt to assume the preference above others, a polite man learns to behave with deference towards his companions, and to yield the superiority to them in all the common incidents of society."

Conversation in France, Hume says, is better than it is in Britain. "In common life, they [the French] have, in a great measure, perfected that art, the most useful and agreeable of any, *L'Art de Vivre,* the art of society and conversation." In the short autobiography he wrote in the final months of his life, Hume praises Paris as the city where he would most prefer to live. "There is . . . a real satisfaction in living at Paris from the great Number of sensible, knowing, and polite Company with which the City abounds above all places in the universe." In the autobiography, and in many letters, Hume implies that the English are not as polite as the French because so many Englishmen are religious zealots.

Hume also liked Paris because learned Frenchmen spent a great deal of time in the conversible world. (Hume thought too many learned Englishmen—though not learned Scotsmen—avoided the conversible world.) The separation of the learned world from the conversible world, Hume says, has a negative effect on both worlds, but it is especially bad for the learned world. Hume acknowledges that scholars and thinkers require periods of solitude, but he thinks the learned need to discuss their ideas in the conversible world. Learning, he says, "has been as great a Loser by being shut up in Colleges and

Cells, and secluded from the World and good Company." As a result, "*Belles Lettres* became totally barbarous, being cultivated by Men without any Taste of Life or Manners, and without that Liberty and Facility of Thought and Expression, *which can only be acquir'd by Conversation*" (emphasis mine). The separation of the two worlds, Hume says, has been bad for philosophy. "Philosophy went to Wrack by this moping recluse Method of Study, and became as chimerical in her Conclusions as she was unintelligible in her Stile and Manner of Delivery."

Hume thought women should play the dominant role in the conversible world. Women, he says, "are the Sovereigns of the Empire of Conversation." He also says they are "much better Judges of all polite Writing than Men of the same Degree of Understanding." Attacking "the common Ridicule that is level'd against Learned Ladies," he argues that "all Men of Sense, who know the World, have a great Deference for their Judgment of such books as ly [*sic*] within the Compass of their Knowledge, and repose more Confidence in the Delicacy of their Taste, tho' unguided by Rules, than in all the dull Labours of Pedants and Commentators."

Hume does not explain why he thinks women are better judges of polite writing than men. He does argue that women play—or should play—a central role in the formation of knowledge, but he does not clarify what this role is. He also seems to be saying that women belong only to the conversible world, yet he notes that "in a neighbouring Nation [France] . . . the Ladies are, in a Manner, the Sovereigns of the *learned* World, as well as of the *conversible;* and no polite writer pretends to venture upon the Public, without the Approbation of some celebrated Judges of that Sex." What does he mean when he says women are "sovereigns of the learned world"?

If Hume's view of the role of women in the production of knowledge is unclear, it is clear that he thinks women are intellectual underachievers. They read too many bad books, especially "Books of Gallantry and Devotion." He wishes they would read "Mr. Addison's elegant Discourses of Religion" rather than "Books of mystic Devotion." Women, he says, should "accustom themselves to Books of all Kinds." In "Of the Study of History" he says women should read more works of history. "I must think it an unpardonable ignorance in persons of whatever sex or condition, not to be acquainted with the history of their own country, together with the histories of ancient Greece and Rome. A woman may behave herself with good manners, and have even some vivacity in her turn of wit; but where her mind is so unfurnished, 'tis impossible her conversation can afford any entertainment to men of sense and reflection."

Hume seems to be of two minds when it comes to the question of women's intelligence. In "Of Essay Writing" he implies that women's intelligence is different from men's, but he does not say it is inferior. In "Of the rise and progress of the arts and sciences," which appeared in the same year, he says: "Nature has given *man* the superiority above *woman* by endowing him with greater strength both of mind and body." Hume thinks authority should reside with men, but women should be treated with respect. "But the male sex, among a polite people, discover their authority in a more generous, though not a less evident manner; by civility, by respect, by complaisance."

Whatever we make of Hume's view of women's intelligence, he always argues that polite conversation is successful only when it includes women. In praising Paris Hume undoubtedly was thinking of the many hours of pleasurable conversation he had in Parisian salons when he lived there in the mid-1760s. Salons, which were private social gatherings, could be found in many European cities, but the salons of Paris were the most famous. They attracted France's greatest writers and thinkers, including Montesquieu, Voltaire, and Diderot. Brilliant foreigners were also invited, including Hume, Gibbon, and Adam Smith.

The main activity of the salons, which were presided over by women—who were called *salonnières*—was conversation, though occasionally guests played cards or other games, listened to music, and even danced. According to Dena Goodman, most eighteenth-century salons took the form of weekly dinners (some met more frequently) that would last all afternoon, but "discourse, not dining, was their defining function."

Benjamin Franklin attended the salon of Helvétius's widow (outside of Paris, in Auteuil), to whom he wrote: "I see that statesmen, philosophers, historians, poets, and men of learning of all sort are drawn around you, and seem as willing to attach themselves to [you] as straws about a fine piece of amber." Franklin proposed marriage to her, but she declined. Hume, as far as we know, did not propose marriage to a *salonnière*, but he was on close terms with several leading *salonnières*. They include Madame Geoffrin, about whom he said, "There are few heads naturally better than hers"; Mademoiselle de Lespinasse, who "is really one of the most sensible Women in Paris"; and the Comtesse de Boufflers, with whom he maintained a correspondence for the rest of his life. Hume also enjoyed "symposia"—lavish evening dinner parties—at the house of the Baron d'Holbach. He met the leading philosophes at Holbach's house and at the salons. "Those whose Persons & Conversation I like best," Hume says, "are d'Alembert, Buffon, Marmontel, Diderot, Duclos, [and] Helvétius."

By 1760 the salons of Paris were a venerable institution
that had been in existence for more than a century. The first
salon was started early in the 1610s by Madame de Rambouil-
let. (At roughly the same time a prosperous merchant founded
a salon in Amsterdam; it was presided over by his two daughters.) Seventeenth-century salon culture reached its high point
in the 1660s, when the salon of Madame de Sablé flourished.
Attending her salon were some of the greatest writers of the
period, including Madame de Sévigné, a brilliant letter writer;
Madame de La Fayette, the author of *The Princess of Clèves*
(1678), which has been called the first great French novel; and
the Duc de La Rochefoucauld, the author of the celebrated
Maximes, which many admired for their elegance and psychological penetration. (Both Swift and Johnson praised La
Rochefoucauld.) At Madame de Sablé's salon La Rochefoucauld's aphorisms were refined and polished. He would read
them aloud, and members of the salon would offer advice and
criticism.

In a self-portrait La Rochefoucauld indirectly praises
salon culture when he says that he prefers the conversation of
women to men. "When they are intelligent I prefer their conversation to men's, for there is a kind of smooth ease about it
that is not found in us men, and moreover it seems to me that
they express themselves more clearly and give a more graceful
turn to what they say." La Rochefoucauld also says how much
he enjoys conversation. "The conversation of well-bred people
is one of the pleasures I enjoy most keenly. I like talk to be serious and mainly concerned with moral questions, but I can
enjoy it when it is amusing."

What did people talk about at the salons? In the seventeenth-century salons the talk was mainly about the passions
that drive humankind, perhaps because Descartes had written

an influential study, *Traité des passions de l'âme* (1649). Religion and politics generally were avoided, especially the latter because some attendees could be informers for Louis XIV. W. G. Moore says they did not talk about business, military affairs, political questions, or religious doctrine because they were dangerous topics, nor did they discuss other subjects that would be of interest to just a few of the participants. Literature and, especially, language were often topics of conversation. In two plays, *Les Précieuses ridicules* (1659) and *Les Femmes savantes (1672)*, Molière makes fun of the salon world's interest in language.

In both the mid-seventeenth-century and the mid-eighteenth-century salons there was a good deal of light conversation—what La Rochefoucauld calls *conversation galante*. Friedrich Grimm, the German man of letters, says with tongue-in-cheek exaggeration that "*Mother* Geoffrin could so manage things that the conversation in her *salon* never touched upon domestic news or foreign news; news of the Court or news of the city; news of the North or news of the South; news of the East and the West; topics of politics or of finance; of peace or of war; of religion or of government; of theology or of metaphysics; of grammar or of music, or, in general, any topic whatsoever." Gibbon also thought Geoffrin controlled the conversation too much; he spoke of her "capricious tyranny."

The salons of Paris could hardly have attracted the leading thinkers and writers of Britain and France if the conversation had mostly been about trivial topics. The entry for *conversation* in the famous *Encyclopedia* says: "The laws of conversation generally discourage leaning too heavily on any subject; it should flow lightly, effortlessly, and without affectation from one subject to another; it should be possible to speak of the frivolous and the serious."

Suzanne Necker, a *salonnière*, implies that salon conversation is a serious business (not a solemn business) that requires intellectual preparation. "One is most ready for conversation when one has written and thought about things before going into society." At Lespinasse's salon, Grimm says, "nothing was excluded from the conversation." Politics, religion, philosophy, the latest news—all were discussed.

Lespinasse was an extraordinary woman. An illegitimate child, she was raised in a convent. Working as a governess, she was befriended by Madame du Deffand, who was a leading *salonnière*. She quarreled with Deffand and began her own salon, which Hume and Adam Smith attended. (Lespinasse could speak English, Italian, and Spanish, and she was well-versed in philosophy, literature, and science.) According to Jean-François Marmontel, "Nowhere was conversation more lively, more brilliant, or better regulated than at her house." After she died at age forty-four, Suzanne Necker wrote to Grimm: "The movement that she gave to her society has slowed down greatly. . . . Everyone in these assemblies is [now] convinced that women fill the intervals of conversation and of life like the padding that one inserts in cases of china; they are valued at nothing, and [yet] everything breaks without them."

Writing in 1814, Madame de Staël argues that "the development of ideas [in France] has, for a century, been entirely directed by conversation." Since the Parisian salons played a major role in French literature and thought, were they a breeding ground for revolutionary ideas? Describing the salon of Lespinasse, the authors of *Salons: The Joy of Conversation* say: "People came to her small apartments to gossip, to challenge, and to be inspired. They left fired up with hope for revolution." This view of salon culture is wrong. Those who attended the salons were not interested in radical change. William Doyle, a leading historian of the period, says that "hardly anybody, and certainly not the philosophes, dreamed of revolution, or would even have understood the idea." Though the writers who attended the Parisian salons were critics of French society, most hoped France would evolve into a constitutional monarchy.

The patron saint of the French Revolution was Rousseau—a man who hated salon culture. Rousseau thought it was unnatural for men to be under the dominance of women. Speaking of the Parisian salons, he says: "Every woman in Paris gathers in her apartment a harem of men more womanish than she." Rousseau sneers at his former Parisian friends. "What can be the temper of the soul of a man who is uniquely occupied with the important business of amusing women, and spends his entire life doing for them what they ought to do for us?" He thought the men who frequented the salons were emasculated, decadent, and hypocritical.

There were other critics of salon culture. Traditional religious thinkers attacked them. So did Horace Walpole, the English man of letters. He thought salon conversation was overrated: "The style of conversation [in the salons of Paris] is solemn, pedantic, and seldom animated, but by a dispute." But Walpole took a dim view of all the leading writers of the age, including Rousseau, Voltaire, Diderot, Hume, and Johnson. The English essayist William Hazlitt, who was greatly interested in the art of conversation (see Chapter Six), rightly said that "Walpole never speaks with respect of any man of genius or talent. . . . He envied all great minds; and shrunk from encountering them, lest his own should suffer by the comparison."

In the decade before the French Revolution salon culture waned. The men who joined the new clubs and societies—men who wanted radical change—were more influenced by Rousseau than by Hume or Diderot. They decided that women should not have a large role in intellectual life—or any role whatsoever. According to Goodman, "They denied the need for women as a civilizing force."

Fueled by secular enthusiasm and paranoia, the Jacobins, who came to power during the Revolution, had nothing in common with the world of salon culture. Robespierre revered Rousseau. As Jean Starobinski says: "Like Rousseau, he [Robespierre] used eloquence in two ways: to accuse others and to promulgate his own views. He accused his enemies of creating factions and being self-interested while the moral goals he proclaimed were always of the loftiest kind." The humorless Robespierre was not interested in the pleasures of conversation. For him and for most Jacobins, disagreement was a sign of treason. Instead of conversation, the Jacobins preferred patriotic speeches and fervent denunciations.

The paranoid Rousseau wrongly thought the salon world wanted to destroy his reputation, but he was right to say that salon culture was a coterie. It was a coterie of men and women of intelligence and learning who took the art of conversation seriously. According to Deffand, Gibbon at first cut a poor figure in the salon he attended because he tried so hard to speak in polished sentences. Apparently he improved because she later said that Gibbon is "a very sensible man, who has much conversation [and] infinite knowledge."

Salon culture was not based on class; it was a meritocracy. Madame Geoffrin would not let her husband participate in the salon because she thought he was not up to the mark. According to Grimm, Monsieur Geoffrin "was permitted to sit down to dinner, at the end of the table, upon condition that he never attempted to join in conversation."

It was not easy to get an invitation to a salon. Hume told his friend Hugh Blair that it was "impracticable" for him (Hume) to try to wangle for a fellow Scotsman an invitation to the salon Hume attended. It is a "ridiculous Idea," Hume says, to assume that he could introduce the Scotsman "to the good Company of Paris." He could not "present such a man, silent, grave, awkward, speaking ill the Language, not distinguished by any Exploit or Science or Art. ... No people are more scrupulous of receiving Persons unknown." Hume would advise the Scotsman that "as soon as he has seen Paris, to go to a Provincial Town, where People are less shy of admitting new Acquaintance, and are less delicate Judges of behaviour."

If the awkward Scotsman wanted to participate in a conversation, he would have been better off in London. All he need do was enter a coffeehouse—as Boswell did when he first came to London in 1763. According to most Continental visitors, London was a city where conversation flourished in coffeehouses and clubs (and in other venues as well), especially during the first half of the eighteenth century.

IV

The Age of Conversation: Eighteenth-Century Britain

The importance of conversation to eighteenth-century Britons—I speak of Britons because England and Scotland were united in the Act of Union in 1707—can be gauged by Defoe's travel book, *A Tour Through the Whole Island of Great Britain* (1724–26). Defoe rates the conversation of many of the towns and cities he visited. He says of Lime: "While we stayed here some time viewing this town and coast, we had opportunity to observe the pleasant way of conversation, as it is managed among the gentlemen of this county, and their families, which are without reflection some of the most polite and well bred people in the isle of Britain." He also thinks highly of the conversation in Lichfield (Johnson's birthplace): it is "a place of good conversation and good company, above all the towns in this county or the next."

Defoe accords the highest praise to Greenwich. It possesses "the best air, best prospect, and the best conversation in England." If Defoe has a low opinion of a town's conversation, he usually says nothing, though—like Johnson and Hume—he criticizes the conversation of the people who live in the

Western Highlands of Scotland, saying they are "desperate in fight, cruel in victory, fierce even in conversation."

Defoe's interest in conversation was not unusual. Fielding calls conversation "this grand Business of our Lives, the Foundation of every Thing, either useful or pleasant." In Frances Burney's novel *Evelina* (1778), the first thing the heroine says of Lord Orville, the man she will eventually marry, is: "His conversation was sensible and spirited." Boswell was preoccupied with the quality of his own conversation. Summing up his own life when he was forty years old, he says: "I have a variety of knowledge and excellent talents for conversation." Boswell also hoped to achieve literary fame by recording the conversation of the great men whom he sought out. He says in his journal: "We [Boswell and two friends] talked of the great advantage of keeping a journal so as to preserve conversations in which knowledge and wit and anecdote occur."

During the first half of the eighteenth century more than fifty works on conversation were published. One of the most popular was the French writer P. Ortigue de Vaumorière's *The Art of Pleasing in Conversation,* which appeared in four English translations between 1691 and 1736. Joshua Reynolds, whose conversation was admired by Johnson, Boswell, and Edmund Burke, copied many remarks from it when he was a young man. Boswell praised Reynolds's "equal and placid temper . . . variety of conversation . . . [and] true politeness," which makes him "so amiable in private society."

There is an odd scene in Boswell's *Life of Johnson* that suggests how highly the art of conversation was valued. "Mrs. Thrale mentioned a gentleman who had acquired a fortune of four thousand a year in trade, but was absolutely miserable, because he could not talk in company; so miserable, that he was impelled to lament his situation in the street to ****, whom he hates, and who he knows despises him. I am a most un-happy man (said he). I am invited to conversations. I go to conversations; but, alas! I have no conversation."

Johnson thought the man was being too hard on himself. "Man commonly cannot be successful in different ways. This gentleman has spent, in getting four thousand pounds a year, the time in which he might have learnt to talk; and now he cannot talk." Because the man devoted himself to becoming a successful businessman, he lacked the time to learn the art of conversation.

Why was there such a strong interest in the art of conversation? The Puritan Revolution, Hume says in the *History of England,* led Englishmen to develop a "propensity for political conversation." The interest in political conversation probably abetted the growth of coffeehouses and clubs, though conversation in these venues was by no means confined to politics. Another reason was the growth of luxury, which expanded the conversible world. An increasing number of Britons aspired to be polite. Finally, there was the general openness of British society, which had a flourishing periodical press after the Licensing Act lapsed in 1695, though many observers, including Defoe, Swift, and Addison, worried that the press inflamed public opinion.

Whatever the reason, the interest in the art of conversation was so great that Swift made fun of it in a mock guide-book entitled *A Compleat Collection of Genteel and Ingenious Conversation, According to the Most Polite Mode and Method, Now Used at Court, and in the Best Companies of England* (1738). This work, which probably was begun in 1704, begins with a lengthy introduction written by one Simon Wagstaff, Esq. Wagstaff, who does not reflect Swift's views, is ludicrously hyperbolical. His *Compleat Collection,* he says, offers a "complete system [of conversation] to the world."

Wagstaff acknowledges that he is perfecting an art that has already advanced far in England. "I cannot but with some pride, and much pleasure congratulate with my dear country, which hath outdone all the nations of Europe in advancing the whole art of conversation to the greatest height it is capable of reaching." His "treatise" will serve as a summary of what is best about conversation in England. "And therefore being entirely convinced that the collection I now offer to the public is full and complete, I may at the same time boldly affirm, that the whole genius, humour, politeness and eloquence of England are summed up in it."

The treatise will also offer traditional proverbs and sayings, which are more interesting than the modish sayings heard in London's coffeehouses and clubs. "As for phrases invented [discovered] to cultivate conversation, I defy all the clubs and coffee houses in this town to invent a new one equal in wit, humour, smartness, or politeness, to the very worst of my set." Wagstaff recommends that his guide to conversation "be carried about as a pocket companion, by all gentlemen and ladies, when they are going to visit, or dine, or drink tea . . . to prepare themselves for every kind of conversation that can possibly happen."

Wagstaff's hyperbole knows no limits. In this work he has "subdued barbarism, rudeness, and rusticity . . . [and has] fixed for ever, the whole system of all true politeness and refinement in conversation." He asks: "For, who can contest it [the treatise] to be of greater consequence to the happiness of these kingdoms, than all human *knowledge* put together?" His treatise is indispensable. "Whatever person would aspire to be completely witty, smart, humorous, and polite, must by hard labour be able to retain in his memory every single sentence contained in this work, so as never to be once at a loss in applying the right answers, questions, repartees, and the like, immediately and without study or hesitation."

Wagstaff calls himself a "projector," which is a word Swift often uses to describe someone with a foolish scheme—usually with the idea of making a lot of money. Wagstaff wants to found schools that teach the art of conversation by studying his book, and he hopes to have the power of licensing them. "Neither shall I be so far wanting to myself, as not to desire a patent granted of course to all useful projectors: I mean, that I may have the sole profit of giving a license to every school to read my *grammar* [this book] for fourteen years."

Wagstaff even wants to trademark his conversation, so that his name would be mentioned every time one of his conversational gems is employed. When "lords, ladies, and gentlemen . . . are entertaining and improving each other with those polite questions, answers, repartees, replies, and rejoinders, which I have with infinite labour, and close application, during the space of thirty six years, been collecting for their service and improvement, they shall, as an instance of gratitude, on every proper occasion, quote my name, after this or the like manner: 'Madam, as our Master Wagstaff says,' 'My Lord, as our friend Wagstaff has it.'"

In creating Wagstaff Swift is making fun of the age's preoccupation with conversation, but the editors of the *Oxford Swift* rightly say that "Swift's theme [in this work] is a serious one, the importance for civilization of the supreme social art of conversation; it occupied him all his life." *Polite Conversation* also includes three silly dialogues composed of formulaic phrases. They seem as if they were written by an eighteenth-century cross between Harold Pinter and Groucho Marx.

Any discussion of conversation in eighteenth-century Britain must take into account the *Spectator*—the influential journal founded in 1711, by Joseph Addison and Richard Steele, largely to promote the art of conversation. (It ran for roughly two years; it was revived again by Addison for a short period in 1714.) According to Mr. Spectator—the persona Addison and Steele use in the journal—those "needy Persons" who don't know what to talk about "should not . . . stir out of their Chambers till they have read this Paper." Mr. Spectator promises his readers "that I will daily instil into them such sound and wholesom Sentiments, as shall have a good Effect on their Conversation for the ensuing twelve Hours."

The *Spectator* was Addison's brainchild though Steele wrote many essays for it. (Steele was the main writer for the *Tatler,* the journal that preceded the *Spectator.*) Addison hoped that a journal devoted to nonpolitical topics might help mitigate what he called "the rage of Party." Mr. Spectator says: "My Paper has not in it a single Word of News, a Reflection in Politicks, nor a Stroke of Party; . . . nor [is there] any thing that may tend to the Defamation of particular Persons, Families, or Societies."

When the *Spectator* appeared Britain had been embroiled in the War of the Spanish Succession for roughly nine years. The war, Defoe says, polarized "publick society," making political conversation very difficult. "Unhappy Nation! What End can these Things lead us to? Not a Publick Society, not a Coffee-house, not a meeting of Friends, not a Visit, but like *Jehu* to *Jezabel, who is on my side?* Who? Who is for Peace? Who is for carrying on the War?"

Addison wanted Britons to spend less time having conversations about politics. "As these Politicians of both Sides have already worked the Nation into a most unnatural Ferment, I shall be so far from endeavouring to raise it to a greater Height, that, on the contrary, it shall be the chief Tendency of my Papers to inspire my Countrymen with a mutual Good will and Benevolence." Thus the *Spectator* was Addison's prescription for Britain's political sickness—its "furious Party-Sprit, [which] when it rages in its full Violence, exerts it self in Civil War and Bloodshed."

Addison, a Whig Member of Parliament, is being disingenuous when he says that he will not take a party line. The *Spectator* does advocate Whiggish views, albeit in an understated way. Brian Cowan says Addison's goal "was to construct a social world that was amenable to the survival of Whig politics during a time in which the future of Whiggery was unclear." Yet in several essays Addison warns that it is foolish to assume that one party has the moral high ground. "A man must be excessively stupid, as well as uncharitable, who believes that there is no Virtue but on his own Side, and that there are not Men as honest as himself who may differ from him in political Principles."

In several *Spectator* essays, written mainly by Addison, Mr. Spectator describes a club where good-humored conversation occurs even though the two leading club members have opposing political views. Sir Roger de Coverley is a Tory and Sir Andrew Freeport is a Whig. Though Addison implies that Sir Roger's views are misguided, he treats him with respect. Moreover, he makes it clear that Sir Roger and Sir Andrew like each other. Addison implies that one should not demonize people who have different political views.

In promoting conversation, Addison was exhorting Britons to make a better effort to control their passions, for conversation can take place only when people are good-natured. "There is no Society or Conversation to be kept up in the World without Good-nature." According to Addison, by an effort of the will we can discipline ourselves to appear good-

natured. "Mankind have been forced to invent a kind of artifi-
cial Humanity, which is what we express by the Word Good-
Breeding ... [which is] nothing else but an Imitation and
Mimickry of Good-nature, or in other Terms, Affability, Complaisance and Easiness of Temper reduced into an Art."

If we cultivate good nature, we are also more likely to
enjoy life in general. "There is nothing ... which we ought
more to encourage in our selves and others than that Disposition of Mind which in our Language goes under the Title of
Good-Nature."

Addison also spoke of the need for cheerfulness, which is
essentially the same trait as good nature. Cheerfulness now
connotes mindless pleasantness, but in the eighteenth century it
was a more admirable and serious trait—a disposition that one
should cultivate in order to cope with life's inevitable setbacks.
Cheerfulness, Addison says, is a *"Moral* Habit of the Mind."

Addison worried that too many Britons were melancholy. "Melancholy is a kind of Demon that haunts our Island." Britons, he said, could make it more likely that they
would become cheerful by enjoying "the several Entertainments of Art ... the pleasures of Friendship, Books, Conversation, and other accidental Diversions of Life," all of which are
"Incitements to a Chearful Temper." Addison argues that cheerfulness is easier to achieve if one is religious: "The true Spirit
of Religion cheers, as well as composes, the Soul; it banishes
indeed all Levity of Behaviour ... but in exchange fills the
Mind with a perpetual Serenity, uninterrupted chearfulness,
and an habitual Inclination to please others."

Addison's notion of cheerfulness struck a chord with
many people. Writing to her future husband in August 1712,
Lady Mary Wortley Montagu praises "Cheerfulnesse," remark-
ing that "one of the Spectators is very Just, that says a Man

ought allways to be on his guard against Spleen and too severe a Philosophy." In his *Autobiography* Franklin echoes Addison when he speaks of his lifelong attempt to acquire that "Evenness of Temper, & that Chearfulness in Conversation which makes his Company still sought for, & agreeable even to his younger Acquaintance."

Did the *Spectator* succeed in lowering the political temperature in Britain? It certainly was widely read. Addison thought there were roughly twenty readers for each copy printed. Yet the political situation in Britain became even more heated in 1714, when Queen Anne was nearing death. A foreign observer said that "affairs are moving in such a manner that civil war is becoming inevitable in England." In the short run the *Spectator* did little to mitigate the rage of party. Yet it may have had a long-term impact. After Anne's death the transfer of power to a new royal family took place without violence. And though eighteenth-century Britain would suffer periodically from riots that occasionally turned violent—the worst being the Gordon Riots in 1780, when 285 persons died in London—Britain did not become embroiled in a civil war.

Johnson thought the *Spectator* was very influential. Referring to both the *Tatler* and the *Spectator* (though he is mainly talking about the *Spectator*), Johnson says that they "were published at a time when two parties, loud, restless, and violent, each with plausible declarations, and each perhaps without any distinct termination of its views, were agitating the nation; to minds heated with political contest, they supplied cooler and more inoffensive reflections." The two journals, he says, "adjusted . . . the unsettled practice of daily intercourse by propriety and politeness."

Johnson specifically praises the two journals for the effect they had on conversation. "Before the *Tatler* and *Spectator* . . .

England had no masters of common life. No writers had yet undertaken to reform either the savageness of neglect, or the impertinence of civility [that is, either rudely ignoring someone or presumptuously addressing someone]; to shew when to speak, or to be silent; how to refuse, or how to comply. We had many books to teach us our more important duties and to settle opinions in philosophy or politicks; but . . . a judge of propriety was yet wanting, *who should survey the track of daily conversation, and free it from thorns and prickles*" (emphasis mine). Johnson also notes—obviously with approval—that Addison himself said of his essays "that they had a perceptible influence upon the conversation of that time."

The *Spectator* was also widely admired on the Continent. In Milan in 1764 several Italian writers published the journal *Il Caffè*, which they modeled after the *Spectator*. Markman Ellis points out that "all over Europe, groups of young reformers clubbed together to produce progressivist 'Spectatorial' essays, designed to be read in the coffee-houses for entertainment and instruction."

Coffeehouses, "Free Conversation," and Liberty

In London the *Tatler* and the *Spectator* were popular with coffeehouse patrons, who often read the journals aloud. The poet and dramatist John Gay said that many people went to coffeehouses to read the *Tatler*, which he enjoyed. He also liked the *Spectator*, which he said was "in every ones Hand, and a constant Topick for our Morning Conversation at Tea-Tables, and Coffee houses." By "tea-table" Gay means a private conversational setting—one mainly but not exclusively for women.

The writings of Addison and Steele were an extended advertisement for coffeehouses: the *Tatler* mentions seventeen coffeehouses, the *Spectator* forty-eight. In the first issue of the *Tatler* Steele says his essays will emanate from different coffeehouses, depending on the topic being discussed. "*All accounts of* Galantry, Pleasure, *and* Entertainment, *shall be under the Article of* White's Chocolate-house; Poetry, under that of Will's Coffee house; Learning *under the Title of* Graecian; Foreign *and* Domestick News, *you will have from* St. James's Coffee house."

In the first issue of the *Spectator,* written by Addison, Mr. Spectator says he goes regularly to several coffeehouses. "Sometimes I am seen thrusting my Head into a Round of Politicians at *Will's,* and listening with great Attention to the Narratives that are made in those little Circular Audiences." He also goes to Child's as well as to St. James's, the Grecian, the Cocoa Tree, and Jonathan's. The *Spectator's* readers would know about many of these coffeehouses; Dryden had made Will's famous, and the Royal Society often met at the Grecian. Addison used to hold court at Button's. The St. James was popular with Whigs, White's with Tories.

Both Addison and Steele speak of the hours of conversation they have had at various coffeehouses. "It is very natural for a Man . . . to delight in that sort of Conversation which we find in Coffee-houses." Men go to coffeehouses to discuss foreign affairs, to engage in business, or simply to enjoy conversation. Mr. Spectator says he passes "the evening at *Will's* in attending the Discourses of several Sets of People, who relieved each other within my Hearing on the Subjects of Cards, Dice, Love, Learning and Politicks."

In the first decades of the eighteenth century many foreigners were impressed by the wide-ranging conversation they heard in English coffeehouses. A Swiss visitor said that in coffeehouses "the English discourse freely of everything." According to a French visitor, "the coffee-houses, which are very numer-

ous in London, are extremely convenient. You have all manner
of news there; you have a good Fire, which you may sit by as
long as you please; you have a Dish of Coffee; you meet your
Friends for the transaction of Business, and all for a penny, if
you don't care to spend more."

The mingling of different classes in coffeehouses also impressed many visitors. "What a lesson," the Abbé Prévost said,
"to see a lord, or two, a baronet, a shoemaker, a tailor, a wine-
merchant, and a few others of the same stamp poring over the
same newspapers. Truly the coffee houses . . . are the seats of
English liberty."

Britons, especially Londoners, praised coffeehouses for
similar reasons. A Londoner wrote that coffeehouses "particularly are very commodious for a *free Conversation,* and for
reading at an easie Rate all manner of printed News, the Votes
of Parliament when sitting, and other Prints [newspapers] that
come out weekly." By "free conversation" he means a conversation that is open to anyone who enters the coffeehouse.

Londoners praised the coffeehouse for being an island of
equality in a sea of class. A broadside for a London coffeehouse, written in 1674, announced:

> Enter sirs freely, But first if you please,
> Peruse our Civil-Orders, which are these.
> First, Gentry, Tradesmen, all are welcome hither,
> And may without Affront sit down Together:
> Pre-eminence of Place, none here should Mind,
> But take the next fit Seat that he can find.

Samuel Butler, the author of the satirical poem *Hudibras* (1663–
78), said that a coffeehouse was a place "where people of all
qualities and conditions meet to trade in foreign drinks and

newes, ale, smoak, and controversy. He (the coffee-man) admits of no distinction of persons." In the early days coffeehouses consisted of one long table, but in later years there were cubicles and booths.

Coffeehouse conversation, unlike the conversation in the salons of Paris, was often about politics. Though Addison hoped that the *Spectator* would furnish nonpolitical topics of conversation for coffeehouse patrons, Mr. Spectator says that "when any Publick Affair is upon the Anvil"—has become an important question—he goes to coffeehouses to sample public opinion, since "every Coffee house has some particular Statesman belonging to it, who is the Mouth of the Street where he lives." Mr. Spectator also says he enjoys coffeehouse political debates as an intellectual exercise: "Coffee houses have ever since been my chief Places of Resort, where I have made the greatest Improvements; in order to which I have taken a particular Care never to be of the same Opinion with the Man I conversed with. I was a Tory at *Button's* and a Whig at *Childe's*. . . . In short, I wrangle and dispute for exercise." It is useful, he says, to learn how to defend an opinion you disagree with, but when you achieve mastery in conversation you should refrain from this practice.

In recent years there has been a great deal of scholarly interest in the rise of coffeehouses in Britain—spurred to some degree by Jurgen Habermas's *The Structural Transformation of the Public Sphere* (published in 1962, translated into English in 1989). Habermas associates coffeehouses with "a public sphere that . . . arose first in Great Britain at the turn of the eighteenth century." By public sphere Habermas means a public space that has no connection with the state—a space where, among other things, people from various walks of life can discuss politics without fear of arrest.

But coffeehouses were flourishing in England long before the turn of the eighteenth century. Most observers say that
the first English coffeehouse opened in Oxford in 1650, but in
The Coffee House: A Cultural History (2004) Markman Ellis plau-
sibly argues that the Oxford coffeehouse opened in 1655, and
that the first coffeehouse opened in London in 1652. (Ellis says
it was the first coffeehouse in Christendom.) By the mid-1660s
there were hundreds of coffeehouses in London. By 1707 there
may have been as many as 2,000 coffeehouses in London, though
a survey taken in 1739 lists only 551. There were also coffeehouses in many other cities in England. According to one observer (writing in 1681), they could be found in "most cities
and boroughs of the nation."

At first coffeehouses did not serve alcoholic beverages, but
in the eighteenth century many began to serve wine, brandy,
and punch as well as tea, chocolate, and a cheap beverage called
bocket (or saloop), which was a decoction of sassafras and sugar.
Coffee was for many decades far more popular than tea, probably because it was much cheaper, but by the 1710s tea gradually became more popular because the British East India Company began importing huge amounts from China and India.
Though coffeehouses served alcoholic beverages, they generally were places for conversation rather than heavy drinking.
Some coffeehouses served food. Boswell says that on two occasions he "supped" with Johnson at the Turk's Head Coffee
House. To relieve a hangover, Boswell once went to the King's
Arms Coffee House, where he ate "a basin of gravy soup, and a
basin of pease soup."

Coffee first became popular in the Near East in the middle
of the sixteenth century. A century later it was fast becoming a
popular drink throughout Europe, and by the turn of the eighteenth century there were coffeehouses in all the major Euro-

pean cities. In Britain coffee cost less than beer or ale. A pamphleteer argues that in a coffeehouse "for a penny or two you
may spend 2 or 3 hours, have the shelter of a house, the warmth
of a fire, the diversion of company and conveniency if you please
of taking a pipe of tobacco." Another pamphleteer notes that in
coffeehouses you can read newspapers for free: "He that comes
often [to the coffeehouse] saves two pence a week in Gazettes,
and thus has news and his coffee for the same charge." Johnson
defined a coffeehouse as "a house of entertainment where coffee
is sold, and the guests are supplied with newspapers."

Many people thought coffee was healthful. A broadsheet
speaks of "that Sober and wholesome Drink, called Coffee, and
its Incomparable Effects in Preventing or Curing Most Diseases
incident to Humane Bodies." Coffee, a pamphleteer writes,
"cannot but be an incomparable remedy to dissolve crudities,
comfort the brain, and dry up ill humors in the stomach."
Coffee, it was said, clears the mind; it is "a wakeful and civil
drink." By contrast, "ale, beer, or wine . . . make many unfit for
business."

Some observers—especially owners of taverns and alehouses—said coffee diminishes the sexual drive and causes im-
potence. One pamphleteer argues that "the excessive use of
that newfangled, abominable, heathenish liquor called coffee . . .
[has] so eunuched our husbands, and crippled our more kind
gallants, that they are become as impotent as age."

The attacks on coffee did not succeed. Pope, Voltaire, and
Bach—among others—disagreed with the notion that coffee
was bad for you. In the *Coffee Cantata* (1734) Bach makes fun
of those who think women should abstain from coffee because
it is unhealthful (it was thought that coffee made women
sterile). A father threatens to prevent a daughter from getting
married unless she agrees to stop drinking coffee. She prom-

ises to obey his wishes, but when he leaves she sings: "No suitor gets in my house unless he has promised me . . . that I can brew coffee whenever I wish."

In Britain a growing commercial society liked a drink that made one energetic and alert. Defoe notes that Man's Coffee House is "perpetually thronged with men of business, as the others are with men of play and pleasure." At Lloyd's Coffee House, founded in 1668, merchants and maritime insurance agents conducted business; several decades later it became Lloyd's of London. The Jerusalem Coffee House became the London Shipping Exchange; the modern stock market began in Jonathan's Coffee House. Other coffeehouses catered to lawyers, booksellers (the eighteenth-century word for publishers), writers, and singers. Some coffeehouses restricted entry to certain professions. Alice's Coffee House was open only to Lords, Members of Parliament, and barristers.

A British defender of coffeehouses says: "A well-regulated coffeehouse . . . is the sanctuary of health, the nursery of temperance, the delight of frugality, an academy of civility, and free-school of ingenuity." However, the writer admits that some coffeehouses are not "well-regulated." In 1726 a French visitor to London said: "Some coffee houses are a resort for . . . scholars and for wits; others are the resort of dandies or of politicians, or again of professional newsmongers; and many others are temples of Venus."

Edward "Ned" Ward, a turn-of-the-century satirist, describes a "beau" who frequents coffeehouses to pick up women. "He is as constant a visitor of a coffee-house as a Drury Lane whore is of Covent Garden Church, where he cons over the newspapers with as much indifference as the other prays, reading only for fashion's sake, and not for information." Ward, a tavernkeeper, also describes the clientele of a coffeehouse he visits as "a parcel of muddling muckworms [who] were as busy as so many rats in an old cheese-loft; some going, some coming, some scribbling, some talking, some drinking, others jangling, and the whole room stinking of tobacco. . . . Indeed, had not my friend told me 'twas a coffee-house I should have took it for Quacks' Hall, or the parlour of some eminent mountebank."

It is hard to generalize about coffeehouses. If some were haunts of prostitutes, others were "penny universities" where there were conversations about philosophy or literature or the latest scientific developments. Samuel Pepys discussed Plato and Machiavelli at both Miles's Coffee House and Garraway's Coffee House. In the 1670s the extraordinary polymath Robert Hooke—architect, chemist, biologist, inventor, astronomer—discussed his work at more than sixty coffeehouses. Dryden discussed drama and poetry at Will's Coffee House. In 1713 William Whiston, a protégé of Newton, often lectured about science and mathematics at Douglas's Coffee House or the Marine Coffee House. In 1738 Hume, who lived in London at the time, discussed philosophical questions with other Scotsmen and with exiled French Protestants at the Rainbow Coffee House.

Coffeehouses were attacked not only by the owners of taverns and alehouses. In the three decades before the Glorious Revolution many High Church Tories (Anglican Royalists who were strong supporters of Charles II) regarded coffeehouses as "direct seminaries of sedition." The coffeehouses, one writer says, were responsible for turning "every porter" into a "statesman." The coffeehouse, another writer claims, is "midwife to all false intelligence." According to a government loyalist, "at those tables our superiours are dissected; calumny and treason are the common, are indeed the more peculiar entertainments of those places." A pamphleteer calls a coffeehouse "an *Exchange* where Haberdashers of *Political small wares* meet, and mutually abuse each other, and the Publique, with bottomless stories, and headless notions."

According to a pro-government writer, the alehouse denizen "is one of the quietest subjects his Majesty has, and most submissive to monarchical government." Manly men (and loyal men) drink ale and beer, not coffee. Charles II thought Englishmen should spend more time in alehouses and taverns than in coffeehouses. On 29 December 1675, he issued an edict calling for the suppression of coffeehouses, but the popular outcry was such that the edict was withdrawn in less than two weeks. The king saved face by issuing an unenforceable requirement that coffeehouse proprietors "take care to prevent treasonable talk in their houses."

In the *History of England* Hume explains why the king acted as he did. He says there was in England at the time a "propensity for political conversation, and as the coffee-houses in particular were the scenes, where the conduct of the king and the ministry was canvassed, with great freedom, a proclamation was issued to suppress these places of rendezvous." Hume points out that Charles II did not act solely on the basis of royal prerogative. "Such an act of power, during former reigns, would have been grounded entirely on the [royal] prerogative," but Charles II sought judicial support for his action. The king, Hume says, was not satisfied with the arguments the judges advanced to defend his edict so he rescinded it, but the main reason he changed his mind was public opinion. As Hume puts it: "The king, therefore, observing the people to be much dissatisfied, yielded to a petition of the coffee-men, who promised for the future to restrain all seditious discourse in their houses; and the proclamation was recalled."

Though Hume calls the whole affair a "trivial" incident, he implies it was a significant development in the history of

English liberty, for he says that the incident "tends strongly to mark the genius of the English government, and of Charles's administration, during this period." The "genius"—meaning the distinctiveness—of the English government was its realization that, as a contemporary writer put it, "a convulsion and discontent would immediately follow" if the anti-coffeehouse edict were not withdrawn.

According to Stephen Pincus, many supporters of Charles II were in favor of coffeehouses. Sir William Coventry, an advisor to the government, argued that coffeehouses should be allowed because they "had been permitted in Cromwell's time, and that the King's friends had used more liberty of speech in those places than they durst in any other." Coffeehouses made sedition less likely because in coffeehouses radical ideas, as one writer put it, were often criticized by "experienced gentlemen, judicious lawyers, able physicians, ingenious merchants, and understanding citizens." Or, as Andrew Marvell put it in a poem attacking the king's edict:

> It is wine and strong drinks [that] make tumults
>   increase;
> Choc'late, tea, and coffee are liquors of peace . . .
> Then, Charles, thy edicts against coffee recall:
> There's ten times more treason in brandy and ale.

Ellis rightly says that "the emergence of the coffee-house transformed the social organization of the city, bringing with it a new principle of convivial sociability based on conversation and discussion." At the turn of the eighteenth century John Houghton, a member of the Royal Society, was probably uttering a commonplace opinion when he said that "coffee-houses make all sorts of people sociable. The rich and the poor meet together, as also do the learned and unlearned: it [the coffee-house] improves arts, merchandise, and all other knowledge."

In the first half of that century coffeehouses were so popular that they often were given as places of address. A visitor to London in the 1720s said "a man is sooner asked about his coffee house than his lodging." When the poet Thomas Gray came back from a two-year trip to the Continent in 1741, he found mail waiting for him at Dick's Coffee House. In a letter to her future husband, Lady Mary Wortley Montagu asks him to leave a letter for her "at Mr Foulks, a Coffee house at the three Lions in Salisbury, Wiltshire."

How could Lady Montagu expect to pick up a letter at a coffeehouse if, as many historians have argued, women were barred from them? Pincus disagrees with this view. "There is little warrant for the claim that women were excluded from coffeehouses. . . . There is every reason to believe that women frequently attended the newly fashionable coffeehouses, places that celebrated sober discourse rather than inebriated play, cultural exchange rather than social status." Robert Hooke and the famous chemist Robert Boyle dined at Man's Coffee House with Boyle's sister. And the sister of Sir William Temple, Swift's patron, frequented coffeehouses. Yet prints of eighteenth-century coffeehouses do not show any women present except for the "coffee-woman" who managed the coffeehouse (she often wore an outlandish headdress), so it is likely that coffeehouses were mainly for men, which is what Addison and Steele imply in the *Spectator*.

In the major cities of the Continent there also were coffee-houses where people read newspapers, discussed politics, and conducted business, but London was widely considered to be the European city with the most interesting coffeehouses because the conversation there was the freest. By the early eighteenth century the London press was the most extensive and most diverse in Europe. After the lapse of the Licensing Act in 1695, the London press grew rapidly. The first modern daily newspaper appeared in 1702; by the 1730s there were six London dailies and nine by the 1770s. London coffeehouses subscribed to many journals, which they offered to their clients.

The press flourished in large part because of the high level of literacy—especially in London. In central London in the mid-eighteenth century the literacy rate was 92 percent for men and 74 percent for women. A French writer visiting London in the 1730s said: "All Englishmen are great newsmongers. . . . Workmen habitually begin the day by going to coffee-rooms in order to read the latest news."

In Paris coffeehouse subscriptions to leading newspapers were not as widespread as they were in London. Moreover, the French press was more limited in its coverage of politics, especially during the first half of the century, and it lagged behind the English press in its coverage of commerce and manufacturing. Focusing on literature, art, and philosophy, most French journals were written for an elite readership that frequented salons rather than coffeehouses.

According to John Brewer, in their writings about the coffeehouse Addison and Steele shaped "an exemplary institution, fabricating an ideal of polite conduct and good taste developed in a convivial environment." Yet Addison and Steele occasionally describe coffeehouse conversation in negative terms. In one essay Mr. Spectator complains that many coffeehouse conversations are confusing. "I, who hear a Thousand Coffee house Debates every Day, am very sensible of this Want of Method in the Thoughts of my honest Countrymen."

Addison worried that coffeehouse patrons often became obsessed with politics. In the *Tatler* he writes about an upholsterer who has become so consumed with the news, especially foreign affairs, that he neglects his own business and impoverishes his family. Addison closes the essay with the following warning: "This paper I design for the particular Benefit of those worthy citizens who live more in a Coffee-house than in their Shops, and whose Thoughts are so taken up with the Affairs of the Allies, that they forget their Customers."

For the most part the *Tatler* and the *Spectator* take a positive view of coffeehouse conversation. Mr. Spectator calls coffeehouses "very good Institutions" that are "our *British* Schools of Politics." At coffeehouses Britons could become informed about current events, hear a variety of political views, and learn how to discuss political questions without letting their passions boil over. According to Mr. Spectator, "there may be something very useful in these little Institutions and Establishments," where men are "combined for their own Improvement, or for the Good of others, or at least to relax themselves from the Business of the Day, by an innocent and cheerful Conversation."

Swift and Shaftesbury disagreed. They thought coffeehouses were places where superficial opinions and fashionable ideas were aired. When Swift was a propagandist for the Tory government of Robert Harley, he attacked coffeehouses as centers of Whig opinion. Speaking of "the obscene, ominous bird" of faction, he says: "She intruded into all companies at the most unseasonable times . . . haunted every coffee-house and bookseller's shop." In "The Conduct of the Allies," which appeared in November 1711, Swift says it is a mistake to assume that what is said in coffeehouses reflects public opinion in general. "It is the folly of too many to mistake the echo of a London coffee-house for the voice of the kingdom."

Swift also wrote that "the worst Conversation I ever remember to have heard in my Life, was that at *Will's* Coffeehouse, where the Wits (as they were called) used formerly to
assemble; that is to say, five or six Men, who had writ Plays, or
at least Prologues, or had Share in a Miscellany, came thither,
and entertained one another with their trifling Composures,
in so important an Air, as if they had been the noblest Efforts
of human Nature or that the Fate of Kingdoms depended on
them." At Will's Coffee House—Swift says—smug men of wit
dazzle "an humble audience of young Students from the Inns
of Courts, or the Universities." As a result, the young men return home "with great Contempt for their Law and philosophy, their Heads filled with Trash, under the Name of Politeness, Criticism and Belles Lettres." Will's Coffee House, Swift
implies, is a school for foolish thinking and foppery.

Swift also betrays a certain disdain for the people who
frequent coffeehouses. The coffeehouse is a world that has
little in common with the world of "the great"—the Tory lead-
ers Swift worked for. Swift thought public policy should be the
preserve of the landed interest. In his early days in London
Swift frequently went to coffeehouses, but when he became the
leading Tory propagandist he gave them up. In April 1711 he
writes Esther Johnson: "I go to no coffeehouse at all."

Johnson's view of coffeehouses is more positive than
Swift's. He told Boswell: "For spending three pence in a coffee
house, you may be for hours in very good company." Yet, like
Swift, he satirizes coffeehouse writers. He creates a fatuous literary critic, Dick Minim, who sits in a coffeehouse and pontif-
icates about literature. "When he entered his coffee-house, he
was surrounded by circles of candidates, who passed their
noviciate of literature under his tuition; his opinion was asked

by all who had no opinion of their own." Johnson also criticizes coffee-house learning: "There are many who, instead of endeavouring by books and meditation to form their own opinions, content themselves with the secondary knowledge which a convenient bench in a coffee-house can supply." He tells Hester Thrale: "To study manners ... only in coffee-houses, is more than equally imperfect; the minds of men who acquire no solid learning, and only exist in the daily forage that they pick up by running about, and snatching what drops from their neighbors as ignorant as themselves, will never ferment into any knowledge valuable and durable."

After mid-century the number of coffeehouses declined. Many were converted to clubs and many became chophouses and taverns. Yet coffeehouses remained part of the London scene until well into the nineteenth century. In 1754 a magazine described the Bedford—a coffeehouse frequented by Fielding, David Garrick, and Oliver Goldsmith—as a place that is "crowded with men of parts. Almost everyone you meet is a polite scholar and a wit. . . . Every branch of literature is critically examined, and the merit of every production of the press, or performance at the theatres, weighed and determined." In 1791 a foreign observer said that "the English live in a very remarkable manner. They rise late, and spend most of the morning, either in walking about town or sitting in the coffeehouse." But by 1791 there was little conversation in coffeehouses (see Chapter Six). The Age of Conversation was over.

Boswell and Coffeehouses

In 1762, when Boswell first came to London, he often went to a coffeehouse. On 4 December 1762 he wrote a memorandum to himself about how he should spend the day. "Go to Child's, take dish coffee, read *Auditor, Monitor, Briton.*" In his journal Boswell mentions several London coffeehouses, but Child's is the only one he went to regularly, and it is the only coffeehouse where he recorded conversation. Boswell liked Child's because he associated it with the *Spectator.* "The Spectator mentions his being seen at Child's, which makes me have an affection for it. I think myself like him, and am serenely happy there. There is something to me very agreeable in having my time laid out in some method, such as every Saturday going to Child's." Boswell could have chosen Will's as his favorite, for it too is frequently mentioned in the *Spectator,* as he notes in his entry for 28 June 1763: "Temple [a Scottish friend] and I drank coffee at Wills, which is often mentioned in *The Spectator.*"

Boswell hoped that if he went to coffeehouses regularly, he would become a polite Londoner. Soon after he arrived in London he wrote in his journal: "I felt strong dispositions to be a Mr. Addison." He exhorts himself to exercise self-restraint so that he might achieve "constant useful conversation, with mild and grave dignity," yet he worries that he is an uncultivated Scotsman. "Indeed, I had accustomed myself so much to laugh at every thing that it required time to render my imagination solid and give me just notions of real life and of religion. But I hoped by degrees to so attain some degree of propriety. Mr. Addison's character in sentiment, mixed with a little of the gaiety of Sir Richard Steele and the manners of Mr. Digges, were the ideas which I aimed to realize." West Digges was a well-known Scottish actor whom Boswell admired for his sexual triumphs with genteel women. It is characteristic of Boswell that thoughts of politeness slide into thoughts of seducing women.

On Boswell's first trip to Child's he "read the political papers, and had some chat with citizens." Breakfasting at Child's would soon become a Saturday ritual for him—a way of disciplining himself and also cheering himself up. "It is quite a place to my mind; dusky, comfortable, and warm, with a society of citizens and physicians who talk politics very fully and are very sagacious and sometimes jocular." After quoting some snatches of conversation that he heard at Child's, he says: "I shall hereafter . . . throw our conversation in my journal in the form of a dialogue. So that every Saturday this my Journal shall be adorned with A DIALOGUE AT CHILD'S."

The snatches of conversation Boswell records from his visits to Child's cover a number of topics. The first one is about the peace treaty that Britain recently concluded with France to end the Seven Years' War; others are about a recent work of literary criticism, the weather, and a new play. Boswell stopped going to Child's regularly, but in March he returned in the hope that it would cheer him up. "I again went to my good Child's, which gave me some comfort. I felt a warmth of heart to it after so long an absence."

Meeting with his polite London acquaintances, Boswell would often talk about literature or philosophy. He reports that he went with a new acquaintance to Tom's Coffee House, where we "had a pot of coffee, and sat there for two hours. Our conversation took a literary turn. We talked of Helvétius, Voltaire, Rousseau, Hume." Boswell frequently complains that the presence of his Scottish friends makes it difficult for him to have such conversations. When a number of Scotsmen visit him, he says: "I was vexed at their coming." Seeing them "hurt my grand ideas of London." On another occasion, he says: "I find that I ought not to keep too much company with Scotch people, because . . . they prevent my mind from being filled with London images." In March 1772 he speaks of the "hearty draught of free and friendly conversation" he was having with his friend George Dempster. Unfortunately, several Scotsmen showed up—putting an end to the conversation.

In later years Boswell seems to have spent less time at coffeehouses, no doubt because he was now a member of London's polite world and had a wide circle of acquaintances. Coffeehouses no longer loomed so large in his imagination, though a coffeehouse's removal to a new location occasioned a melancholy thought: "I breakfasted at the Smyrna Coffee house, now removed to St. James's Street. . . . I thought its being removed a striking instance of the instability of human affairs." In his entry for 17 November 1789 he says he breakfasted at the Chapter Coffee House, where he read the Scottish newspapers.

On 4 July 1786 there is a haunting journal entry about coffeehouses. Upset because he was not having much luck in his attempt to practice law in England as well as feeling guilty about remaining in London while his wife and children were in Scotland, Boswell hoped to raise his spirits by having dinner with a friend. Unable to find anyone to dine with, he spent the evening going from one coffeehouse to another—in search of conversation. "I sauntered into various coffee houses 'seeking rest and finding none' [Luke 11:24]. The Virginia, Maryland, and *Greenland* Coffee house attracted my curiosity, but I found nothing particular in it. I walked on beyond Cornhill to see if there are any coffee houses so far east. I grew somewhat weary, perceived *Aldgate Coffee house*. Went into it and had tea and dry toast and butter. This was a poor relief. When I got out into the streets again I was so depressed that the tears run down my cheeks."

What Boswell was seeking that night was what he had sought at coffeehouses when he was a young man: free conversation. At this stage in his life he didn't need conversation to improve his politeness; he needed it to restore his spirits. The death of Johnson in 1784 had left a great gap in his life. On 24 July 1790 a journal entry reveals another failed attempt to have a coffeehouse conversation. "Was warmed, and wished to have a social evening at a coffee-house. Tried the Grecian, Temple, and George's, Temple Bar; hardly a soul there or at Nando's. Read the Scotch newspapers at Peele's, which was pretty full. But I knew nobody. The Bedford was empty, and one solitary gentleman sat in the Piazza."

Clubs and Clubbability

Coffeehouses were not the only venue for conversation in eighteenth-century Britain. Conversations took place in clubs as well. If many foreigners admired London's coffeehouses, many also admired the variety of clubs in London and elsewhere in Britain. In 1724 the author of a *Journey Through England* said London had "an infinity of clubs or societies for the improvement of learning and keeping up good humor and mirth." On a tour of England in the 1790s a French writer said that clubs and societies are "one of the most sensible institutions."

In *Rambler* 23 (written in 1750) Johnson says that one of his critics "admonished him to have a special eye upon the various clubs of this great city, and informed him that much of the *Spectator*'s vivacity was laid out upon such assemblies." In effect, the critic is saying to Johnson: Addison wrote about clubs, which are an important part of London life, so you should write about them too.

Johnson defines a club as "an assembly of good fellows, meeting under certain conditions." In Britain there were many different kinds of clubs—clubs for scientific discussion, clubs mainly for "modern midnight conversation" (heavy drinking), and clubs for sexual "conversation." The members of the Roaring Boys Club met in a tavern, got drunk, and went to the brothels of Covent Garden. The Hell-Fire Club's main activities were heavy drinking, reading pornographic literature, and engaging in orgies. The Mollies Club was for male crossdressers. There were also clubs (usually called societies) for philanthropic purposes: the Anti-Slavery Society, the Society for Charitable Purposes, the London Society for the Discharge and Relief of Persons Imprisoned for Small Debts.

Clubs were almost as old as coffeehouses, but it was not until after the Glorious Revolution that they became widespread. By the end of the first decade of the eighteenth century there were approximately two thousand clubs in London. The *Spectator* refers to "a young man of very lively Parts, and of a sprightly Turn in Conversation, who . . . was initiated into a Half a Dozen Clubs before he was One and twenty." A number of coffeehouses became venues for clubs. The "Honest Whigs" Club first met at St. Paul's Coffee House and later at the London Coffee House. White's began as a coffeehouse; three decades later it became an exclusive club for the aristocracy.

There were clubs throughout England and Scotland. In Newcastle alone there were approximately fifty clubs and societies. Glasgow and especially Edinburgh had many clubs. In the first two decades of the century three influential clubs were founded in Edinburgh: the Grotesque Club, the Easy Club, and the Rankenian Club. The Grotesque Club hoped to promote "Virtue, Learning, and Politeness." The founders of the Easy Club said the "first thing that induced us to join in a society was the reading of . . . *Spectators.*" The Rankenian Club's function was to promote "mutual improvement by liberal conversation and rational inquiry." There was also the Poker Club, founded by Adam Ferguson, the champion of Spartan values.

Named after the fire poker, the club hoped to stir up support for a Scottish militia. Hume, Adam Smith, and the historian William Robertson were members.

Clubs were not an alternative to coffeehouses. Many people who went to coffeehouses regularly also belonged to several clubs. In the first issue of the *Spectator* Mr. Spectator says that he is only a spectator at coffeehouses, but he participates in the conversation at "my own Club." The second issue, written by Steele but in conjunction with Addison, describes the six members of the club Mr. Spectator belongs to: a country squire, a rich merchant, a retired military officer, a student of the law who is a devoted theatergoer, an elderly fop, and a clergyman. In subsequent issues of the *Spectator,* Mr. Spectator's club is not featured prominently. The only club member who is the subject of many essays is the country squire, Sir Roger de Coverley, but Mr. Spectator often writes about other clubs.

Clubs became popular because of their restricted membership. Becoming a member of a club was often a sign that one had gained entry into the polite world. According to Peter Clark, the leading historian of British clubs, "in London the big bourgeoisie—overseas merchants, bankers, wholesale traders . . . sought social recognition, not through migration to a country estate, but through polite socializing in town, rubbing shoulders with the landed elite at assembly rooms, coffee houses, and above all, at clubs and societies." Clubs were obviously good places for merchants to make contacts. According to a contemporary observer, "the Use of *Clubs,* so frequent in London, especially among Traders, is a good way to improve a diverting and useful Correspondence. The way of 'em, is for a select Company of Men to meet at a certain Hour in the Evening at a publick House, where they talk of Trade, News. & etc."

The popularity of clubs, like the popularity of coffee-houses, was a sign for Addison of humankind's sociability. "Man is said to be a Sociable Animal, and, as an Instance of it, we may observe, that we take all Occasions and Pretences of forming our selves into those little Nocturnal Assemblies, which are commonly known by the Name of *Clubs*."

Addison's phrase "little Nocturnal Assemblies" suggests that he will treat the topic of clubs in a lighthearted fashion. *Spectator* 72 describes a fictitious club—the so-called Everlasting Club because it is always in session, providing sociability twenty-four hours a day seven days a week. A friend tells Mr. Spectator that the club "consists of an hundred Members, who divide the whole twenty four Hours among them in such a Manner, that the Club sits Day and Night from one End of the Year to another. . . . By this Means a member . . . never Wants Company."

In the Everlasting Club the main activities are drinking, smoking, and playing cards. There is no mention of food, but there are references to the staggering amount of ale, port, brandy, and beer the members have consumed over the years. Needless to say, the members of this fictitious club are not interested in conversation. According to Addison, "their ordinary Discourse (as much as I have been able to learn of it) turns altogether upon such Adventures as have passed in their own Assembly; of Members who have taken the Glass in their Turns for a Week together without stirring out of the Club; of others who have smoaked an Hundred Pipes at a Sitting."

Addison and Steele refer to many fictitious clubs. There is the Widow-Club, where the conversation "often turns upon their former Husbands, and it is very diverting to hear them relate their several Arts and Stratagems, with which they amused the Jealous, pacified the Cholerick, or wheedled the Good-natured Man, 'till at last, to use the Club-phrase, They sent him out of the House with his Heels foremost." There is the Lawyers Club, whose members discuss "several Ways of abusing their Clients, with the Applause . . . given to him who has done it most Artfully."

In *A Compleat and Humorous Account of all the Remarkable Clubs and Societies in the Cities of London and Westminster*, which went through seven editions between 1709 and 1759, Edward Ward (the same writer who ridiculed coffeehouses) describes such nonsensical fictional clubs as the No-nose, Man-killing, Surly, and Farting clubs. A number of writers spoke of a Quidnunc Club. A quidnunc—the Latin for "what now"—is a person obsessed with knowing the latest news. The modern reader is likely to find these satirical efforts thin, but they were popular with eighteenth-century readers.

Though many clubs mentioned by the *Spectator* were fictitious, some were not. The correspondent of a club devoted to reading the *Spectator* writes: "To speak plain, there are a number of us who have begun your Works afresh, and meet two Nights in the Week in order to give you a Rehearing." *Spectator* 9 refers to the Kit-Cat Club, whose fame was such that Fielding mentions it in *Tom Jones*. Its members included Addison, Steele, and many leading Whig politicians. Concerned about the influence of the Whig Kit-Cat Club, Swift founded a Tory counterpart—the Society or Brothers' Club in June 1711. Three years later it became the Scriblerus Club—its purpose to combat pedantry and dullness. *Spectator* 9 also mentions the October Club, which was composed of Tories with Jacobite leanings. It also refers to the apolitical Beef-Steak Club (also known as the Sublime Society of Beefsteaks), which was still in existence fifty years later, when Boswell came to London.

A reader of the *Spectator* may come away with the impression that clubs were mainly for eating and drinking. Addison implies as much when he says that "our Modern celebrated Clubs are founded upon Eating and Drinking, which are Points wherein most Men agree." Enjoying food and drink was an important aspect of club life, yet Clark says that "what was central to the life of many . . . clubs . . . was not drinking *per se,* nor feasting, singing, or the various ceremonies, but conversation."

According to Thomas Bewick, Swarley's Club of Newcastle was "the most rational Society or meeting I ever knew. . . . It was expected that every member should behave with decorum & like a Gentleman. . . . Conversations among the friends, thus associating, consisting of Merchants or respectable Tradesmen, was [*sic*] carried on without restraint." James Watt, the inventor of the steam engine, remembered the conversations he had at the Anderston Club in Glasgow. "Our conversations then, besides the usual subjects with young men, turned principally on literary topics, religions, belles-lettres, &c.; and to those conversations my mind owed its first bias towards such subjects, I never having attended a college, and being then but a mechanic." Watt and Benjamin Franklin were occasional visitors to the Oyster Club in Edinburgh, which was founded by the chemist Joseph Black, the geologist James Hutton, and Adam Smith. Hume, Ferguson, and William Robertson were also members. The discussions, Hutton says, were "informal and amusing."

According to Sir John Hawkins, Johnson founded the Ivy Lane Club in 1748 because of "his love of conversation." The Ivy Lane Club disbanded in 1756. Eight years later Johnson and Reynolds founded the Literary Club—also known as Johnson's Club, the Turk's Head Club, or simply The Club. Its sole purpose was "solid conversation," as Johnson put it, while eating and drinking. It began with nine members and gradually expanded to thirty-five. The members met, Boswell says, "one evening in every week, at seven, and generally continued their conversation till a pretty late hour."

The club continued to meet for two decades into the nineteenth century, but Boswell thought the conversation became less interesting after Johnson's death in 1784. (Boswell died in 1795.) In his journal entry for 13 February 1786, Boswell says: "Dined at the Literary Club. . . . The want of Johnson was much felt. There was no vigorous exertion of intellect." He makes the same point eight years later—in his journal entry for 1 March 1794: "Dined at the LITERARY CLUB. . . . It was not as in the days of Johnson."

The Literary Club had an extraordinarily distinguished membership. It included two of the leading writers of the age (Johnson and Goldsmith); the leading painter (Reynolds); the leading actor (David Garrick); the leading English historian (Edward Gibbon); the leading political economist (Adam Smith); the leading political writer (Edmund Burke); a major politician (Charles James Fox); the leading playwright (Richard Sheridan); and one of the leading scientists (Joseph Banks). It also included other distinguished scholars of law, literature, and music. In 1778 Sir William Jones, a club member who was the leading orientalist—he was the first to describe the connection between Sanskrit and modern Indo-European languages—wrote to a former pupil: "Johnson says truly that Europe cannot produce another such club, and that there is no branch of human knowledge, concerning which we could not collectively give the world good information."

The Literary Club was not the only distinguished club in eighteenth-century Britain. At least two others deserve mention. In Edinburgh there was the Select Society. Founded in

1754, the club included among its members Hume, Smith, Robertson, Black, Ferguson, Blair, and virtually all the leading lights of what has come to be known as the Scottish Enlightenment. The Select Society was not an informal club for conversation, but rather a debating society that in five years expanded to 135 members. Unlike the Literary Club, the Select Society discussed political questions. It was in some respects the forerunner of a modern policy-oriented think tank, for it hoped by "reasoning and eloquence, and by the freedom of debate, to discover the most effectual methods of promoting the good of the country." Scotland's polite world all clamored to get into the Select Society. Hume complained that "young and old, noble and ignoble, witty and dull, laity and clergy, all the [Scottish] world are ambitious of a place amongst us, and on each occasion we are as much solicited by candidates as if we were to choose a Member of Parliament."

Another important club was the Lunar Society of Birmingham, founded in 1765. Its fourteen members included Watt, Josiah Wedgwood, and Matthew Boulton, a leading manufacturer. The club also included two leading scientists: Priestley and Erasmus Darwin—the latter a botanist, poet, and inventor who was the grandfather of Charles Darwin (Wedgwood was Darwin's other grandfather). The club formally met once a month at full moon, but many members met more frequently to discuss the scientific work they were doing. Calling themselves "lunaticks," they were interested in basic science but also in the application of science to manufacturing, mining, transportation, and medicine. Ten club members were fellows of the Royal Society.

The French Revolution put a great strain on the club, and after Priestley emigrated to America in 1794 the club rapidly declined. As one member put it: "The Members are to a Man

either too busy, too idle, or too much indisposed to do anything; and the interest wch [sic] everyone feels in the state of
public affairs draws the conversation out of its proper course."
Priestley was also a member of a club that Boswell belonged to: the "Honest Whigs" Club. (Franklin was also a member.) The "Honest Whigs" Club, Boswell says, "is composed
principally of physicians, dissenting clergy, and masters of acad-
emies." At one meeting Priestley told a story about a Methodist
sailor who tried in vain to explain the doctrine of the Trinity—
Priestley's point being that the doctrine is absurd (he was a
Unitarian). Describing a meeting, Boswell says: "We have wine
and punch upon the table. Some of us smoke a pipe, conversation goes on pretty formally, sometimes sensibly and sometimes furiously."

In March 1772 Boswell was invited by his friend Sir John
Pringle to dine at another club that took conversation seriously: the Royal Society Club. Pringle was the President of the
Royal Society as well as a distinguished physician who in 1774
became physician to the king. What did the club members talk
about? Boswell says only that "there was little conversation that
I could learn, from the company being numerous."

Boswell himself founded two clubs. In 1760, while he was
studying for the law in Edinburgh, he and several friends
founded the Soaping Club; its motto was "let every man soap
his own beard," which roughly means do whatever you want to
do. The club, which included several medical students, an army
officer, and an Anglican priest, met every Tuesday evening at a
tavern in order to drink, sing, and rattle, which means to "talk
rapidly in a noisy, lively, or inane manner." They also played a
card game: snip-snap-snorum. In 1768 he founded the Corsican Club, which met annually on the birthday of the Corsican
general, Pasquale di Paoli, the leader of the Corsican independence movement. (Boswell had just published *Account of*

Corsica, in which he called for Corsican independence.) Horace Walpole and Franklin attended the founding meeting.

In November 1762 Lord Eglinton, a Scottish aristocrat and family friend who served as a mentor to Boswell while he was in London, invited him to attend a meeting of the Beef-Steak Club. (Eglinton hoped to use his connections to help Boswell secure a commission in the Foot Guards.) The club, which met in a room above a theater in Covent Garden, had the vague mission of celebrating British culture. "The president," Boswell says, "sits in a chair under a canopy, above which you have in golden letters, *Beef and Liberty.* . . . We had nothing to eat but beefsteaks, and had wine and punch in plenty and freedom. We had a number of songs."

In 1791 Boswell became a member of the Royal Academy Club, which he was eligible to join because Reynolds had arranged for him to be elected Secretary for Foreign Correspondence in the Royal Academy. Frank Brady, Boswell's biographer, mentions several other clubs that Boswell frequented: "The occasional lonely evening [in London] could be filled in at several other clubs: the Free and Easy (whist); the Eumelian, which had a distinguished membership, and the lively Friends round the Globe."

It was commonplace in Britain's polite world to belong to several clubs. Gibbon was a member of the Literary Club as well as Boodles, Atwoods, Brooke's, Almack's, and the Catch Club, whose members sang catches. According to Patricia Craddock, "Gibbon remained 'clubable' throughout his life."

Being clubbable, a word coined by Johnson, was a widely admired trait. Johnson said that Boswell was "a very clubable man," but he said that Sir John Hawkins was "a most unclubable man." Johnson respected Hawkins, who was a lawyer and musicologist, and he made Hawkins one of his literary executors, but he thought Hawkins's conversation was marked by "brutality" and "savagery." Hawkins, who would publish the first biography of Johnson in 1787, was banished from the Literary Club because he had been rude to Burke. (Hawkins claimed he had "seceded" from it.)

Reynolds was considered the most clubbable member of the Literary Club. Boswell hoped to write a biography of the painter but he gave up because, as Burke put it, "the very qualities which made the society of our late friend so pleasant to all who know him are [the] very things that make it difficult to write his Life, or to draw his Character." Reynolds helped his reputation for clubbability by avoiding conversations about politics. According to an early biographer, "Politics never amused him nor ever employed his thought for a moment." Though Johnson complained that Reynolds didn't read his political pamphlets, he was very attached to Reynolds. When he learned that Reynolds had suffered a minor stroke, he wrote to him: "Your Country has been in danger of losing one of its brightest ornaments, and I, of losing one of my oldest and kindest friends."

Clubs—unlike coffeehouses—were mainly places where political passions were left at the door. In 1762 the membership of the Beef-Steak Club included Lord Eglinton, who was close to the Earl of Bute, the chief minister in George III's government. It also included John Wilkes, the editor of *The North Briton,* a strongly anti-Bute journal. Eglinton and Wilkes remained on good terms, but in 1763 another club member, the Earl of Sandwich, accused Wilkes of obscene and seditious libel. Because the Earl attacked a club member, he was expelled from the club. (When the Earl once said to Wilkes: "You will die, sir, either on the gallows or from the pox," Wilkes replied: "That depends, sir, on whether I embrace your principles or your mistress.")

Is being clubbable the same thing as being polite? It would seem so, since being clubbable means succeeding at the art of pleasing in conversation. Being clubbable, however, was not the main requirement for gaining membership in Johnson's Literary Club. One had to be a man of learning or accomplishment in some field or walk of life. (Women could not become members.) Boswell knew that his high rank in society had nothing to do with his becoming a member.

Ten years before Boswell was admitted into the Literary Club, he implied in his journal that rank was an important aspect of politeness. "But I must find one fault with all the *Poker Club,* as they are called; that is to say, with all that set who associate with David Hume and Robertson. They are doing all that they can to destroy politeness. They would abolish all respect due to rank and external circumstances, and they would live like a kind of literary barbarians." Boswell is wrong to connect politeness with rank. For Hume and all the eighteenth-century writers on conversation, politeness was an acquired trait. Boswell probably was annoyed because Hume and Robertson did not take him seriously, for he was not yet a man of any accomplishments.

It is hard to overestimate the importance of clubs in Britain. According to John Brewer, "some of the finest works and most important ideas of the Scottish Enlightenment" emerged from conversations held at Edinburgh's clubs and at dinner parties thrown by David Hume, who bragged of his "great Talent for Cookery."

The leading eighteenth-century clubs were far more intellectually lively than Oxford or Cambridge. In *Memoirs of My Life* (1796), Gibbon offers a sarcastic view of the intellectual activity of the "monks" of Oxford and Cambridge (fellows were not allowed to get married): "The fellows or monks of my time were decent easy men who supinely enjoyed the gifts of the founder [meaning a lifetime fellowship]. Their days were filled by a series of uniform employments: the chapel and the hall, the coffee house and the common room, till they retired, weary and well-satisfied, to a long slumber. From the toil of reading or thinking or writing they had absolved their conscience."

Britain's clubs not only promoted the advancement of knowledge, they also reduced the likelihood of violent political discord. Members of the same club who disagreed about politics were unlikely to demonize each other. Johnson disliked Burke's politics (he thought Burke's pose of disinterestedness was humbug), and Burke disliked Johnson's politics (two years after Johnson died Boswell reported that Burke "was violent against Dr. Johnson's political writings"), yet Johnson and Burke remained close friends and fellow club members for many years.

Roy Porter describes the Anglo-Scottish Enlightenment as "more like a communing of clubbable men than a conspiracy or clique." The point should be made more strongly. It *was* a communing of clubbable men. When the Italian poet Alessandro Verri visited London's clubs and the House of Commons in 1767, he thought the House of Commons resembled a club. According to Paul Langford, he found "the same strange mixture of drinking, cheerfulness, and serious debate in both."

Clubbability continued to remain a trait the English admired. Writing in the early Victorian period, the Baron d'Haussez said: "Club habits have necessarily a very considerable influence on the national manners. They are a sort of initiation to political life, less by means of discussions, which are rarely entered within their walls, than by conversations, in which the most important affairs, relating to the general interests of the country, are treated with depth and justness of view."

V

Samuel Johnson:
A Conversational Triumph;
Lady Mary Wortley Montagu:
Conversation Lost

With its lively coffeehouses and flourishing clubs, Britain's conversible world was larger than that of any other European nation. Moreover, the major British writers on conversation were known for the high quality of their conversation. According to Franklin, Hume "is a very pleasant Gentleman in Conversation." The Scottish novelist Henry Mackenzie agreed: "Of all men I ever knew, his ordinary conversation was the least tinctured with pedantry, or liable to dissertation [argument]." Reviews were mixed, however, about Johnson's conversation. Some people regarded Johnson as the greatest conversationalist of the age; others thought he was deficient in politeness.

Hume, who met Johnson briefly, disliked his conversation. "Johnson is abusive in Company," he said. Horace Walpole, who refused to be introduced to Johnson, said that his "manners were sordid, supercilious and brutal." The poet Thomas Gray, who also declined to meet Johnson, once saw him walking in London and exclaimed to his companion: "The great bear . . . there goes *Ursa Major!*" Johnson was also called the old growler and the old elephant.

Even Johnson's admirers acknowledged that sometimes Johnson failed at the art of pleasing in conversation. Though Boswell said that Johnson's "conversation was, perhaps, more admirable than even his writings, however excellent," he also spoke of Johnson's "dogmatic roughness of manners." In *Anecdotes of Samuel Johnson*, Mrs. Piozzi (Hester Thrale) quotes with approval William Hogarth's remark that "Mr. Johnson's conversation was to the talk of other men like Titian's painting compared to Hudson's [a minor British painter]," yet she also gave Johnson zero points for good humor.

Johnson himself admitted that he was occasionally "somewhat rough in conversation," but he tried to be polite. In *Rambler* 98 a letter writer who is clearly speaking for Johnson says: "Politeness is one of those advantages which we never estimate rightly but by the inconvenience of its loss. Its influence upon the manners is constant and uniform, so that . . . it escapes perception." Both Johnson and Hume were acquaintances of Colonel James Forrester, who was the author of a popular manual on politeness, *The Polite Philosopher* (1738).

Like Addison and Hume, Johnson often uses good breeding and good humor as synonyms for politeness. "Wisdom and virtue are by no means sufficient without the supplemental laws of good-breeding to secure freedom from degenerating to rudeness, or self-esteem from swelling into indolence." Johnson defines good humor as the "habit of being pleased; a constant and perennial softness of manner, easiness of approach, and suavity of disposition." Good humor is essential for "free and easy conversation."

Johnson often attacks ill humor or peevishness. Ill humor "wears out happiness by slow corrosion." Ill humor is the "canker of life, that destroys its vigour, and checks its improvement." This "unsocial quality," he warns, is often contracted by "those who have long lived in solitude." According to Johnson, men who "have not mingled much in general conversation, but spent their lives amidst the obsequiousness of dependants, and the flattery of parasites" tend to be ill-humored—"not only careless of pleasing, but studious to offend." Johnson puts considerable emphasis on the will—on a conscious decision to regulate one's ill humor. "No disease of the mind can more fatally disable it from benevolence, the chief duty of social beings, than ill humour or peevishness."

According to Johnson, one's natural passions are antisocial, which is why the will to please is so important. In his biography of the poet Isaac Watts, Johnson says: "By his natural temper he was quick of resentment; but, by his established and habitual practice, he was gentle, modest, and inoffensive." Politeness, he tells Boswell, "is . . . fictitious benevolence. . . . Depend upon it, the want of it never fails to produce something disagreeable to one or other."

Though Johnson often talked about the importance of politeness, he disliked some types of politeness. In *Rambler* 194 a young nobleman is a master of "puerile politeness." The young nobleman thinks the art of pleasing in conversation means knowing everything about the latest fashions, gossip, and language. The nobleman, who has an "eagerness to lead the conversation," thinks he is greatly admired for his dress and his conversation, but he is merely indulged in because of his youth and deferred to because of his rank. Confident that he

possesses the art of pleasing in conversation, the young nobleman has no idea that the polite world considers him a fool.

At times Johnson's praise of politeness seems grudging,
for he dislikes people whose only trait is their good humor. In
Rambler 72 the letter writer at first praises good humor, but
then argues that some good-humored persons please us only
because they are inoffensive. They are people who are mindlessly polite. Aware that he seems to have changed his opinion
of good humor, the letter writer says he has not done so. "You
may perhaps think this account of those who are distinguished
for their good humor, not very consistent with the praises
which I have bestowed upon it. But surely nothing can more
evidently show the value of this quality, than that it recommends those who are destitute of all other excellencies, and
procures regard to the trifling, friendship to the worthless, and
affection to the dull." Politeness, Johnson suggests, is a necessary quality in the conversible world, but it is far from sufficient by itself.

Johnson describes with a certain disdain three innocu-
ous and insipid persons who are reputed to excel at the art of
conversation. There is the "merry fellow, whose laugh is loud
and whose voice is strong; who is ready to echo every jest with
obstreperous approbation." There is the "modest man . . .
whose only power of giving pleasure is not to interrupt it. The
modest man satisfies himself with peaceful silence." And there
is the "good-natured man"—the lengthiest portrait. He is "a
being generally without benevolence or any other virtue, than
such as indolence and insensibility confer."

The good-natured man, Johnson suggests, raises no objection to anything. "The characteristic of a good-natured man
is to bear a joke; to sit unmoved and unaffected amidst noise
and turbulence, profaneness and obscenity." The good-natured

man is good-humored but in an undiscriminating way. It is all the same to him whether the conversation is "honest" or immoral. He does not even take offense at insults. "The good-natured man is commonly the darling of the petty wits, with whom they exercise themselves in the rudiments of raillery." Why are such mindlessly good-natured persons popular? According to Johnson, people like them because they pose no threat to anyone's self-esteem. "That companion will be oftenest welcome, whose talk flows out with inoffensive copiousness, and unenvied insipidity." Envy, Johnson says, is a strong passion, and many people are envious of those whose conversation is superior to their own. He tells Boswell: "There is nothing by which a man exasperates most people more, than by displaying a superiour ability or brilliancy in conversation. They seem pleased at the time; but their envy makes them curse him at their hearts." The best way to avoid stirring up envy, he says, is to tell stories. "He who has stored his memory with slight anecdotes, private incidents, and personal particularities, seldom fails to find his audience favourable. . . . Narratives are for the most part heard without envy, because they are not supposed to imply any intellectual qualities above the common rate."

Johnson, though, never condemns good humor. Good humor should not be looked down on simply because it is "considered as a cheap and vulgar quality." Perhaps chiding himself for his own occasional lack of good humor, he says that good humor is often neglected by superior people who "perhaps imagine that they have some right to gratify themselves at the expense of others."

Johnson, like Addison, thinks mindless politeness is good insofar as it promotes cheerfulness. Describing several men who amuse their fellow club members by being silly—one

yelps like a hound, another sits among them with his wig reversed—Johnson says: "Such are the arts by which cheerfulness is promoted, and sometimes friendship established; arts,
which those who despise them should not rigorously blame,
except when they are practised at the expense of innocence."
    Johnson says that we should not judge the conversible
world too harshly. If we do not expect too much from conversation, we will enjoy it more. Those "with delicate and tender
minds" who become disillusioned by the conversible world are
"always expecting from the conversation of mankind, more
elegance, purity and truth than the mingled mass of life will
easily afford." Johnson is saying to his readers—and also I
think to himself: lower your expectations and you will enjoy
the conversible world more. The point is: one should try to
enjoy the conversible world, despite its inanities, because re-
moving oneself from it is dangerous to one's mental health.
    Johnson's biography of Swift offers a cautionary tale
about living without conversation. When Swift was a young
man in London, he was noted for his conversation. (In August
1714, when Swift was leaving London for Dublin, Dr. John Arbuthnot, a noted physician, told Swift: "I am sure I never can
forget you, till I meet with . . . another whose conversation I
can so much delight in as Dr. Swift's.") Yet, according to Johnson, when Swift left London he gradually lost his politeness.
"In the intercourse of familiar life, he indulged his disposition
to petulance and sarcasm, and thought himself injured if the
licentiousness of his raillery, the freedom of his censures, or
the petulance of his frolicks, was resented." Moreover, Swift
became hard of hearing, which "made conversation difficult."
He also became so frugal that he refused to offer his guests
wine, "and in Ireland no man visits where he cannot drink."
    Johnson sees a connection between Swift's gradual with-

drawal from the conversible world and his descent into madness. "Having thus excluded conversation, and desisted from study [his vision was bad yet he refused to wear glasses], he had neither business nor amusement. . . . His ideas, therefore, being neither renovated by discourse, nor increased by reading, wore gradually away, and left his mind vacant to the vexations of the hour, till at last his anger was heightened into madness." When a mind is "empty and unoccupied," the dark passions may triumph.

Johnson: Politeness Put to the Test

Johnson always tried to regulate his ill humor, but he often found it difficult to do so. At the famous dinner party of 15 May 1776—where Johnson and John Wilkes finally met—he succeeded in maintaining his politeness, and as a result the dinner party was a success.

In the 1760s and early 1770s Johnson and Wilkes were bitter political enemies. Wilkes, who had attacked Johnson in print, was a rake—one of the founders of the Hell Fire Club. He was also a strident "Patriot"—one who thought the policies of King George III and his chief minister, Lord Bute, were undermining British liberty. Johnson considered Wilkes and his Patriot followers to be demagogues who threatened Britain's constitutional order. He once told Boswell that Wilkes was "an abusive scoundrel." In *The False Alarm* (1770) Johnson calls Wilkes a "retailer of sedition and obscenity." (Johnson mistakenly thought Wilkes had written an obscene parody of Pope's *Essay on Man*.) Johnson was probably thinking of Wilkes and his followers when in November 1775 he made his famous remark: "Patriotism is the last refuge of scoundrels."

(Hume's view of Wilkes was the same as Johnson's. Hume

worried that Wilkes and his Patriot followers were undermining the "mutual confidence" necessary for Britain's political
stability. He especially disliked Wilkes's claim that liberty was
in danger in Britain because Parliament had denied him his
seat. Franklin also disliked Wilkes. He said he was "an outlaw
and an exile, of bad personal character, not worth a farthing.")

Since Johnson and Wilkes had attacked each other in
print, it would seem foolhardy of Boswell to want to arrange a
meeting between the two. When Boswell asked the publisher
Edward Dilly, who was planning a dinner party with Wilkes, to
invite Johnson, Dilly replied: "Not for the world. Dr. Johnson
would never forgive me." Boswell told Dilly not to worry. Not
only would he persuade Johnson to attend the dinner, he
would also "be answerable that all shall go well."

Why was Boswell so confident that he could persuade
Johnson to attend a dinner party with Wilkes—confident also
that the meeting between the two would not result in a nasty
political quarrel? He was confident because he knew Johnson
had a strong sense of politeness. On their trip to Scotland in
1773 Boswell says Johnson "insisted that politeness was of great
consequence in society." On the same trip Johnson told Boswell:
"Sir, I look upon myself as a very polite man." Boswell adds:
"He was right, in a proper manly sense of the word."

Even though Boswell knew that Johnson aspired to be
polite, Boswell worried about the trip to Scotland because
Johnson, a self-proclaimed Tory, would be meeting his father,
an ardent Whig. (They met at Auchinleck, the Boswell family
estate.) Boswell says: "I was very anxious that all should be
well; and begged of my friend to avoid three topics, as to which
they differed very widely; Whiggism, Presbyterianism, and—
Sir John Pringle." (Johnson probably disliked Pringle because
he was a Unitarian.) Johnson replied that a polite man would

never think of getting into an argument with his host, especially if the host is the father of a friend. "I shall certainly not
talk on subjects which I am told are disagreeable to a gentleman under whose roof I am; especially, I shall not do so to
your father."

As it turned out, Johnson did not keep his promise for the
duration of his stay at Auchinleck. One day, when the subject
of Cromwell came up, both men—Boswell says—"became
exceedingly warm, and violent. . . . In the course of their altercation, Whiggism and Presbyterianism, Toryism and Episco-
pacy were terribly buffetted." Johnson despised Cromwell;
Boswell's father admired the Puritan leader. Despite this argument, at the end of Johnson's stay both men strove to be polite
to each another. "Notwithstanding the altercation that had
passed, my father, who had the dignified courtesy of an old
Baron, was very civil to Dr. Johnson, and politely attended him
to the post-chaise, which was to convey us to Edinburgh."

Since Johnson regarded himself as a polite man, it was
impossible for him to turn down Dilly's dinner invitation even
after he learned that Wilkes might be there. If Johnson refused
to attend Dilly's dinner party, he would be impolite because he
would be appearing to dictate to the host whom he should invite. In *Rambler* 98 Johnson says: "The universal axiom in
which all complaisance is included, and from which flow all
the formalities which custom has established in civilized nations, is, That no man should give any preference to himself."
If Johnson turned Dilly down, he would be giving preference
to himself, for he would be implying that he had the right to
choose the guests at someone else's dinner party.

Knowing that Johnson valued politeness, Boswell baited
him. After Johnson said he would be glad to go to a dinner
party at Dilly's, Boswell replied:

BOSWELL: Provided, sir, I suppose, that the company which he is to have is agreeable to you.

JOHNSON: What do you mean, Sir? What do you take me for? Do you think I am so ignorant of the world, as to imagine that I am to prescribe to a gentleman what company he is to have at his table?

BOSWELL: I beg your pardon, Sir, for wishing to prevent you from meeting people whom you might not like. Perhaps he may have some of what he calls his patriotick friends with him.

JOHNSON: What care I for his patriotick friends? Poh!

BOSWELL: I should not be surprized to find Jack Wilkes there.

JOHNSON: And if Jack Wilkes should be there, what is that to me, Sir? My dear friend, let us have no more of this. I am sorry to be angry with you; but really it is treating me strangely to talk to me as if I could not meet any company whatever, occasionally.

Would Johnson have met with "any company whatever, occasionally"? It is impossible to answer this question, but Boswell apparently never tried to arrange a dinner party that included Johnson and Hume.

Arriving at the dinner party, Johnson at first struggled to maintain his politeness. When Dilly informed Johnson that a certain gentleman in the room was "not only a patriot but an American," he muttered under his breath, 'Too, too, too.'" When Johnson learned that another gentleman was the famous Wilkes, "he had some difficulty to restrain himself, and taking up a book, sat down upon a window-seat and read." Nevertheless, Johnson soon managed to control his feelings; he "resolutely set himself to behave quite as an easy man of the world, who could adopt himself at once to the disposition and manners of those whom he might chance to meet." For his part, Wilkes treated Johnson "with so much attention and politeness that he gained upon him insensibly." Out of politeness, both men avoided politics, and the result was an enjoyable evening for Johnson. "I attended Dr. Johnson home," Boswell says, "and had the satisfaction to hear him tell Mrs. Williams how much he had been pleased with Mr. Wilkes's company."

Did the successful dinner party make Johnson and Wilkes more well-disposed toward each other? Boswell thought so. He says the meeting at Dilly's "had the agreeable and benignant effect of reconciling any animosity, and sweetening any acidity, which in the various bustle of political contest, had been produced in the minds of [the] two men." This is wishful thinking on Boswell's part, for one year later Wilkes attacked Johnson in the House of Commons—calling him (and another man) "pensioned advocates of despotism." Johnson did not attack Wilkes in print, but he continued to disapprove of "Patriots." In April 1781, when Johnson was discussing the membership of a new club that he hoped to form, he told a friend: "Don't let them [any new members] be patriots."

Boswell, however, was certain that Johnson's political differences with Wilkes no longer loomed as large in Johnson's mind as they had in the past. Discussing the second dinner that he arranged for them on 8 May 1781, Boswell says that "no negociation was required to bring them together, for Johnson was so well satisfied with the former interview, that he was very glad to meet Wilkes again." The implication is that Johnson was now eager to meet Wilkes because he had enjoyed his first conversation with him.

Johnson may have revised his opinion of Wilkes for another reason; he admired Wilkes's conduct during the Gordon Riots, which erupted in June 1780. At the time a London mob, ostensibly protesting proposed legislation that would give more rights to Catholics, rioted for roughly seven days. When the mob attempted to burn down the Bank of England, it was repulsed by a group of citizens led by Wilkes, who was then City Chamberlain. Writing to Hester Thrale, Johnson notes that Wilkes seized the publisher of a seditious paper; and that he also headed the party that drove the rioters away. According to Johnson, Wilkes saved the day; he was the man who enabled government to "act again with its proper force . . . [so that] we are all again under the protection of the King and law."

Yet in one sense Boswell was right to say that Johnson's view of Wilkes had changed as a result of the famous dinner party, for Johnson greatly valued a good conversationalist and Wilkes clearly was one. Six months after the first dinner party, Johnson summed up his view of Wilkes's conversational skills by offering a tongue-in-cheek criticism of them. "Did we not hear so much said of Jack Wilkes, we should think more highly of his conversation. Jack has great variety of talk, Jack is a scholar, and Jack has the manners of a gentleman. But after hearing his name sounded from pole to pole, as the phoenix of convivial felicity, we are disappointed in his company. He has always been at me; but I would do Jack a kindness, rather than not." In a jesting way Johnson is saying that Wilkes's reputation as a conversationalist is overrated, but he is also implicitly admitting that Wilkes has passed the test of clubbability. He may not be "the phoenix of convivial felicity," but he is a good dinner companion, which is why Johnson says: "I would do Jack a kindness rather than not."

Johnson ends his remarks about Wilkes by saying that "the contest is now over." Johnson is not referring to his political differences with Wilkes but to their respective conversational talents. He is saying that the contest as to who is the better conversationalist is over and he—Johnson—has won. Johnson often thought of conversation as a contest. When Boswell once asked him: "May there not be conversation without a contest for superiority?" Johnson replied: "No animated conversation, for it cannot be but one or other must come off superior. I do not mean that he shall have the better in the argument, for he may take the weak side; but his superiority of parts and knowledge will necessarily appear." By contest Johnson doesn't mean a grim, humorless debate; he means a lively, witty exchange of ideas—an exchange that includes raillery. He liked conversational contests, provided everyone was polite.

Johnson, we might say, has two ways of thinking about Wilkes. On the one hand, he strongly disapproves of Wilkes's Patriot politics and libertine ways. (By the mid-1780s Wilkes said that he was no longer a Patriot.) On the other hand, he enjoys having a conversational contest with Wilkes, so long as it is not about politics. Johnson preferred the company of people who were skilled at the art of conversation even if he did not agree with their political views.

In Johnson's biography of the minor poet Edmund Smith, he says that political differences never prevented him from enjoying the company of a good conversationalist. He praises Gilbert Walmsley, an older man whose conversation he had greatly enjoyed, even though Walmsley was a Whig. "He was a

Whig," Johnson says, "with all the virulence and malevolence of his party; yet difference of opinion did not keep us apart. I honoured him, and he endured me." Johnson then reminisces about the conversations he had at Walmsley's house. "At this man's table I enjoyed many chearful and instructive hours with companions such as are not often found."

For Johnson the pleasures of conversation trump political differences, yet when political questions came up he often found it difficult to maintain his politeness. When Boswell took the side of the American colonists on the question of taxation without representation, Johnson became angry. "The violent agitation into which he [Johnson] was thrown, while answering, or rather reprimanding me, alarmed me so, that I heartily repented of my having unthinkingly introduced the subject. I myself, however, grew warm, and the change was great, from the calm state of philosophical discussion in which we had a little before been pleasingly employed." In the conversation with Boswell about the American colonies, Johnson did not have the time to summon up the will to be polite.

Johnson, like Hume, thought it was profoundly important not to let political differences prevent the art of conversation from flourishing. Politeness was essential because governments that allowed extensive liberty, as Britain did, were in danger of collapsing into violent civil discord if the code of politeness was abandoned.

Johnson thought politeness was so important that he even defended Lord Chesterfield's posthumously published *Letters to His Son* (1774), a book that was attacked by many people for its cynicism and immorality. Chesterfield repeatedly tells his son that the main purpose of pleasing in conversation is to suck up to those who might help one get ahead in life. He also speaks of the pleasures of manipulating other people and the pleasures of adultery with a "polite" mistress. Johnson famously remarked that Chesterfield's *Letters* "teach the morals of a whore, and the manners of a dancing master," yet two years later he said the letters "might be made a very pretty book. Take out the immorality, and it should be put in the hands of every young gentleman." There is a great deal about Chesterfield's letters that Johnson would have liked: Chesterfield's knowledge of the passions, his debunking of the notion that rural people are more virtuous than urban people, and his detailed advice about how to please at the art of conversation.

As Johnson's remarks about Chesterfield suggest, Johnson never equated being skilled at the art of conversation with achieving "moral discipline of the mind." In *Rambler* 188 Johnson says: "The pleasure which men are able to give in conversation, holds no stated proportion to their knowledge or their virtue." Johnson's powerful biography of the minor poet Richard Savage, whom he befriended when he was a young man in London, is a case in point. Savage, he says, "excelled in the arts of conversation," yet Savage lacked any willpower; he suffered from an "habitual slavery to his passions, which involved him in many perplexities." Savage, he says, "was not master of his own motions."

Though Johnson deplores Savage's "irregular and dissipated manner of life," he never tires of praising Savage's conversation. He speaks of "the politeness and variety of his conversation," and he says "his method of life particularly qualified him for conversation, of which he knew how to practise all the graces." Savage was a good listener; "He was naturally inquisitive and desirous of the conversation of those from whom any information was to be obtained." Because he was a good listener, he picked up a great deal of knowledge in coffeehouses. "He mingled in cursory conversation with the same steadiness of attention as others apply to a lecture; and, amidst the appearance of thoughtless gaiety, lost no new idea that was started, nor any hint that could be improved. He had therefore made in coffee-house the same proficiency as others in their closets."

Savage's ability to educate himself by being a good listener in coffeehouses was the reverse side of his inability to spend any time in solitary study. He spent so many hours in coffeehouses (and taverns) because he had no sense of time. "He could not confine himself to any stated hours . . . but would prolong his conversation till midnight, without considering that business might require his friend's application in the morning." Savage was especially undisciplined about his finances—never paying back debts yet taking umbrage if anyone asked to be repaid. His conversational skills enabled him to charm people into giving him money. "Mrs. Oldfield . . . was so much pleased with his conversation, and touched with his misfortunes, that she allowed him a settled pension of fifty pounds a year."

After Mrs. Oldfield died the pension was withdrawn, but Savage continued to make new friends on the strength of his conversation and then cadge money from them. "His conversation was so entertaining, and his address so pleasing, that few thought the pleasure which they received from him dearly purchased, by paying for his wine." They usually paid for more than his wine. But friendships that were quickly gained were just as quickly lost. Describing Savage when he was in desperate straits, which was most of the time, Johnson says: "While he was thus spending the day in contriving a scheme for the morrow, distress stole upon him by imperceptible degrees. His conduct had already wearied some of those who were at first enamoured of his conversation." Savage died in debtor's prison.

Johnson's account of Savage's life does not contradict his view that spending time in the conversible world is likely to help us regulate our passions. The will to reform is necessary, and Savage lacked it. Moreover, Savage always blamed his misfortunes on others. "By imputing none of his miseries to himself, he continued to act upon the same principles, and to follow the same path." What Johnson has to say about the poet Abraham Cowley applies to Savage: "He readily persuaded himself that . . . every alteration would bring some improvement; he never suspected that the cause of his unhappiness was within, that his own passions were not sufficiently regulated."

Though Johnson argues that spending time in the conversible world is not necessarily going to help people strengthen their will, he always wants to improve conversation. In the *Life of Milton* he says: "Those authors . . . are to be read at schools that supply most axioms of prudence, most principles of moral truth, and *most materials for conversation*" (emphasis mine). Johnson hoped his own essays would furnish topics for conversation. In *Rambler* 126 a letter writer speaks of the "topicks of conversation which your papers supply."

Johnson promoted conversation for intellectual reasons as well. Like Hume, he argues that the learned need to test their ideas in the conversible world. "He that never compares his notions with those of others, readily acquiesces in his first thoughts, and very seldom discovers the objections which may be raised against this opinions; he, therefore, often thinks himself in possession of truth, when he is only fondling an error long since exploded." Johnson thought Milton was a great poet, but he says *Paradise Lost* lacks human interest mainly because Milton "had mingled little in the world, and was deficient in the knowledge which experience must confer."

Lady Mary Wortley Montagu:
Shunning the Conversible World

When Lady Mary Wortley Montagu (1689–1762) was in her twenties and thirties, she was a leading figure in England's conversible world. Admired by many for her "Wit and Charming Conversation," she was the friend of several writers, including Addison, Alexander Pope, and the playwright William Congreve. In letters written during this period, she often talks about the pleasures of conversation. She tells her future husband, Edward Wortley Montagu, "I like your conversation." A few years later she notes that her three-year-old son "improves ev'ry day in his Conversation." Staying over in Vienna for two months while she and her husband were on their way to Istanbul (he had been appointed British ambassador to Turkey), she says she has enjoyed the kind of conversation that is "the greatest happynesse of Life": the "chosen conversation compos'd of a few that one esteems."

Yet in 1739, at age fifty, Lady Mary in effect said goodbye to the conversible world. She left London for the Continent—ostensibly for her health but really to pursue a man she had fallen in love with: Francesco Algarotti, an Italian intellectual who was more than two decades younger. Two years later, after Algarotti made it clear that he was no longer interested in her, she did not return to her husband in England. Instead, she lived in France and Italy for more than twenty years—for the most part shunning the conversible world. In 1753 she writes her daughter, Lady Bute, that "since my last return to Italy [from France] . . . I have liv'd in a solitude not unlike that of Robinson Crusoe. Excepting for short trips to Louvere [*sic*], my whole time is spent in my Closet and Garden, without regretting any Conversation but that of my own Family." ("Louvere" is Lovere—an Italian spa town that Lady Mary went to for her health.)

Why did Lady Mary choose to live like Robinson Crusoe? She frequently implies that she did so in large part because the conversible world does not respect learned women. Writing her daughter about how to educate her granddaughter, Lady Mary says it is absolutely necessary "to conceal whatever Learning she attains, with as much solicitude as she would hide crookedness or lameness. The parade of it can only serve to draw on her the envy, and consequently the most inveterate Hatred, of all he and she Fools, which will certainly be at least three parts in four of all her Acquaintance."

Lady Mary is bitter that most Englishmen do not respect learned women. And she is bitter, it seems, because the world is dominated by men. "A studious Life . . . may be . . . preferable even to that Fame which Men have engross'd to themselves and will not suffer us to share." Anticipating her daughter's objection that Lady Mary did not conceal her own learning, Lady Mary says: "You will tell me I have not observ'd this rule [concealing her learning] my selfe, but you are mistaken; it is only inevitable Accident that has given me any Reputation that way."

Lady Mary's claim that she had tried to conceal her learning is puzzling, for when she was in her early twenties she was known for being a learned woman. She was the author of poems and essays that circulated in manuscript, and she was also the translator of Epictetus's *Enchiridon*. Owing to her literary skills, Addison invited her to contribute an essay for the *Spectator*. No other woman wrote for Addison's journal.

Moreover, Lady Mary did not conceal her dissatisfaction with the way women were educated. When she was twenty-two she wrote Gilbert Burnet, the Bishop of Salisbury, that women "are permitted no Books but such as tend to the weak-

ening and Effeminateing the Mind, our Natural Deffects are
every way indulg'd, and tis look'd upon as in a degree Criminal to improve our Reason, or fancy we have any. We are taught
to place all our Art in adorning our Outward Forms, and permitted . . . to carry that Custom even to Extravagancy, while
our Minds are entirely neglected." Forty years later she would
make roughly the same remark to her daughter: "There is
hardly a character in the World more Despicable or more liable to universal ridicule than that of a Learned Woman."

Lady Mary claims that she is not arguing "for an Equality for the 2 sexes." Her main point is that women are easily
corrupted because of their lack of education. To support this
point—as well as to show that she is educated—she ends the
letter with a lengthy Latin quotation from Erasmus, who also
is in favor of educating women. "It is proper," Erasmus says,
"for a woman born in Germany to learn French so that she can
talk with those who know French. Why then is it considered
indecorous if she learns Latin so that she can converse daily
with so many eloquent, learned and wise authors and trustworthy counselors?" Lady Mary agrees with Erasmus that a good
education may help women regulate their passions. (Lady Mary
did not think highly of Bishop Burnet. "I knew him in my very
early Youth, and his condescension in directing a Girl in her
studies is an Obligation I can never forget.")

Though Lady Mary speaks of a general European contempt for learned women, her quarrel is mainly with the view
of women that she thinks is commonplace in England. In 1753
she writes her daughter: "To say Truth, there is no part of the
World where our Sex is treated with so much contempt as in
England." After saying that women "are educated in the gross-
est ignorance, and no art omitted to stifle our natural reason,"
she adds that "I am now speaking according to our English no-

tions, which may wear out (some ages hence) along with others equally absurd." She says that Longinus, a Greek author of the third century AD, was more enlightened on these matters than most contemporary Englishmen. "I find him so far superior to vulgar prejudices as to chuse his two Examples of fine Writeing [*sic*] from a Jew (at the time the most despis'd people upon Earth) and a Woman." (In *On the Sublime* Longinus cites Moses and Sappho.)

This angry letter was occasioned by an odd request: an Italian cardinal wanted to have copies of Lady Mary's complete works. When she told the cardinal's representative that "I had never printed a single line in my Life," he did not believe her. Lady Mary was not lying. Her poems occasionally were printed without her name on them, but mostly they were circulated in manuscript. Her essay in the *Spectator* was published anonymously, as were all the *Spectator* essays. (The first edition of her letters was published in 1763, one year after her death.) In the letter she complains about the way her writing has been treated. "Sure no body ever had such various provocations to print as my selfe. I have seen things I have wrote so mangle'd and falsify'd I have scarce known them. I have seen Poems I never read publish'd with my Name at length, and others that were truly and singly wrote by me, printed under the names of others."

Lady Mary, though, is mainly flattered by the cardinal's request, which for her is proof that in Italy learned women are treated with respect. They are even given academic appointments. (She mentions a woman professor of mathematics at the University of Bologna.) "I confess I have often been complimented (since I have been in Italy) on the Books I have given the Public. I us'd at first to deny it with some Warmth, but finding I persuaded no body, I have of late contented my selfe with laughing when ever I heard it mention'd, knowing the character of a learned Woman is far from being ridiculous in this Country."

Yet if learned women are respected in Italy, why did Lady Mary live a life of semiseclusion in the small city Brescia when she could have lived in such intellectual centers as Milan or Bologna? Did she really lose interest in conversation, since in many letters she speaks of the pleasures of solitude? Perhaps, but in 1748 she writes her daughter: "I enjoy every amusement that Solitude can afford . . . [but] I confess I sometimes wish for a little conversation." In another letter she writes her good friend Lady Oxford that "if I could have your Ladyship's dear Conversation, I may truly say my Life would be very comfortable."

In 1755 Lady Mary describes a "Conversation" held by an Italian intellectual, the Marquis Maffei, at his palazzo in Verona—pointing out that the conversation "allways turn'd upon some point of Learning, either Historical or Poetical, Controversie and Politics being utterly prohibited." But apparently she never attended another "conversation." She says: "I have had many honourable invitations from my old Freind [sic] Maffei to make one of this Society; some accident or other has allwaies prevented me [from attending]."

In 1756 Lady Mary moved to Venice, which offered more opportunities for conversation. Unfortunately, she became the bitter enemy of the British consul in Venice, who continually derided her, but in 1758 she befriended Sir James Steuart and his wife. Steuart was a Scottish intellectual living in exile because he was a Jacobite. Far from ridiculing her because she was a learned women, Steuart enjoyed her conversation, and he asked her to read his manuscript on political economy in the hope that she would make suggestions for improving it. In 1759 she writes a long letter to Steuart and his wife (they had left Venice), at the end of which she says: "I experienced last year how much happiness may be found with two amiable friends . . . and 'tis as hard [now] to return to political or gallant conversations as it would be for a fat prelate to content himselfe with the small beer he drank at college." In other words, she misses Steuart's conversation, which she greatly enjoyed. Steuart was Scottish, so perhaps Lady Mary's strictures against "English notions" did not apply.

It is hard to know how much weight to give Lady Mary's claim that in England learned women were regarded as figures of ridicule. As we have seen, many writers on conversation admired learned women. Swift admired the learned Esther Johnson; Hume was the friend of several learned *salonnières;* Johnson praised a number of learned women, including Elizabeth Carter. (Carter would translate the book on Newton that Algarotti, Lady Mary's lover, had written.) Lady Mary herself was admired for her learning and wit.

When Lady Montagu was in her twenties and thirties her greatest admirer probably was Alexander Pope. When she was traveling to Turkey, Pope wrote her a flirtatious letter—stressing how much he misses her conversation. "There is not a day in which your Figure does not appear before me, [and] your Conversations return to my thought." In another letter he says that by going to Turkey, she has robbed him "of the most valuable of his enjoyments, your Conversation." In 1718 he writes that he wants to see her as soon as she returns to England. Writing about living in the countryside and translating Homer, he says: "You will not wonder I have translated a great deal of Homer in this Retreat; Any one that sees it will own, I could not have chosen a fitter or more likely place to converse with the Dead. As soon as I return to the Living, it shall be to converse with the best of them"—meaning Lady Mary.

A few years later Pope came to detest Lady Mary. He blames the break on her "dangerous" conversation—saying that Lady Mary was intent on slandering him, "though my only fault towards her was, leaving off her conversation when I found it dangerous." By dangerous Pope meant that Lady Mary's wit had turned ugly and that she now enjoyed libeling people. Pope warned Robert Walpole, the prime minister, that he might be her next victim. "I have seen Sir R[obert] Walpole. . . . I made him then my confidant in a complaint against a lady, of his, and once of my, acquaintance, who is libelling me, as she certainly one day will him, if she has not already. You'll easily guess I am speaking of Lady Mary."

Pope's concern for Walpole's reputation cannot be taken seriously, for Pope disliked Walpole's politics—and soon he himself would attack Walpole in his poetry. Moreover, Lady Mary was a strong supporter of Walpole, so it is unlikely that she would libel him. Pope was furious with Lady Mary because he thought she had written—in collaboration with Lord Hervey—several nasty poems about him that circulated in manuscript. (One poem refers to his "wretched little Carcass.") In the advertisement to "An Epistle from Mr. Pope, to Dr. Arbuthnot," Pope says that he is publishing this poem because "it pleas'd some Persons of Rank and Fortune . . . to attack in a very extraordinary manner, not only my Writings . . . but my Person, Morals, and Family." He is referring to Lady Mary and Lord Hervey. According to Maynard Mack, Pope's biographer, Pope "seems to have convinced himself that either by her encouragement or by her pen she was covertly responsible for certain of the attacks made on him."

The change in Pope's view of Lady Mary is dramatic. In "On Lady Mary Wortley Montagu's Portrait," a poem composed when he still admired her, he praises her learning and

wit while talking about how difficult it is for a painter to show
Lady Mary's extraordinary traits:

> The Equal Lustre of the Heavnly mind
> Where every grace with every Virtue's join'd
> Learning not vain, and wisdom not severe
> With Greatness easy, and with wit sincere.

By contrast, in "To Ld. Hervey & Lady Mary Wortley," a poem
written roughly a decade later (and circulated only in manuscript), he calls her "a flagrant Whore" in the first stanza. The
second stanza begins with a sarcastic "Thanks, dirty Pair!" He
is saying that their cruel attacks have given him ideas about
how to attack them.

> Thanks, dirty Pair! You teach me what to say,
> When you attack my Morals, Sense, or Truth,
> I answer thus—poor Sapho [sic] you grow grey,
> And sweet Adonis—you have lost a Tooth.

Everyone in London's polite world knew that by Sappho Pope
meant Lady Mary.

In other poems Pope implies that Lady Mary is slovenly
and sexually promiscuous. He also implies that she and her
husband are tightfisted. In "Epistle To A Lady: Of the Characters of Women," he refers to her "dirty smock." He describes
the contradiction between

> Sappho at her toilet's greasy task,
> With Sappho fragrant at an ev'ning Mask:
> So morning Insects that in muck begun,
> Shine, buzz, and fly-blow in the setting-sun.

In short, she is a disgusting creature.

The nastiest attack is a couplet that appears in the "First Satire of the Second Book of Horace Imitated":

From furious *Sappho* scarce a milder Fate,
P—x'd by her Love, or libell'd by her Hate.

Lady Mary, Pope implies, has two ways of destroying you; she can libel you or she can give you syphilis. Poxed also refers to smallpox, from which Lady Mary suffered from 1715—leaving her face pitted and without eyebrows. It may also refer to Lady Mary's campaign, which she began when she returned from Turkey, to promote inoculation for smallpox—a campaign that many physicians initially attacked though inoculation gradually gained acceptance.

Lady Mary tried to enlist Pope's friends to persuade him to stop attacking her. Pope told his friends that Lady Mary was imagining the whole thing—that he was not thinking of her when wrote about Sappho; he had no one in particular in mind. His defense is not credible.

With the help of Lord Hervey, whom Pope attacked as harshly as he attacked Lady Mary, Lady Mary now tried to fight fire with fire. She began a poetic and pamphlet war with Pope—also attacking his friend Swift. This war, which was political as well as personal (Pope and Swift were allied with the anti-Walpole Tories), lasted roughly five years. She scored some hits, but she could hardly win a war against the age's most renowned poet—one who had many influential friends. According to Isobel Grundy, Lady Mary's biographer, "in every department of Lady Mary's life, Pope's blasting of her name would come to be felt more and more; her husband must have hated this, but his responses are not recorded. . . . Her bitterness about Pope rankled for years, in many contexts."

Grundy also implies that although Lady Mary left Britain in pursuit of Algarotti, she stayed abroad because her reputation had been sullied by Pope's "sustained vilification." (It is also possible, Grundy says, that Lady Mary stayed abroad because she had lost ten thousand pounds in financial speculations, and her husband refused to pay the debt. It was settled that he would give her an annuity.) Did Lady Mary think of returning to London after she learned that Pope had died? We do not know, but we do know that Lady Mary had few friends left in London's conversible world. Several had died, including her closest female friend, and several male friends had sided with Pope.

The extent to which Lady Mary's reputation was damaged by Pope's attacks can be inferred by a comment that Johnson makes in his biography of Pope, which was written roughly a half-century after Pope's campaign against Lady Mary. Johnson, who probably never met Lady Mary, writes that Pope and Lady Mary were guests at Lord and Lady Oxford's. "The table," he says, "was indeed *infested* by Lady Mary Wortley, who was the friend of Lady Oxford, and who knowing his [Pope's] peevishness could by no intreaties be restrained from contradicting him, till their disputes were sharpened to such asperity, that one or the other quitted the house" (emphasis mine). (The story is probably apocryphal. Lady Mary's daughter flatly denied it.)

Why did Johnson use the word "infested"—a very hostile word—to describe Lady Mary's presence? After all, the main point of the paragraph is to show that Pope "was fretful, and easily displaced, and allowed himself to be capriciously resentful." Did Johnson remember that in Pope's "Of the Characters of Women" Sappho is compared to an insect? Hence "infested." Johnson has no reason to be hostile to Lady Mary. He seems to be conveying the standard opinion of Lady Mary in London's polite world—that she was a difficult person, even a disgusting person. Johnson, who elsewhere speaks of Pope's "tedious malignity," implies that Pope and Lady Mary deserved each other.

Thus when Lady Mary says that learned women are ridiculed in England, we should keep in mind that she was burned badly by her quarrel with Pope. Other learned women were not subjected to such vicious abuse.

One should note, though, that even Lady Mary's friends thought that at times she lacked politeness. Lord Hervey complained about her talking "so fast, so incessantly, and so loud," though he also she said she was a civilized conversationalist. Grundy says that "Lady Mary's strong feelings and tendency to self-righteousness made her very prone to quarrels." She also speaks of Lady Mary's "ease and outspokenness in male company"—adding that "apparently she cracked jokes about forbidden subjects, and chose or wore her clothes in a manner to give offence."

Lady Mary enjoyed being crude at times. In Venice in 1758 she first tells a British visitor that Pope, Swift, and Bolingbroke were rascals. Then she shows him "her Commode, with false back of books"—the works of Pope, Swift, and Bolingbroke, whom she called "the greatest Rascals." This arrangement, she says, gave her "the satisfaction of shitting on them every day."

Lady Mary could also be arrogant—expecting a certain deference that she felt was owed to a woman of her class. Writing to her daughter, she complains that "the confounding of all

Ranks and making a Jest of order has long been growing in England, and I perceive, by the Books you sent me, has made a very considerable progress." In her view "it has long been the endeavor of our English Writers to represent people of Quality as the vilest and silliest part of the Nation." They take this view, she says, because they are generally "very low born themselves." Defending her class, she says that "the greatest examples I have known of Honor and Integrity has been amongst those of the highest Birth and Fortunes."

Yet it was the English aristocracy that was most likely to be against the education of women—and most likely to ridicule learned women. The aristocrat Shaftesbury did not think women belonged in the conversible world. The lower-middle-class Defoe and Johnson thought they did. Defoe and Johnson also agreed with Lady Mary that learning promotes morality. "I have often thought," Defoe says, "of it as one of the most barbarous customs in the world . . . that we deny the advantages of learning to women."

Why did Lady Mary return to England in 1761, after an absence of more than two decades? (Because her reputation was still under a cloud, her son-in-law, Lord Bute, who was now prime minister, did not want her to return.) Perhaps she returned because she knew she was dying; in late 1760 she had discovered a lump on her breast. (Seven months after she returned, she died of cancer.) More likely, she returned because her husband had died in January 1761 and she was worried that if she were not in London her dissolute and wayward son would try to deprive her and her daughter of their inheritance. (Her son did contest the will.) But she was not looking forward to her return. While still in Venice, she writes Steuart that "the few friends I esteemed are now no more; the new set of people who fill the stage at present are too indifferent to me even to raise my curiosity." Soon after she returned, she received many visitors. One said that Lady Mary "neither thinks, speaks, acts, or dresses, like any body else."

Lady Mary and Johnson are not usually twinned, but they have some things in common. Both suffered from smallpox, which disfigured their faces. Both were somewhat slovenly in their dress. More important, both valued politeness but had trouble being polite. Lady Mary sounds like Johnson when she writes her daughter that "I have seen Ladys indulge their own ill Humour by being very rude and impertinent, and think they deserv'd approbation by saying, I love to speak Truth." And she sounds like Johnson when she says there is "no such thing as being agreeable without a thorough good humour . . . enliven'd by Cheerfullnesse."

Reading a collection of Johnson's essays from the *Rambler* that her daughter had sent her, Lady Mary gives them a mixed review. "He allwaies plods in the beaten road of his Predecessors, following the Spectator (with the same pace a Pack horse would do a Hunter)," yet she thinks the essays provide moral instruction. She concludes by saying: "I should be glad to know the name of this Laborious Author." (Johnson's essays were published anonymously.)

Finally, both Lady Montagu and Johnson were frequently attacked. He was often criticized for accepting a government pension from George III in 1762. (Lord Bute, Lady Mary's son-in-law, recommended the pension.) But Johnson's attackers were not of the stature of Pope. And they were not as clever—or as nasty.

Perhaps the memory of her quarrel with Pope made Lady Mary reluctant to enter into the conversible world on the Continent, for fear that a similar quarrel might occur. Yet her letters make it clear that, despite her praise of solitude, she never lost interest in conversation. On her way back to England in 1761, she comments that in Rotterdam she found "neither amusement nor conversation." An English traveler who met her in the late 1750s, when she was living in Venice, said that "her letters were, like her conversation; natural, lively, gay; full of reason, wit, and interest."

VI

Conversation in Decline: From Raillery to Reverie

In the first two decades of the eighteenth century, as we have seen, many foreigners praised the conversation in English coffeehouses and clubs. Yet when a German baron visited Britain in the 1790s, he noted that the clients of coffeehouses read their newspapers in silence, and a few years later an Italian visitor complained that whispering was the norm in English coffeehouses. Moreover, a Spanish visitor said that the typical English club member prefers to avoid conversation. "If the Englishman be the most clubbable of men, according to Johnson's expression, it is not so much because he likes to speak, as that he possesses the art of holding his tongue. He respects your silence, but he expects you to respect his." In *Democracy in America* (1835) Alexis de Tocqueville speaks of the "strange unsociability and reserved and taciturn disposition of the English."

The comments were about Englishmen, not Scotsmen. The *Edinburgh Review* agreed with Tocqueville. "There is nothing which an Englishman enjoys more than the pleasure of sulkiness,—of not being forced to hear a word from any body which may occasion to him the necessity of replying." Scotsmen, it appears, had not changed.

Why had Englishmen changed? Perhaps a better question to ask is: Had they changed very much? Even during the heyday of the Age of Conversation there was a strong anti-conversation countercurrent. Many Englishmen regarded the good conversationalist with distrust. In a *Spectator* essay written by Steele, a letter writer says: "the greatest part of the Conversation of Mankind is little else but driving a Trade of dissimulation." It would make a man, he says, "heartily sick and weary of the World, to see the little Sincerity that is in Use and Practice among Men." Even Hume admitted that "modern politeness . . . runs often into affectation and foppery, disguise and insincerity."

Perhaps because the famous books on conversation were written by Italians and Frenchmen, being a good conversationalist was often regarded as a foreign trait. Was the good conversationalist like a courtier—practicing the art of pleasing in conversation in order to further his own interest? In *Amelia* (1751), Henry Fielding's last novel, politeness is connected with the deception practiced by courtiers. Describing a polite character, the narrator says that he possesses "that noble art which is taught in those excellent schools called the several courts of Europe. By this men are enabled to dress out their countenances as much at their own pleasure, as they do their bodies; and to put on friendship with as much ease as they can a laced coat."

Though Fielding extolled the pleasures of conversation, he was also preoccupied with the question of hypocrisy in conversation. In "On the Knowledge of the Characters of Men" (1743), Fielding discusses hypocrisy—"that detestable Fiend" which is "a great Evil . . . the Bane of all Virtue, Morality, and Goodness." In his view "a little reflection will convince us, that most Mischiefs (especially those which fall on the worthiest Part of Mankind) owe their Original to this detestable Vice," which is commonplace. People who are good-natured—Fielding, unlike Johnson, thinks of this trait as an innate quality—and possess an "open Disposition" are especially vulnerable to being "imposed on by Craft and Deceit."

In Fielding's novels the good conversationalists often are unscrupulous. In *Tom Jones* (1749) a captain who is Miss Bridget Allworthy's suitor is noted for his conversation, but we soon learn that he is a dishonest man. The narrator says: "Such were the charms of the captain's conversation, that she [Miss Bridget] totally overlooked the defects of his person."

Polite hypocrites are pervasive in *Amelia*. When the narrator calls a character polite, he is usually saying to the reader: don't trust him (or her). A minor character takes a very critical view of politeness. "'For my own part,' said she, 'I have not the least relish for those very fine gentlemen; what the world generally calls politeness, I term insincerity.'" Mr. Booth, the central character, defends politeness: "To say the truth, politeness carries friendship far enough in the ordinary occasions of life, and those who want [lack] this accomplishment rarely make amends for it by their sincerity; for bluntness, or rather rudeness, as it commonly deserves to be called, is not always so much a mark of honesty as it is taken to be." His point is: don't assume that a blunt man is an honest man. Yet Booth suffers because the polite Colonel James, who he assumes is his friend, turns out to be unscrupulous.

In *Amelia* the polite characters seem to enjoy deception for its own sake. Booth says: "Sometimes one would be almost persuaded that there was a pleasure in lying itself." A central event in the novel is a masquerade, which (as David Blewett says) "functions as a microcosm . . . of a world characterized by artifice, deception, hidden identity, seduction, betrayal, and adultery." Why are there so many polite schemers in Britain? Fielding implies that Britain is a corrupt society in which the selfish passions have become predominant.

Fielding's view of Britain is not uniformly bleak. Booth, his wife (Amelia), and another couple spend an evening "in great mirth and festivity" with Doctor Harrison, about whom the narrator says: "For the doctor was one of the best companions in the word; and a vein of cheerfulness, good-humour and pleasantry, ran through his conversation, with which it was impossible to resist being pleased." Doctor Harrison is polite yet he is also a good man. He is Fielding's ideal—the cheerful, good-natured conversationalist. Nevertheless, the novel leaves the reader with a warning. most polite men and women are not to be trusted.

The Pleasures of Solitude: In Search of the Sublime

If many English men and women were wary of polite people, many also were not interested in the conversible world. They preferred solitude, especially rural solitude. In "A Nocturnal Reverie," which was written in the first decade of the eighteenth century, Anne Finch, Countess of Winchilsea—one of the earliest published women poets in England—speaks of the tranquility of solitude. The poem begins with a dreamlike description of a rural evening where the only sounds are those that emanate from the natural world. As night arrives the speaker is free from the tyranny of the day, with its "fierce light [that] disturbs," and is at one with the "inferior world" of Nature. In eight powerful lines she describes her state of mind.

> When a sedate content the spirit feels,
> And no fierce light disturbs, whilst it reveals;
> But silent musings urge the mind to seek

Something, too high for syllables to speak;
Till the free soul to a composedness charmed,
Finding the elements of rage disarmed,
O'er all below a solemn quiet grown,
Joys in th' inferior world, and thinks it like her
   own.

She knows that her reverie cannot last.

In such a night let me abroad remain,
Till morning breaks, and all's confused again;
Our cares, our toils, our clamors are renewed,
Or pleasures, seldom reached, again pursued.

In her "nocturnal reverie" she experiences a feeling of "composedness" that she cannot define—a feeling that is "too high for syllables to speak." It goes without saying that this state of mind cannot be achieved in coffeehouses and clubs.

In "Ode on Solitude," which Pope claimed he wrote when he was twelve, he implies that solitude promotes tranquility. The poem describes a self-sufficient farmer who is "blest" because he

can unconcernedly find
Hours, days, and years slide soft away,
In health of body, peace of mind,
Quiet by day,

Sound sleep by night; study and ease,
Together mix'd; sweet recreation;
And innocence, which most does please,
With meditation.

In this pastoral fantasy the farmer has no worries about making a living. He spends his leisure hours in "sweet recreation" and meditation. He does not engage in conversation. Many years later Pope referred to the poem in a letter: "You may perceive how long I have continued in my passion for a rural life." Yet Pope occasionally complained about his solitary rural existence. "Retiring into oneself," he says in a letter, "is generally the *Pis-aller* of mankind." In another letter he is upset because he has gone several weeks without conversation. "I have now past [*sic*] five weeks without once going from home, and without any company but for three or four of the days. . . . I never pass'd so melancholy a time."

In "Windsor-Forest" (1713) Pope describes the life of a retired public servant who has moved to the country. Alluding to a Roman literary tradition that praised rural retirement, Pope refers to two famous Roman retirees: Scipio, the Roman general who retired to his estate, and Atticus, the friend of Cicero who left public life to devote himself to study. Pope's retired gentleman lives a natural life: "He gathers Health from Herbs the Forest yields." He also lives an intellectual life—studying the heavens as well as the natural world. His retirement, Pope suggests, is satisfying because he is following Nature.

> T'observe a Mean, be to himself a Friend,
> To follow Nature, and regard his End.

Far from the conversible world, the gentleman enjoys "wandering thoughtful in the silent wood." The line echoes a line in Horace's *Epistles* (I-iv): "walking in silence through the healthy woods, pondering questions worthy of the wise and good."

James Thomson, the author of the popular poem *The Seasons* (1730), also associates rural life with tranquility and

virtue. In "Hymn on Solitude" he addresses Solitude as if he
were a companion:

> Hail mildly pleasing Solitude,
> Companions of the wide and good;
> But from whose holy piercing eye
> The herd of fools and villains fly . . .

In the last stanza Thomson addresses Solitude as if it were a
place. He admits that he is still interested in London life, but he
hopes Solitude will shield him from its temptations.

> Oh, let me pierce thy secret cell!
> And in thy deep recesses dwell!
> Perhaps from Norwood's oak-clad hill,
> When meditation has her fill,
> I just may cast my careless eyes
> Where London's spiry turrets rise,
> Think of its crimes, its cares, its pain,
> Then shield me in the woods again.

Thomson, who lived in London for most of his adult life, is not
exhorting the reader to move to the country. (Norwood is the
seat of Gilbert West—a retired friend.) He is giving the reader
advice: if you live in London meditate about rural solitude in
order to inoculate yourself against London's dark passions.

"Hymn on Solitude" also has a quasi-political message.
Thomson implies that the ideal civic-minded gentleman—the
man most likely to defend liberty—is not the Londoner who
frequents the coffeehouse or club. It is the man who has retired
from London to enjoy the solitude of rural life. In *The Seasons*
he says:

> The happiest he! Who far from public rage,
> Deep in the vale, with a choice view retir'd,
> Drinks the pure pleasures of the rural life . . .

According to Thomas, one has a better chance of living a virtuous life in the country, where the pleasures are "pure."

During the ministry of Robert Walpole, which lasted
from 1721 to 1742, many writers argued that London was a center of corruption. In "London," a poem Johnson wrote when
he was twenty-nine, the main character flees from the corrupt
city to the "wilds of Kent"

> To breathe in distant fields a purer air . . .
> And, fixed on Cambria's solitary shore,
> Give to St. David one true Briton more.

(Cambria is Wales, and St. David is the patron saint of Wales.)
By leaving London, he becomes an honest citizen: a "true
Briton." It is unlikely that Johnson really held such a view of
London. He was a young writer trying to impress the leading
writers of the age, and the notion that London was a den of
corruption was commonplace in English literary circles.

Fifteen years later Johnson attacked the vogue for rural
solitude. "These specious representations of solitary happiness, however opprobrious to human nature, have so far
spread their influence over the world, that almost every man
delights his imagination with the hopes of obtaining some
time an opportunity of retreat." He also argued that solitude
is dangerous for the mind. "Many have no happier moments
than those that they pass in solitude, abandoned to their own
imagination, which sometimes puts scepters in their hands
or mitres on their heads, shifts the scene or pleasure with end-

less variety, bids all the forms of beauty sparkle before them, and gluts them with every change of visionary luxury." By "visionary luxury," he means mental extravagance—an imagination slipping into madness. Johnson also says that rural solitude is boring. In another essay a woman who had hoped to find felicity in the country complains: "I am condemned to solitude; the day moves slowly forward, and I see the dawn with uneasiness, because I consider that night is at a great distance."

Johnson was not opposed to occasional periods of solitude. He would probably agree with Burke, who in *A Philosophical Enquiry into the Origin of Our Ideas of the Sublime and Beautiful* (1757) says that "solitude as well as society has its pleasures." In Burke's view "good company, lively conversations, and the endearments of friendship, fill the mind with great pleasures; a temporary solitude, on the other hand, is itself agreeable." Burke, though, did not approve of "absolute and entire *solitude,* that is, the total and perpetual exclusion from all society."

No eighteenth-century English writer praised absolute solitude, but by the middle of the century many writers argued that solitude not only was the path to tranquility and virtue, it was also requisite for experiencing the sublime pleasures of the imagination. These writers were influenced—surprisingly— by the work of Addison, who argued in several essays that the pleasures of the imagination complement the pleasures of conversation. The pleasures of the imagination, Addison says, promote cheerfulness. Speaking about "Beauty," whether in Nature or in art, he says: "The very first Discovery of it strikes the Mind with an inward Joy, and spreads a Cheerfulness and Delight through all its Faculties." These pleasures should also be re-

garded as a kind of conversation. "A man of a Polite Imagination ... can converse with a Picture, and find an agreeable
Companion in a Statue."

Addison argues that the pleasures of imagination are of
two kinds: enjoying a "beautiful prospect" or appreciating a
great work of art. "Delightful Scenes, whether in Nature, Painting or Poetry, have a kindly Influence on the Body, as well as
the Mind, and not only serve to clear and brighten the Imagination, but are able to disperse Grief and Melancholy." Referring to "huge Heaps of Mountains, high Rocks and Precipices,
or a wide Expanse of Waters," Addison asks: What is the effect
of viewing "that rude kind of Magnificence which appears in
many of these stupendous Works of Nature?" According to
Addison, "we are flung into a pleasing Astonishment at such
unbounded Views, and feel a delightful Stillness and Amazement in the Soul at the Apprehension of them." He says that "a
beautiful Prospect delights the soul."

Literary descriptions of landscapes, Addison argues, also
delight the soul. They are "apt to raise a secret Ferment in the
Mind of the Reader, and to work, with Violence, upon his Passions." Reading the *Iliad* is like "traveling through a Country
uninhabited, where the Fancy [Addison uses "imagination"
and "fancy" interchangeably] is entertained with a thousand
Savage Prospects of vast Desarts, wide uncultivated Marshes,
huge Forests, mis-shapen Rocks, and Precipices." Homer, Addison says, "fills his readers with Sublime Ideas."

Sublime had been an English word for more than a century, but it gained a new life by way of France. In the late seventeenth and early eighteenth centuries Boileau's French translation of Longinus's *On the Sublime* (written around AD 200)
was then translated into English. In the *Dictionary* Johnson de-

fines the noun "sublime": "The grand or lofty stile. *The sublime*
is a Gallicism, but now naturalized." At first sublime referred to
a literary style that could be called "high," but English critics
expanded the meaning of the word to signify any work of art
or literature that has a powerful effect upon the viewer or
reader. Experiencing the sublime was good for the psyche. In
Essay on the Sublime (1747), John Baillie says that sublimity
"extends [man's] very Being."

In *A Philosophical Enquiry* Burke argues that sublime
works of art as well as sublime landscapes have a terrifying aspect; they are scenes of darkness, solitude, silence, vacuity,
vastness. The sublime causes "delightful horror" in the viewer
or reader. The sublime is different from the beautiful, which is
smooth, delicate, sweet, and feminine. Some writers also spoke
of the picturesque, which is closer to the sublime than it is to
the beautiful though it lacks the element of terror.

Hugh Blair, Hume's friend and a leading Scottish literary
critic, tried to define the sublime in nature. "What are the
scenes of nature that elevate the mind in the highest degree,
and produce the sublime sensation? Not the gay landscape, the
flowering field, or the flourishing city; but the hoary mountain, and the solitary lake; the aged forest, and the torrent
falling over the rock." In the late eighteenth century, it became
fashionable to go to the mountain districts in England, Scotland, and Wales, where there were many sublime and picturesque landscapes. A popular guide to the Lake District says:
"Picture the mountains rearing their majestic heads with native sublimity." Many people also associated the sublime with
ruins. In the popular poem "Ruins of Rome" (1740), John Dyer
calls Rome a "solitary, silent, solemn scene."

The poets and tourists who were in search of the sublime
admired the sounds of the natural world, especially the sound

of running water, which was a symbol of the creative imagination. The sounds that human beings make are sublime only if they are experienced as sounds. Blair, who says that "mighty force or power . . . [is] the fundamental quality of the sublime," associates the sublime with "the burst of thunder or cannon, the roaring of winds, the shouting of multitudes, [and] the sound of vast cataracts of water." What the "shouting multitudes" are saying is irrelevant.

If it was relatively easy to define the sublime in nature, it was difficult to define the sublime in art. In *Essay on Original Genius* (1767), William Duff says: "The sublime is the proper walk of a great Genius, in which it delights to range, and in which alone it can display its power to advantage." Sublime poetry was supposed to thrill and astonish the reader. It was not supposed to make the reader laugh or smile. The sublime world is a world without wit and raillery. It is also a melancholy world. In *The Seasons* Thomson says:

The desolated prospect thrills the soul.
He comes! He comes! In every breeze the Power
Of philosophic Melancholy comes.

Needless to say, the sublime could not be found in coffeehouses or clubs. In search of the sublime, one should read poetry, especially ancient poems, one should gaze at ruins, or one should take solitary walks in the countryside—preferably in the mountains. To quote *The Seasons* again:

Now the soft hour
Of walking comes to him who lonely loves
To seek the distant hills, and there converse
With nature.

In 1780 the poet William Cowper was uttering a commonplace when he said: "O! I could spend whole days and moonlight nights in feeding upon a lovely prospect!"

The vogue for lovely prospects was abetted by the popularity of Jean-Jacques Rousseau. In Britain Rousseau was almost as influential as he was in France. John Brewer says that in the last quarter of the eighteenth century Rousseau was "one of the most popular and controversial authors" in Britain. Rousseau's *La Nouvelle Héloïse* (1761), which celebrates rustic life and indirectly attacks the salons, was the most popular eighteenth-century novel. According to Maurice Cranston, Rousseau's biographer, the novel "transformed Rousseau from a celebrated author into the object of a cult. . . . The success of the novel was such as to modify prevailing tastes radically."

Rousseau was praised by Boswell, who saw no contradiction between admiring Johnson, who championed conversation, and admiring Rousseau, who attacked the conversible world. When Rousseau was living in Switzerland, Boswell hoped to gain an interview with him. "Enlightened Mentor!" Boswell wrote. "Eloquent and amiable Rousseau! I have a presentiment that a truly noble friendship will be born today." Trying to ingratiate himself with Rousseau, Boswell speaks of "the silence and the solitude of your sacred retreat." Boswell did manage to meet Rousseau, but no friendship came of it.

Rousseau's first "sacred retreat" was the Hermitage, which he moved to after he left Paris in 1756. The Hermitage was a spacious farmhouse that was isolated—a mile from the nearest neighbor and even farther from the nearest road. Life at the Hermitage suited him: "I delight in living like a peasant, which I feel is my true vocation." Rousseau was hardly a typical peasant. In the mornings he copied music, in the afternoons he took a walk, and in the evenings he wrote. Thérèse Levasseur, his common-law wife, provided for all his needs, and the house was given to him rent-free by his patron, Madame d'Épinay. She confided to a friend that there was only one way to deal with Rousseau, "and that is to pretend to leave him alone entirely but actually to be fussing over him all the time."

Rousseau's decision to leave Paris disturbed his philosophe friends. Diderot wrote a play in which a character comments on someone who has decided to live in rustic solitude: "Only the bad man is alone." Rousseau complained to Diderot that the remark was cruel. Diderot offered an apology: "I ask your forgiveness for what I said about the solitude in which you live." But Diderot signed off his letter with the line: "Adieu, Citizen—and yet a hermit makes a very peculiar citizen." Diderot thought Rousseau was being irresponsible as well as misanthropic in choosing to live in rural solitude.

Rousseau did not think he was a misanthrope. About the time he left Paris, he wrote that he had adopted a motto, *Vitam impendere vero:* To risk one's life for the truth. Unlike his Parisian friends, who were quickly becoming ex-friends, he thought he was committed to telling the truth rather than practicing the art of pleasing in conversation. According to Rousseau, the truth is simple: luxury has turned men and women into servile and hypocritical creatures animated by self-love. In *Discourse on the Origins and Foundations of Inequality Among Men* (1755), he contrasts the savage man with the social man: "Savage man lies within himself; social man knows only how to live beyond himself in the opinion of others, and it is, so to speak, from their judgment alone that he derives the sentiment of his own existence." The implication is that the social man is someone who cares only about appearances.

According to Rousseau, the more polite a society is, the more corrupt it is. A man of integrity and civic virtue—a man like himself—cannot flourish in such an environment, which is why he left Paris. Summing up his view of the modern age, Rousseau says: "We have only a deceptive and frivolous outward appearance, honor without virtue, reason without wisdom, and pleasure without happiness. It suffices for me to have proved that this is not the original state of man, and that it is only the spirit of society and the inequality it engenders which thus transform and corrupt all our natural inclinations."

Rousseau says "we," but he doesn't consider himself to be part of the world that he attacks. He shuns the conversible world. If Hume thinks sociability nourishes the benevolent passions, Rousseau argues that sociability prevents the benevolent passions from flourishing. In the posthumously published *Reveries of the Solitary Walker* (1782) he says: "The taste for solitude and contemplation grew up in my heart along with the expansive and tender feelings which are best able to nourish it. Noise and turmoil constrain and quench them, peace and quiet revive and intensify them. I need tranquility if I am to love." To love modern—that is, corrupt—men and women, he needs to be removed from them. "I have never been truly fitted for social life, where there is nothing but irksome duty and obligation, and that my independent character has always made it impossible for me to submit to the constraints which must be accepted by anyone who wishes to live among men."

Rousseau wants it both ways: he says that a man of integrity chooses solitude, and he also says that a man of integrity will be rejected by the conversible world. He begins the *Reveries* with a famous sentence: "So now I am alone in the word, with no brother, neighbour or friend, nor any company left me but my own. The most sociable and loving of men has . . . been cast out by all the rest." Telling the truth, moreover, has made him many enemies. "I used once to enjoy living in society, when I saw only friendship in all eyes, or at worse indifference in the eyes of those to whom I was a stranger. . . . Is it surprising that I love solitude? I see nothing but animosity in the faces of men, and nature always smiles on me."

Animosity? Rousseau was disliked by his former friends, but he was regarded by many as a great sage and he was often surrounded by adoring women—and often pestered by uninvited visitors, even when he lived on an island in the middle of Lake Geneva. He preferred to avoid his worshipers. As he said: "My whole life has been little else than a long reverie divided into chapters by my daily walks."

Rousseau had a profound effect on European culture. Many nineteenth-century writers and readers came to the conclusion that in a corrupt materialistic age the noble soul should seek solitude—or at least dream of solitude. They preferred reverie to raillery. Yet salon culture did not die. In 1835 Tocqueville, who became a literary celebrity after he published *Democracy in America,* was invited to attend the salon of Madame Récamier. He confides to Gustave de Beaumont (his traveling companion in America): "I found there a parcel of celebrities, in bud or already in bloom, a small *salon* very well composed."

Thomas Gray: The Anti-Conversationalist

Thomas Gray, the most popular English poet during the second half of the eighteenth century, held views that were similar to Rousseau's. He too disliked the conversible world (though he thought *La Nouvelle Héloïse* was boring). London, he said, is a "tiresome, dull place."

In both his letters and his poetry Gray seems to be proud of his lack of sociability. In several letters he refers to the "sulkiness of my disposition," and he complains that being sociable wears out his spirits "especially in a situation where one might sit still, and be alone with pleasure." He also expresses irritation that when he sits in the new British Museum (it opened in 1753) an acquaintance often interrupts his solitude: "I often pass four hours in the stillness & solitude of the reading room, which is uninterrupted by anything but Dr Sukeley the Antiquary, who comes to talk nonsense, & Coffee-house news."

Coffeehouse news held no interest for the reclusive Gray. Though he occasionally went to coffeehouses in Cambridge, where he lived for most of his adult life, he had a low regard for the conversations that took place in them. Writing to his friend Horace Walpole about how a new poetry anthology (it included several of his poems) would be received by Cambridge acquaintances, he says: "Our people . . . wait till some bold body saves them the trouble, and then follow his opinion; or stay till they hear what is said in town, that is at some bishop's table, or some coffee-house about the Temple."

Gray disliked coffeehouses mainly because he was uncomfortable with most people. As a contemporary of Gray's said: "It is clear from all testimonies that in the society of strangers or of those whom he was not on easy terms, Gray was shy, reserved and sometimes silent; and that he often appeared fastidious and affected." Gray enjoyed conversing only with close friends or with those who shared his interests.

Aside from academic research (mainly about ancient verse), translating the classics, writing letters to his small circle of friends, and occasionally composing a poem, Gray liked to walk—often alone—in a rural setting. Robert Mack, Gray's biographer, speaks of Gray's "life-long affinity for the sights and sounds of the rural countryside." Gray's letters are filled with accounts of trips to the Alps, the Scottish Highlands, and the Lake District.

Gray is always reverential about mountains. Crossing the Alps when on the Grand Tour, he writes: "Not a precipice, not a torrent, not a cliff, but is pregnant with religion and poetry. There are certain scenes that would awe an atheist into belief, without the help of other argument." Visiting the Scottish Highlands more than two decades later, he says: "Since I saw the Alps, I have seen nothing sublime till now."

Gray's interest in sublime natural prospects began when he was a young man. When he was twenty he wrote Walpole about walking in an English forest. "I spy no human thing in it [the forest]." He admires the "crags, that give the eye as much pleasure, as if they were more dangerous," and he compares the "venerable Beeches" of the forest to "ancient People [who] are always dreaming out their old Stories to the Winds." After alluding to Milton's "Il Penseroso," a poem about melancholy, he refers to his good friend: "in this situation I often converse with my Horace aloud too, that is, talk to you."

The subject matter of the letter would be repeated in many other letters: the love of solitude, the pleasure of a sublime prospect, the interest in the stories of ancient people, the allusion to Milton, and the notion of conversation at a distance— by letter. Gray also speaks of how much he enjoys "conversing with the dead"—reading ancient writers.

According to Walpole, Gray was a terrible conversationalist. Writing to a friend who complained about Gray's lack of conversational skills, Walpole says: "I agree with you most absolutely in your opinion about Gray; he is the worst company in the world—from a melancholy turn, from living reclusively, and from a little too much dignity, he never converses easily—

all his words are measured, and chosen, and formed into sentences; his writings are admirable; he himself is not agreeable."
Norton Nicholls, a young man who befriended Gray, disagreed with Walpole's assessment. Praising Gray, Nicholls says: "What I could chiefly observe in him was vast politeness, great Good-nature, and the most elegant accuracy of Phrase in the World." Nicholls, who was twenty-six years younger than Gray, was not an objective observer; he said he had the "most awful respect" for Gray's "Sublime Genius." Yet even he acknowledges that Gray often showed no interest in conversation. On a trip with Gray to Worcestershire, he says Gray was delighted with the scenery but he was not delighted "with the numerous society assembled at the long table where we dined every day. . . . He had neither inclination to mix much in conversation on such occasions, nor I think much facility, even if he had been willing. This rose perhaps partly from natural reserve . . . & partly from having lived retired in the University during so great a part of his life."

Another contemporary makes a similar point. At a dinner party he observes Gray in conversation with Thomas Percy—a man whose company Gray enjoyed because they both were scholars of ancient verse: "One [Percy] was a chearful, companionable, hearty, open, downright Man, of no great Regard to Dress or common Forms of Behavior; the other [Gray], of a most fastidious & recluse Distance of Carriage, rather averse to all Sociability." Gray often implies that a poet is likely to be a solitary and melancholy contemplative who has nothing in common with those who lead an active and unreflective life.

In the *Life of Gray* Johnson says that Gray "was fastidious and hard to please." In conversation Johnson offered a blunter assessment. He called Gray a "dull fellow." Boswell was willing to concede that Gray may have been dull, but he defended Gray's poetry. "I understand he was reserved, and might appear dull in company, but surely he was not dull in poetry." Johnson disagreed. "Sir, he was dull in company, dull in his closet, dull every where. He was dull in a new way, and that made people think him GREAT. He was a mechanical poet."

Johnson, though, admired Gray's most popular poem—the "far-famed" (as Johnson puts it) "Elegy Written in a Country Church Yard" (1751). The poem is about a solitary and melancholy contemplative. In the first stanza the speaker says:

> The ploughman homeward plods his weary way
> And leaves the world to darkness and to me.

In this world of darkness and "solemn stillness," the speaker is like a "moping owl" who complains to the moon

> Of such, as wand'ring near her secret bower,
> Molest her ancient solitary reign.

The speaker then contemplates the lives of those who are buried in the churchyard: "the rude forefathers of the hamlet."

What conclusions does the speaker reach? Johnson says the poem "abounds . . . with sentiments to which every bosom returns an echo," but the speaker expresses different and even conflicting sentiments. First he implies that the lives the rude forefathers led may have been more rewarding than the lives of the "proud"; he speaks of their "useful toil" and "homely joys." Then he wonders if poverty and the lack of education thwarted the ambition of some of them. This reflection, however, leads to a very different one: their lack of opportunity may have been a blessing in disguise—preventing them not only from achieving great things but also from committing great crimes.

The speaker now implies that the rude forefathers were lucky to have lived simple rural lives.

> Far from the madding crowd's ignoble strife
> Their sober wishes never learn'd to stray;
> Along the cool sequestered vale of life
> They kept the noiseless tenor of their way.

Taken out of context, the stanza rehearses the commonplace notion that it is easier to regulate the passions when one lives in the country. Yet the speaker is not content with this reflection. He is troubled by the thought that the memorials the rude forefathers have are inadequate. He is also troubled by the thought of death itself.

The speaker finally turns to another subject: himself. He wonders what people will say about him after he dies. The speaker thinks of "some kindred Spirit" who "by lonely contemplation led" inquires of his fate. This kindred spirit, he says, may learn about his fate from a "hoary-headed swain." In five stanzas the swain offers a portrait of the speaker that is like the portrait Gray painted of himself in the letter he wrote to Walpole about his walk in the forest. The swain describes an isolated figure lying by a stream at the foot of a beech tree. The swain also implies that the person he sees is half-mad from poverty or from hopeless love. The reader, however, sees a man whose creative imagination is stimulated by nature. The "wayward fancies" he mutters are poems in the making.

The "Elegy" is in many respects an apology for Gray's life of "lonely contemplation." Gray, like the speaker, is a solitary figure who rejects the world of the proud. His isolation and melancholy are signs that he has a different calling than most people. Though he appears half-mad and forlorn, he possesses creative energy.

A few years later Gray wrote "The Bard: A Pindaric Ode," which is about a sublime Welsh bard who stands on a rock above a torrent of water, laments the fate of his people, and curses his English enemies. The poem, which is loosely based on Gray's research into ancient English prosody—especially the poetry of Celtic bards—begins with a legendary account of a confrontation between the last of the ancient Welsh bards and the army of King Edward I on Mount Snowden in 1283.

The "Elegy" and "The Bard" gave Britain's polite world two appealing figures: the melancholy poet who lives far from the madding crowd, and the sublime bard who denounces tyranny. It would be wrong to suggest that Gray had a political project, yet when he was working on "The Bard" he said he hoped "men shall never be wanting [lacking] to celebrate true virtue and valor in immortal strains." Gray was a neo-Spartan like Rousseau; he wanted the polite world to turn away from luxury and embrace ancient virtues.

Like many opponents of luxury, Gray disliked change. Describing a beautiful "white village" that borders a lake and lies beneath "a broken line of crags," he notes that there is no evidence of wealthy newcomers: "Not a single red tile, no flaring Gentleman's house, or garden-walls, break in upon the repose of this little unsuspected paradise, but all is peace, rusticity, & happy poverty in its neatest most becoming attire." Since Gray does not engage the villagers in conversation, how does he know the poor villagers are happy? Gray is not interested in talking to the villagers; he prefers to view them from the distance. For him they are picturesque figures in a sublime landscape.

Gray was not a clubbable person, but many clubbable persons admired his work—including Boswell and Adam Smith. In *The Theory of Moral Sentiments* (1759) Smith says that Gray "joins to the sublimity of Milton the elegance and harmony of

Pope." Moreover, not all writers who preferred the sublime world were as hostile to the conversible world as Gray was. William Cowper praised lovely prospects, but he also enjoyed the pleasures of conversation with "a person who has seen much of the word, and understands it well, has high spirits, a lively fancy, and great readiness of conversation."

In *Conversation* (1782), a long poem in rhymed couplets, Cowper makes a number of remarks about pleasing in conversation: don't be argumentative, don't tell long stories, don't talk about your health. He also argues that pipe smoking ruins conversation.

> The pipe, with solemn interposing puff,
> Makes half a sentence at a time enough;
> The dozing sages drop the drowsy strain,
> Then pause, and puff—and speak, and pause
>   again . . .
> The worst effect is banishing for hours
> The sex whose presence civilizes ours.

The pipe smoker takes too long to say anything; he is often solemn and self-important; and the smell of his pipe keeps away women. Though Cowper enjoyed the pleasures of conversation, he disliked London. He told a friend that a long poem he was writing, *The Task*, has a "political aspect . . . to discountenance the modern enthusiasm after a London life, and to recommend rural ease and leisure, as friendly to the cause of piety and virtue."

William Wordsworth's view of London was roughly the same as Cowper's. Wordsworth does not say that profound thought and feeling can be experienced only on mountains, but in the preface to *Lyrical Ballads* he argues that living in cities is bad for the mind. "The discriminating powers of the mind" are being "blunted" in part by "the increasing accumulation of men in cities, where the uniformity of their occupations produces a craving for extraordinary incident, which the rapid communication of intelligence hourly gratifies."

Like Gray, Wordsworth often associates the sublime with mountains. In 1809 he wrote a *Guide to the Lakes*, which offers rhapsodic descriptions of mountains. He says the traveler to these mountains will experience "sublimity." In *The Excursion* he describes a solitary herdsman in the mountains.

> In the mountains did he feel his faith.
> All things . . . there
> Breathed immortality . . .

No English poet was more entranced with solitude than Wordsworth. In the *Prelude* he speaks of the "awful *solitude*" and the "soul-affecting *solitude*" of the Convent of Chartreuse. His sister Dorothy writes: "I do not think that any one spot which he visited during his youthful travels . . . made so great an impression on his mind."

Wordsworth has many arresting images of solitude. A famous one is in the *Prelude*. He is lying in bed in his Cambridge dorm, looking at a statue of Newton.

> And from my pillow, looking forth by light
> Of moon or favouring stars, I could behold
> The antechapel where the statue stood
> Of Newton with his prism and silent face,
> The marble index of a mind for ever
> Voyaging through strange seas of Thought, alone.

Wordsworth's Newton is a visionary voyager like himself. "Grand thoughts," Wordsworth says, " . . . are most naturally and most fitly conceived in solitude." Newton would have agreed. "Truth," he said, is "the offspring of silence and meditation."

It would be wrong to say that Wordsworth disliked conversation. In a letter to his sister, he writes that Lake Como is a place where "a thousand dreams of happiness . . . might be enjoyed upon its banks, if heightened by conversation and the exercise of social affections." Yet in the "Advertisement" to *Lyrical Ballads* he implies that he is not interested in polite conversation. His poems "were written chiefly with a view to ascertain how far the language of conversation in the middle and lower classes of society is adapted to the purposes of poetic pleasure." The world he likes to describe is a world of uneducated people who struggle to describe feelings that are difficult, if not impossible, to put into words.

Sociability Without Conversation

In the latter half of the eighteenth century, then, the conversible world contracted insofar as an increasing number of Englishmen—and probably Scotsmen as well—spent less time conversing in clubs and coffeehouses and more time enjoying the pleasures of the imagination by viewing lovely prospects. But why did so many Englishmen if not Scotsmen forego the pleasures of conversation when they were in coffeehouses and clubs? Why were they often silent in these places? In 1790 a Russian visitor to London noted: "I have dropped into a number of coffeehouses only to find twenty or thirty men sitting around in deep silence, reading newspapers, and drinking port." A decade later Talleyrand remarked that the members of a London club were suffering from "a very English taciturnity."

What caused sociable Englishmen to become less interested in conversation? The main reason is that in the last three
decades of the eighteenth century the anti-conversation countercurrent that existed earlier in the century became the main
current. The concerns Fielding had raised in his novels and essays about hypocritical and unscrupulous conversationalists
were now being raised by many writers, who also implied that
politeness was a foreign trait. Lord Chesterfield's *Letters* were
attacked in large part because, as one critic put it, Chesterfield
praised a Gallic code of manners that "did much, for a time, to
injure the true national character, and to introduce, instead of
open manly sincerity, a hollow perfidious courtliness." Describing a person who has traveled to France, Arthur Murphy says:
"He has forgot the plainness and honesty of an Englishman."

"Impassiveness," Paul Langford says, "was increasingly
associated with the English speaking manner, especially in polite society." Johnson suggested that many Frenchmen chatter
mindlessly. Alluding to a Frenchman who was "very trouble-
some with many absurd inquiries" when he was being shown
around the British Museum, Johnson said to Boswell: "Now
there, Sir, . . . is the difference between an Englishman and a
Frenchman. A Frenchman must be always talking, whether he
knows any thing of the matter or not; an Englishman is content to say nothing, when he has nothing to say." In Ben Jonson's *Epicene* (1609), a fatuous windbag and lecher named Sir
Amorous La Foole brags of his French ancestry. Listening to
his blather, another character says: "Did you ever hear such a
wind-fucker as this?"

By the late eighteenth century the English increasingly
liked to define themselves by stressing how different they were
from the French. If the French were polite—meaning eager to
please—the English were impolite; they weren't rude but they

didn't make an effort to be cheerful and good-humored. If the French were talkative, the English were taciturn.

For a variety of reasons, English national pride—the feeling that the English had distinctive values and traits—became a strong force in the 1770s. National pride was stoked by the popularity of King George III, who often appeared in public with his children and who often chatted with commoners. National pride was also fostered by several histories of English literature, including Johnson's *Lives of the Poets,* and by Benjamin West's painting *The Death of General Wolfe* (1771), which commemorated the British victory over France in the Seven Years War. An engraving made of the painting became a popular print. In 1787 Horace Walpole wrote: "I do not dislike the French from the vulgar antipathy between neighbouring nations, but for their insolent and unfounded airs of superiority."

In the early stages of the French Revolution there was a strong support for the French in many circles, but after Britain declared war on France in February 1793 enthusiasm for the Revolution fell off quickly. By the end of the eighteenth century many Englishmen thought the French were superficial as well as untrustworthy. And a sign of their superficiality was their love of animated conversation. In an essay on Dickens George Orwell points out that "all through nineteenth-century [English] novels and comic papers there runs the traditional figure of the 'Froggy'—a small ridiculous man with a tiny beard and a pointed top-hat, always jabbering and gesticulating."

It would be wrong to say that the English had completely lost interest in conversation. In his introduction to *Northanger Abbey,* written in the second decade of the nineteenth century, Henry Austen—Jane Austen's brother—sounds like an eighteenth-century writer on conversation when he says that his sister "was formed for elegant and rational soci-

ety, excelling in conversation as much as in composition."
(Yet in *Mansfield Park* the characters who are good conversationalists turn out to be untrustworthy.) Moreover, several
early nineteenth-century writers enjoyed conversation, evaluated each other's conversation, and wrote essays about conversation.

Byron was praised for his conversation, and when he was
in London he hosted dinner parties where the conversation
was filled with raillery. In his epic poem *Don Juan* (1819–24) he
makes fun of Wordsworthian notions of solitude and the sublime, and he also describes several dinner parties. At one party
Don Juan practices the art of pleasing in conversation.

> He did not fall asleep just after dinner,
> But light and airy stood on the alert
> And shone in the best part of dialogue
> By humouring always what they might assert
> And listening to the topics most in vogue;
> Now grave, now gay, but never dull or pert . . .

Byron also gently satirizes a conversationalist who prepares in
advance the "*bon mots*" he plans to use in the evening:

> Kit Cat, the famous conversationalist
> Who in his commonplace book had a page
> Prepared each morn for evenings.

Byron is probably referring to Richard Sharp, a wealthy businessman and politician who was known as "Conversation
Sharp." Byron liked Sharp, who hosted literary gatherings at
his London townhouse. He called Sharp "a man of elegant
mind . . . who has lived much with the best."

The essayist Thomas De Quincey was also known for his conversation. "What would one give," Jane Welsh Carlyle said, "to have him in a box, and take him out to talk!" In "Conversation" (1847) De Quincey says that in his "early years, having been formed by nature too exclusively and morbidly for solitary thinking," he thought conversation was a waste of time. "Loving solitude too much, I understood too little the capacities of colloquial intercourse. . . . *To talk* seemed then in the same category as *to sleep;* not an accomplishment, but a base physical infirmity." Conversation was as pointless as a tennis match. "I cared as little what absurdities men practiced in their vast tennis-courts of conversation, where the ball is flying backwards and forwards to no purpose for ever, as what tricks Englishmen might play with the monstrous national debt."

After reading Bacon's remarks on conversation, De Quincey changed his mind. As he puts it in his ornate and overwrought style: "A feeling dawned on me of a secret magic lurking in the peculiar life, velocities, and contagious ardour of conversation, quite separate from any which belonged to books." He could learn things from conversation that he could not learn from reading.

The second half of De Quincey's essay is mainly an attack on Johnson's conversation, which he thinks is wildly overrated. "Many people think Dr Johnson the *exemplar* of conversational power. I think otherwise." He says that Johnson's "views of all things tended to negation, never to the positive and the creative," and that Johnson never "unmasked" any error or "expanded" any "important truth." De Quincey's critique of Johnson's conversation is so vague and banal that it cannot be taken seriously. He makes the absurd charge that Johnson "had little interest in man"—mainly because he was too melancholic in his temperament. "This gloomy temperament," he says, "is fatal to the power of brilliant conversation."

De Quincey says very little about the nature of conversation, and he doesn't discuss some of the questions that preoccupied eighteenth-century writers on conversation—the pros and cons of politeness, the difference between raillery and argument. He implies that he only likes conversations "where a velocity in the movement of thought is made possible"— whatever that means.

If De Quincey is a pretentious essayist, William Hazlitt is contentious essayist. In "On the Conversation of Authors" (1820) he fires off opinions in scattershot fashion. He begins by arguing that the conversation of "low life"—the laboring class—suffers from a lack of politeness. "They contradict you without giving a reason, or if they do, it is a very bad one— swear, talk loud, repeat the same thing fifty times over, get to calling names, and from words proceed to blows."

If the working classes are impolite, the educated classes are too polite. Hazlitt argues that in contemporary Britain politeness has become a stultifying force—making conversation tedious. "Fashionable conversation," he says, "is a sacrifice to politeness." "The conversation of what we understand by gentlemen and men of fashion . . . is flat, insipid, stale, and unprofitable. . . . Persons in high life talk almost entirely by rote. . . . The studied forms of politeness do not give the greatest possible scope to an exuberance of wit and fancy. The fear of giving offense destroys sincerity, and without sincerity there can be no true enjoyment of society, nor unfettered exertion of intellectual activity." The eighteenth-century writers on conversation would not endorse sincerity but they would agree that an excess of politeness undermines conversation.

The conversation of English women, Hazlitt argues, suffers from an excess of politeness. "It is not easy to keep up a conversation with women in company. It is thought a piece of rudeness to differ from them: it is not quite fair to ask them a reason for what they say. You are afraid of pressing too hard upon them: but where you cannot differ openly and unreservedly, you cannot heartily agree." French women are better conversationalists. "There the women talk of things in general, and reason better than men in this country. . . . They are adepts in all the topics. They know what is to be said for and against all sorts of questions, and are lively and full of mischief into the bargain."

Like his eighteenth-century forebears, Hazlitt makes a distinction between argument and discussion. He implies that discussion is good-humored argument. "Argument . . . is the death of conversation, if carried on in a spirit of hostility; but discussion is a pleasant and profitable thing, where you advance and defend your opinions as far as you can, and admit the truth of what is objected against them with equal impartiality: in short, where you do not pretend to set up for an oracle."

Hazlitt admires Johnson's conversation, but he thinks Coleridge is a monologist, not a conversationalist. Coleridge "is the only person who can talk to all sorts of people on all sorts of subjects, without caring a farthing for their understanding one word he says—and he talks only for admiration and to be listened to, and accordingly the least interruption puts him out." Hazlitt makes fun of Coleridge-worshipers. "I firmly believe he would make just the same impression on his audiences, if he purposely repeated absolute nonsense with the same voice and manner and inexhaustible flow of undulating speech!"

Hazlitt praises the conversation of Charles Lamb, whom he calls "the most delightful, the most provoking, the most witty and sensible of men," but he says that "the best converser I know" is James Northcote, a minor painter who was a disciple of Joshua Reynolds. A great listener, Northcote "lends his ear to an observation as if you have brought him a piece of news and enters into it with as much avidity and earnestness as if it interested himself personally. . . . His thoughts bubble up and sparkle like heads on old wine. The fund of anecdote, the collection of curious particulars, is enough to set up any common retailer of jests that dines out every day; but these are not strung together like a row of galley-slaves, but are always introduced to illustrate some argument or bring out some fine distinction of character." Northcote, though, was not a good writer. As Hazlitt says: "Lively sallies and connected discourse are very different things." (According to James Thurber, Harold Ross, the famous editor of *The New Yorker*, was "an entertaining dinner-table conversationalist" but a wooden writer.)

Hazlitt describes better than any other writer on conversation the feeling of exhilaration that one often has after an evening of good conversation. When he leaves Northcote "I come out into the street with feelings lighter and more ethereal than I have at any other time." Yet Hazlitt thinks the opportunities for good conversation are limited. The only conversation "worth anything" is "between friends, or those who agree in the same leading views of a subject." In other words, conversation can take place only where there is some common ground. But conversation can easily go off the rails, as the combative Hazlitt knew, for he quarreled with most of his friends. Hazlitt suffered for his lack of politeness. He once said: "I want to know why everybody has such a dislike of me."

In sum, although the English were regarded by many as a taciturn people, many Englishmen enjoyed conversation in clubs—and also at the English equivalent of a French salon.

When Darwin was considering marriage, he made a note to himself that remaining unmarried would give him more time to listen to the "conversation of clever men in clubs." Many years later he attended George Eliot's Sunday afternoon salon, which she held with her companion, George Henry Lewes. He asked if he might bring his daughter and son-in-law. Agreeing to his request, Eliot added: "Our hours of reception are from ½ past two till six, & the earlier our friends can come to us, the more fully we are able to enjoy conversation with them."

The English also enjoyed evaluating someone's conversation. In the 1880s Churton Collins, a minor literary critic, notes in his journal that he was disappointed by Browning's conversation: "His conversation, except when he was speaking of his reminiscences about Carlyle—studiously commonplace." In 1932 Winston Churchill wrote that he admired the conversation of Bourke Cockran, an American congressman he met in 1895. "It was not my fortune to hear any of his orations, but his conversation, in point, in pith, in rotundity, in antithesis, and in comprehension, exceeded anything I have ever heard." Churchill himself was considered by many to be a poor conversationalist because he was not a good listener. Herbert Asquith said of him: "He never gets fairly alongside the person he is talking to because he is always much more interested in himself and his own preoccupations and his own topics."

In many memoirs and essays by English writers one often finds discussions of someone's conversation. In his memoirs of Cambridge in the 1930s, Victor Rothschild praises the conversation of Anthony Blunt, the art historian and Soviet spy: "Blunt seemed to me a somewhat cold and ascetic figure but with a sense of humour; . . . he was an excellent conversationalist and habitual party goer."

The intellectual historian Isaiah Berlin—who I interviewed while writing a book on the National Endowment for the Humanities—has often been praised for his conversation. In a recent review of Berlin's letters, Timothy Garton Ash praises the "unforgettable, much-imitated, bubbling, allusive, rapid-fire conversation" of Berlin. He notes that Berlin was "something of a conversational chameleon—agreeing with each inter-locutor, flattering them by that generous agreement, before going on to add something original of his own." In a poem en-titled "A Conversation in Oxford," which is dedicated to Isaiah Berlin, the American poet Jay Parini says: "I mostly listen, / let-ting what you say fill up the hour."

Virginia Woolf: Two Views of Conversation

One cannot talk about conversation in twentieth-century En-gland without discussing Virginia Woolf, for she was regarded by her contemporaries as a great conversationalist. Soon after Woolf died, Christopher Isherwood reminisced: "We are at the tea table, Virginia is sparkling with gaiety, delicate malice, and gossip—the gossip that . . . made her the best hostess in Lon-don." Hermione Lee, Woolf's biographer, speaks of "her amaz-ing flights of fancy, her wonderful performances in conversa-tion, spinning off into fantastic fabrications while everyone sat around and, as it were, applauded." Yet in her novels Woolf implies that conversation is impossible because we are all solipsists—lost in the fog of our own memories and desires.

Woolf, it is clear, loved conversation. When she was con-fined to a private home for the mentally disturbed after having suffered a nervous breakdown, she wrote her sister Vanessa: "I really dont think I can stand much more of this . . . you cant conceive how I want intelligent conversation—even yours."

Woolf wrote many essays about the Age of Conversation. Discussing eighteenth-century writers, she says: "One cannot imagine . . . that writers then retired to their studies or worked by the clock. They seem to have learnt by talk; their friendships thus were important and outspoken. Conversation was a kind of strife, and the jealousies and contradictions which attended the display gave it at least an eager excitement." In an essay on Lord Chesterfield, whose letters she admired, she makes a connection between the art of pleasing in conversation and the art of writing. "It may be that the art of pleasing has some connection with the art of writing. To be polite, considerate, controlled, to sink one's egotism, to conceal rather than to obtrude one's personality may profit the writer even as they profit the man of fashion."

Woolf makes a similar point in an essay on Addison. After quoting Pope's remark that "Addison's conversation has something in it more charming than I have found in any other man," she says that "one can well believe" that Addison was a charming conversationalist "for his essays at their best preserve the very cadence of easy yet exquisitely modulated conversation. . . . He seems to speak what comes into his head, and is never at the trouble of raising his voice."

Woolf also admired Johnson. She speaks of Johnson's "love of pleasure, his detestation of the mere bookworm, his passion for life and society." Discussing Johnson and his friend Hester Thrale, she says: "Of talk they could neither of them ever have enough." In another essay she quotes Johnson's evaluation of the conversation of his friend Giuseppe Baretti: "Sir, I know no man who carries his head higher in conversation than Baretti." Yet she also notes that Johnson and Baretti's friendship collapsed over a trivial dispute. Baretti was incensed because Johnson claimed that Baretti had been beaten in a chess match by a Tahitian. "Do you think I should be conquered at chess by a savage?" he asked Johnson. "I know you were," Johnson replied. According to Woolf, "the two men, who respected each other, parted and never met again." Like Hazlitt, Woolf points out how easily a conversation can became derailed.

In "Dr. Burney's Evening Party," Woolf writes about a failed conversation—or, rather, a conversation that never got off the ground. The party was held by Johnson's friend Charles Burney, a musicologist, because Burney's patron, Fulke Greville, wanted to meet Johnson. At the party were Burney, his four daughters, Johnson, Henry Thrale and Hester Thrale, Gabriel Piozzi (a musician who would become Hester Thrale's second husband), Greville, and his daughter—a Mrs. Crewe. Woolf, whose essay is based on Frances Burney's account of the evening, says that after the guests arrived "nobody said anything. Complete silence reigned." The guests expected Johnson to begin the conversation, but "if there was one thing that Dr. Johnson never did, it was to begin. Somebody had always to start a topic before he consented to pursue it or to demolish it." To ease the tension Dr. Burney invited Piozzi to sing. "He sang beautifully," yet still "nobody spoke."

Soon Hester Thrale, who was irritated that the aristocratic Greville was silent (he was standing on the hearth in front of the fire, staring at everyone sardonically), tried to liven things up by sneaking behind Piozzi and offering "a ludicrous mimicry of his gestures" while he sang. The guests tittered, but not Johnson, who was staring at the fire, and therefore "knew nothing of the scene at the piano." Dr. Burney was annoyed by Hester Thrales's behavior, and he asked her to stop, which she did. After Piozzi stopped singing, two of Burney's daughters began to sing. Piozzi fell asleep. Silence again. "Mr. Greville still stood superciliously," Woolf says, "upon the hearth-rug."

Finally Johnson spoke. He looked fixedly at Greville: "'If it were not for depriving the ladies of the fire, I should like to stand upon the hearth myself!'" Rebuked by Johnson, "Greville did his best to smile—a faint, scoffing smile." But eventually he "slunk away, sloping even his proud shoulders, to a chair," and rang the bell for his carriage. Soon "the party . . . broke up," a party that Hester Thrale called "one of the most humdrum evenings she had passed."

Two decades before Woolf wrote about Johnson's silence, she wrote about the silence of her cousins at a family picnic. "They are able to sit speechless without feeling the slightest discomfort while the whole success of the party they have invited depends on them." Woolf admires her cousins' indifference to the effect of their silence. "They acknowledge that it is drizzling & grey, that their guests are depressed & think the whole party a bore; they can bear the knowledge of these facts & support the discovery without turning a hair." Yet their "kind of heroism . . . is not calculated to smooth a tea party."

Woolf's cousins had a lot in common with her father, Leslie Stephen. Henry James, a family friend, spoke of Stephen's "ineffable and impossible taciturnity." Noel Annan, Stephen's biographer, says that Stephen had the reputation for being "formidably silent." On a twenty-mile walk he spoke only once to his companion. Woolf's grandfather, Jem Stephen, disapproved of purposeless conversation. "Unless I am much mistaken, frivolity of discourse, mere talk for talk's sake, is one of the most besetting sins of our generation."

Woolf enjoyed talk for talk's sake. When her brother Thoby went to Cambridge, she complained about the lack of conversation in her life. "I don't get anyone to argue with me now, and feel the want." In 1905, when Thoby's Cambridge friends, who were members of a semisecret Cambridge society called the Apostles (Thoby was not a member), began coming to her house on Thursday evenings, she poked fun at their "as-

tonishingly abstract" conversation. Because the Apostles disdained small talk, the conversation often languished.
Woolf describes how a conversation finally began. "They came in hesitatingly, self-effacingly, and folded themselves up quietly [in] the corners of sofas. For a long time they said nothing. None of our old conversational openings seemed to do. We sat and looked at the ground. Then at last Vanessa, having said perhaps that she had been to some picture show, incautiously used the word 'beauty.'" An Apostle finally deigned to speak: "It depends what you mean by beauty," he said. The conversation then flowed.

It was always "some abstract question," Woolf says, "that . . . drew out all our forces." The Thursday evening conversations often lasted until two or three in the morning. Eventually, one of the discussants would "pronounce very shortly some absolutely final summing up. The marvellous edifice was complete, one could stumble off to bed feeling that something very important had happened. It had been proved that beauty was—or beauty was not—for I have never been quite sure which—part of a picture." Woolf also says the Apostles "never seemed to notice how we were dressed or if we were nice looking or not." But she noticed what the Apostles looked like. "I have never seen young men so dingy, so lacking in physical splendour as Thoby's friends." She quotes Henry James's comment after he met two of them. "Deplorable! Deplorable! How could Vanessa and Virginia have picked up such friends?"

Woolf also talks about the effect that buggers—the Bloomsbury word for homosexuals—had on conversation. (Many of the Apostles were homosexuals.) "The society of buggers," Woolf says, "has many advantages . . . but it has this drawback—with buggers one cannot, as nurses say, show off. Something is always suppressed, held down. Yet this showing off . . . is one of the great delights, one of the chief necessities of life. Only then does all effort cease; one ceases to be honest, one ceases to be clever. One fizzes up into some absurd delightful effervescence of soda water or champagne through which one sees the world tinged with all the colours of the rainbow." Is she saying that when women know they are in the company of homosexual men, they have no incentive to be flirtatious?

After implying that the Apostles often were pompous bores, Woolf says their conversation improved immeasurably as a result of a peculiar incident, though she jokingly says that she may have invented the incident. One evening Vanessa, who was now married to Clive Bell, "sat silent and did something mysterious with her needle or her scissors. I talked, egotistically, excitedly, about my own affairs no doubt. Suddenly the door opened and the long and sinister figure of Mr Lytton Strachey stood on the threshold. [Strachey was an essayist and biographer.] He pointed his finger at a stain on Vanessa's white dress. 'Semen?' he said." The word changed things utterly, Woolf says. "We burst out laughing. With that one word all barriers of reticence and reserve went down. A flood of the sacred fluid seemed to overwhelm us."

According to Woolf, the Apostles and other visitors to her Thursday evening conversations now talked a great deal about sex. "Sex permeated our conversation. The word bugger was never far from our lips. We discussed copulation with the same excitement and openness that we had discussed the nature of [the] good. It is strange to think how reticent and reserved we had been and for how long. . . . So there was now nothing that one could not say, nothing that one could not do. . . . It was, I think, a great advance in civilisation. It may be true that the loves of buggers are not—at least if one is of the other persuasion—

of enthralling interest or paramount importance. But the fact that they can be mentioned openly leads to the fact that no one minds if they are practiced privately. . . . Indeed the future of Bloomsbury was to prove that many variations can be played on the theme of sex."

Woolf hastens to add that the conversations were not only about sex. They talked about many things: art, literature, education. Woolf mentions several Bloomsbury regulars (aside from Strachey): the art critic Roger Fry, the novelist E. M. Forster ("Morgan"), the economist John Maynard Keynes ("Maynard"), and the mathematician H. T. J. Norton. She says that "Norton was the essence of all I meant by Cambridge; so able; so honest; so ugly; so dry," though she admits that once she "spent a whole night" talking with him.

Woolf also mentions "Ottoline"—Lady Ottoline Morrell, a rich aristocrat who befriended writers and artists (and had affairs with many of them). Lady Ottoline once "swooped down upon one of my own Thursday evenings" and asked for the names of her friends so that she could invite them to her house on Bedford Square. Woolf describes a party at Lady Ottoline's. "I took Rupert Brooke. Soon we were all swept into that extraordinary whirlpool where such odd sticks and straws were brought momentarily together." At Lady Ottoline's she met the painter Augustus John, and she met "Winston Churchill, very rubicund, all gold lace and medals, on his way to Buckingham Palace." She also met Raymond Asquith, the prime minister, who was "crackling with epigrams," and "Bertie Russell," whom Lady Ottoline "was said to be in love with."

Woolf's remarks about her Thursday evening conversations and about Lady Ottoline's party are in "Old Bloomsbury," an essay she read to the Memoir Club in the early 1920s. The Memoir Club, which met periodically for dinner and conversation, was formed in 1920. The members were supposed to be frank in their memoirs, but in the three essays Woolf wrote for the club (they were published posthumously) her main concern is not frankness; it is amusing her audience—and occasionally shocking them. In her first memoir, "Hyde Park Gate" (the address of the house where she grew up), she says in the last two paragraphs that she was sexually abused by her half-brother, George Duckworth. Her tone is jaunty, as if she were trying to show her listeners that she could talk in a detached manner about what had happened to her.

In "Am I a Snob?" which she delivered to the Memoir Club either in late 1936 or early 1937, Woolf says that she is a snob because she seeks out the company of titled aristocrats. Keynes, she says, is not a snob. "Maynard never boasts. It is for me to inform you that he lunched today with the Prime Minister." She learned that the prime minister—Stanley Baldwin— had just asked Keynes to be in his Cabinet, but she did not learn this from Keynes. "Maynard never mentioned it. Pigs, plays, pictures—he will talk of them all. But never of Prime Ministers and peerages. Alas and alas—Maynard is not a snob. I am foiled again [in her search for other snobs like herself]." The essay is informed by a spirit of raillery. Woolf is playful and self-mocking.

Woolf says she likes aristocrats because they are unreflective and because they "don't care a snap what anyone thinks. Here is human nature in its uncropped, unpruned, natural state. They have a quality which we in Kensington [writers and artists and academics] lack. . . . The aristocrat is freer, more natural, more eccentric than we are. . . . If you ask me would I rather meet Einstein or the Prince of Wales, I plump for the Prince without hesitation." Woolf is in effect saying that she likes people who make small talk, superficial talk; she is a "lit up drawing room snob; a social festivity snob. Any group of people if they were well dressed, and socially sparkling and unfamiliar will do the trick."

Woolf is gently mocking Bloomsbury's smugness and earnestness. In an unpublished review she described Oxbridge intellectuals as "pale, preoccupied & silent." But it would be wrong to say that she always preferred the light conversation of aristocrats. In 1924 she writes in her dairy: "Aristocrats, worldlings, for all their surface polish, are empty, slippery, coat the mind with sugar & butter, & make it slippery too."

If in her essays Woolf takes it for granted that one can have a pleasurable conversation; in her novels she seems to agree with Rebecca West that conversation is an illusion. In *The Waves* (1931) the characters seem to be delivering monologues. In *Mrs. Dalloway* (1925) a woman who is an old friend of Mrs. Dalloway thinks: "Are we not all prisoners?" The narrator comments: "She had read a wonderful play about a man who scratched on the wall of his cell, and she felt that was true of life—one scratched on the wall." We are all solipsists, the narrator implies.

In *Mrs. Dalloway* Woolf also implies that we seek out superficial conversation in order to escape from the terrible burden of self-absorption. The narrator describes the thoughts of Peter Walsh, a former suitor of Mrs. Dalloway's who has returned to London after many years in India. "For this is the truth about our soul, he thought, our self, who fish-like inhabits deep seas and plies among obscurities threading her way between the boles of giant weeds, over sun-flickered spaces and on and on into gloom, cold, deep, inscrutable; suddenly she shoots to the surface and sports on the wind-wrinkled waves; that is, has a positive need to brush, scrape, kindle herself, gossiping." We are told that these are Walsh's thoughts but the passage can also be read as Woolf's defense of her own "positive need" for superficial conversation. Gossip is a tonic for the beleaguered soul who "inhabits deep seas and plies among obscurities."

In "Portrait of a Londoner," a witty essay written in 1931 (it was lost but rediscovered seventy years later), Woolf describes a London salon that is devoted to gossip. Mrs. Crowe, the *salonnière*, "disliked tête-à-têtes. . . . The truth was she did not want intimacy; she wanted conversation. Intimacy has a way of breeding silence, and silence she abhorred. There must be talk, and it must be general, and it must be about everything. It must not go too deep, and it must not be too clever, for if it went too far in either of these directions somebody was sure to feel out of it, and to sit balancing with his tea cup, saying nothing."

In the following three sentences Woolf sounds more like Evelyn Waugh than the author of *Mrs. Dalloway.* "Thus Mrs. Crowe's drawing room had little in common with the celebrated salons of the memoir writers. Clever people often came there—judges, doctors, members of parliament, writers, musicians, people who traveled, people who played polo, actors and complete nonentities, but if anyone said a brilliant thing it was felt to be rather a breach of etiquette—an accident that one ignored, like a fit of sneezing, or some catastrophe with a muffin. The talk that Mrs. Crowe liked and inspired was a glorified version of village gossip." The list of people is amusing: "people who played polo . . . complete nonentities." And the remark about "some catastrophe with a muffin" recalls the conversation about muffins in Wilde's *The Importance of Being Earnest.*

Did a Mrs. Crowe really exist? If she didn't she would have to be invented because she fills a need. "Thus to know London not merely as a gorgeous spectacle . . . but as a place where people meet and talk, laugh, marry, and die, paint, write and act, rule and legislate, it was essential to know Mrs Crowe. It was in her drawing-room that the innumerable fragments of the vast metropolis seemed to come together into one lively, comprehensible, amusing and agreeable whole." Woolf tried to be a *salonnière* herself at her Thursday evening conversations. "Bloomsbury conversations," Hermione Lee says, "were often compared to 'orchestral concerts,' with Virginia Woolf as conductor."

Woolf knew T. S. Eliot and she admired *The Waste Land* (1922), which was first published in book form by the Hogarth Press—the publishing firm that Woolf and her husband, Leonard Woolf, had begun in 1917. One can say there are two Woolfs. There is the Woolf-the-novelist. She is like the woman in *The Waste Land* who says:

'My nerves are bad tonight. Yes, bad. Stay with me.
'Speak to me. Why do you never speak. Speak.
'What are you thinking of? What thinking? What?
'I never know what you are thinking. Think.'

But Woolf-the-essayist implies that conversation is not only possible, it is often pleasurable. Woolf-the-essayist looks back to the Age of Conversation. The last piece she published in her life—it appeared three weeks before her death—was a review-essay of a biography of Hester Thrale.

VII

Conversation in America: From Benjamin Franklin to Dale Carnegie

Until roughly a decade before the American Revolution, most Americans thought of themselves as Britons. Those who belonged to the polite world went to coffeehouses, joined clubs, and read the *Spectator*. (Ellis points out that "coffee-houses in Boston and New York had hosted auctions of commodities and real estate . . . since the seventeenth century.") A club member in colonial Maryland says: "We meet, converse, laugh, talk, smoke, drink, differ, agree, argue, philosophize, harangue, pun, sing, dance and fiddle together. . . . We are really and in fact a club." When James Madison was eighty he recommended the *Spectator*, especially Addison's contributions, to a young nephew. The *Spectator*, he says, is "peculiarly adapted to inculcate in youthful minds, just sentiments, an appetite for knowledge, and a taste for the improvement of the mind and manners." It also encourages "a lively sense of the duties, the virtues and the proprieties of life."

Franklin also admired the *Spectator*. In his *Autobiography*, which was published posthumously, he says he considered the *Pennsylvania Gazette*—the newspaper he published—"as another means of communicating instruction, and in that view frequently reprinted in it extracts from the *Spectator*." Revolutionary Frenchmen called Franklin the "American Rousseau," but there is no evidence that Franklin ever read Rousseau. The gregarious Franklin, who belonged to several clubs when he lived in London and attended several salons when he lived in Paris, had nothing in common with Rousseau. He enjoyed raillery, not reverie.

In "How to Please in Conversation," an essay Franklin wrote when he was twenty-four, he says "raillery is a part of conversation," though he acknowledges that "it is highly entertaining or exceedingly disobliging, according as it is managed, and therefore we ought to use it with all the caution possible." Like the British writers on conversation, Franklin speaks of the importance of good humor, warns about the danger of "*talking overmuch*," and says that "*story-telling* is another mistake in conversation." He also thinks "a spirit of *wrangling and disputation*" is a "disagreeable error." Like Addison, Hume, and Johnson, he says that the art of pleasing in conversation does not come naturally. One needs to "command" one's temper.

Is Franklin really interested in conversation as I have defined it—talk without a purpose? It does not seem so because Franklin talks about pleasing others in order to further one's career. To please one's fellow conversationalists, one should avoid showing one's own "perfections." One should also let them talk as much they like. "Such is the vanity of mankind, that minding what others say is a much surer way of pleasing them than talking well our selves." Three years before he wrote "How to Please in Conversation" he founded The Junto—

a club for tradesman and artisans. It was a vehicle for what we would call networking, but it was also devoted to solid conversation.

In the *Autobiography* Franklin suggests that conversation plays an important part in improving one's mind. He says his father "liked to have [at his table], as often as he could, some sensible friend or neighbor to converse with, and always took care to start some ingenious or useful topic for discourse, which might tend to improve the minds of his children." Franklin, who founded the first American circulating library, also says that reading makes one a better conversationalist. "These Libraries," he writes, "have improv'd the general Conversation of the Americans."

When Franklin retired from business, he told an acquaintance that he now had "leisure to read, study, make experiments, and converse at large with such ingenious and worthy Men as are pleased to honour me with their Friendship or Acquaintance on such Points as may produce something for the common benefit of Mankind, uninterrupted by the little Cares and Fatigues of Business." Even before he retired, he was interested in the conversation of distinguished men and women. On his first trip to London in 1726 he met "Dr. Mandeville, author of *The Fable of the Bees,* who had a club there, of which he was the soul, being a most facetious, entertaining companion." (Hume and Johnson both admired Mandeville because he was a strong defender of luxury.) Franklin also met a Dr. Pemberton at Batson's Coffee House. Pemberton "promised to give me an opportunity sometime or other of seeing Sir Isaac Newton, of which I was extremely desirous."

Franklin did not meet Newton, but when he moved to London three decades later he attended meetings of the Royal Society and he joined the "Honest Whigs" Club (the same club that Boswell belonged to), which met at Saint Paul's Coffee House. He became a close friend of another club member: Joseph Priestley. He also went to the British Coffee House, where many Scottish intellectuals congregated. Six months after he arrived in London, he wrote his wife that "the conversation of ingenious men" gives me "no small pleasure." In Edinburgh in 1759 he met Hume, whose writing he admired. Three years later, when he was about to return to America, he wrote Hume that he regretted "leaving a country in which I have received so much friendship, and friends whose conversation has been so agreeable and so improving to me."

The clubbable Franklin, who lived in England and France for roughly twenty-five years, enjoyed the pleasures of conversation—and pleasure in general. In a letter that was suppressed in Victorian editions of Franklin's work because it was considered bawdy, Franklin outlines a number of reasons for choosing an older mistress. One is: "Because as they have more knowledge of the world and their minds are better stored with observations, their conversation is more improving and more lastingly agreeable." Here conversation means what we mean by it, but it may also mean sexual intimacy.

In the *Autobiography* Franklin presents himself as a man who always tries to use his time wisely, so he says: "Avoid trifling Conversation." But Franklin did not avoid trifling conversation. In his fifties he told a friend: "I find I love Company, Chat, a Laugh, a Glass, and even a Song, as well as ever." Describing Franklin when he was the American representative in France, Edmund Morgan says: "He cannot do without conversation. . . . He cannot do without fun."

John Adams, who was impatient with light conversation, disapproved of Franklin's easygoing way of running the American legation in Paris. Adams said later that "the life of Dr.

Franklin was a Scene of continual dissipation." Adams complained that he could never meet with Franklin because "as soon as Breakfast was over, a crowd of Carriages came to . . . his [Franklin's] Lodgings, with all sorts of People . . . but by far the greater part were Women and Children." Adams, like the Scotsman Adam Ferguson, was suspicious of politeness, which he thought was a trait fostered by monarchies. A republic, Adams says, would foster other qualities. "It would produce Strength, Hardiness, Activity; Courage, Fortitude and Enterprise; the manly noble and Sublime Qualities in Human Nature."

Franklin, who wrote a number of playful essays, including one that gives 228 synonyms for being drunk, thought the earnest and blunt Adams was a disaster as a diplomat. (The French foreign minister refused to negotiate with the difficult Adams.) Franklin also thought Americans in general were too grave. In an essay he says: "Be not thou disturbed, o grave and sober reader, if among the many serious sentences in my book, thou findest me trifling now and then, and talking idly."

In "How to Write an Almanac" Franklin sounds like Swift—offering an ironic defense of gravity. "The next talent requisite in the forming of *a complete almanac-writer* is a sort of gravity, which keeps a due medium between dullness and nonsense. . . . Now you know, sir, that grave men are taken by the common people always for wise men. Gravity is just as good a picture of wisdom, as pertness is of wit, and therefore very taking." An almanac-writer, he says, "should write sentences . . . that neither himself nor any body else can understand or know the meaning of." In short, gravity is a way of sounding profound without being profound.

Franklin also worried that the Puritans of Boston and the Presbyterians of Philadelphia were dogmatic. "In the present weak state of humane nature, surrounded as we are on all sides with ignorance and error, it little becomes poor fallible man to be positive and dogmatical in his opinions." Six weeks before he died, Franklin outlined his religious views, which were similar to those of Priestley and other English Unitarians. "I have, with most of the present Dissenters in England, some Doubts as to his [Jesus'] Divinity; tho' it is a question I do not dogmatize upon, having never studied it." Franklin agreed with his British counterparts that religious enthusiasm is the enemy of conversation.

Who is the more representative American—the polite Franklin or the plain-spoken Adams? Adams was probably more representative, since most American men would probably agree with Adams that Franklin had become too French in his manners. Most would also agree with the legendary Paul Bunyan, who said: "Since becoming a Real American, I can look any man straight in the eye and tell him to go to hell!" A "real" American man was blunt and laconic. He looked down on those who cultivated the art of pleasing in conversation.

Trollope, Dickens, and Tocqueville: Conversation and Commercial Man

According to many foreign observers, American men often were not polite and they generally were not interested in conversation—mainly because they were preoccupied with business. In *Domestic Manners of the Americans* (1832) Frances Trollope says: "I heard an Englishman, who had been long resident in America, declare that . . . at the theater, the coffee-house, or at home, he had never overhead Americans conversing without the word DOLLAR being pronounced between them."

Mrs. Trollope acknowledged that she enjoyed the conversation of several people in Cincinnati, where she lived for more than half of her four-year stay in the United States. She praises the "conversational powers" of Timothy Flint, a Harvard-educated writer and editor, as well as the conversation of Flint's family, especially his daughter. But the Flints, she says, were an anomaly. "The pleasant, easy, unpretending talk on all subjects, which I enjoyed in Mr. Flint's family, was an exception to every thing else I met at Cincinnati."

The people of Cincinnati, Mrs. Trollope says, were not only poor conversationalists; they were averse to pleasure in general. "I never saw any people who appeared to live so much without amusement as the Cincinnatians. Billiards are forbidden by law, so are cards. . . . They have no public balls, excepting, I think, six during the Christmas holidays. They have no concerts. They have no dinner parties." This lack of interest in pleasure, she says, is not limited to Cincinnatians. "I never saw a population so totally divested of gaiety; there is no trace of this feeling from one end of the Union to the other."

Mrs. Trollope had many complaints about Americans. The Puritan heritage, she says, makes many Americans grave and prudish. She refers to a "serious gentleman"—by serious she means humorless—who became "strongly agitated" when she mentioned Pope's *The Rape of the Lock*. "He muttered, with an indignant shake of the handkerchief, 'The Very Title!'"

Mrs. Trollope also says American men have poor table manners and they put their feet on their desks. Worst of all, they spit continually, which makes it difficult to have a conversation with them. American women are not crude, but they are insipid. They talk about clothes, charitable work, and religion. America is a country "where religion is the tea-table talk"— the conversation of women. American men, she says, are not interested in religion.

Summing up social life in Cincinnati, Mrs. Trollope spares no one. "The gentlemen spit, talk of elections and the price of produce, and spit again. The ladies look at each other's dresses till they know every pin by heart, talk of Parson Somebody's last sermon on the day of judgment, [and] on Dr. T'Otherbody's new pills for dyspepsia, till the 'tea' is announced."

Like Swift and Hume, Mrs. Trollope thinks the separation of the sexes has had a detrimental effect on conversation. "But, whatever may be the talents of persons who meet together in society, the very shape, form, and arrangement of the meeting is sufficient to paralyze conversation. The women invariably herd together at one part of the room, and the men at the other." She complains that "mixed dinner parties of ladies and gentlemen are very rare, and unless several foreigners are present, but little conversation passes at table. It certainly does not, in my opinion, add to the well ordering [of] a dinner table, to set the gentlemen at one end of it, and the ladies at the other; but it is rarely that you find it other wise."

It is not clear why Mrs. Trollope thinks that in America mixing the sexes would improve conversation, for she repeatedly says that most Americans—women as well as men—are dull and narrow-minded. "The want of warmth, of interest, of feeling, upon all subjects which do not immediately touch their own concerns, is universal, and has a most paralyzing effect upon conversation."

Mrs. Trollope describes in withering terms one day in the life of a Philadelphia businessman's wife. After a breakfast spent in silence while "her husband reads one newspaper, and puts another under his elbow," the wife does minor household chores and spends her afternoon in charitable activities. The dinner hour arrives. Her husband "comes, shakes hands with her, spits, and dines." Sarcastically understating her point, Mrs. Trollope says: "The conversation is not much."

Conversation would improve, Mrs. Trollope says, if Americans read more. "I conceive that no place in the known world can furnish so striking a proof of the immense value of literary habits as the United States, not only in enlarging the mind, but what is of infinitely more importance, in purifying the manners." American literary men don't have the "degrading habits" that other American men have. They don't drink whiskey or chew tobacco. And they don't spit.

Though Mrs. Trollope makes suggestions for reforming American conversation, she is not very hopeful that reform will occur. She implies that most American men will continue to be preoccupied with making money—with what she snobbishly calls "the petty soul-degrading transactions of everyday life." (Did she forget that in her years in Cincinnati she was a businesswoman?) In the fifth edition of her book, which appeared in 1839, she contrasts Americans with Austrians. She speaks of "the bustling, struggling, crafty, enterprising, industrious, swaggering, drinking, boasting, money-getting Yankee, who cares not who was his grandfather, and meditates on nothing, past, present, or to come, but his dollars, his produce, and his slaves." By contrast, the Austrian is "contented, sober, tranquil, yet gay-spirited."

Mrs. Trollope may have had second thoughts about some of her generalizations. In the 1839 edition she adds a qualifying footnote to her remark that "there is no charm, no grace in their [the Americans'] conversation." She says: "Many of these observations are inapplicable to the higher classes of society in the Atlantic cities." But her main point is that the art of conversation languishes in the United States. She tells her readers:

if you want to enjoy the pleasures of conversation, go to Austria, not the United States.

Domestic Manners was a great success. In the first year of publication it went through four English and four American editions; it was also translated into French, Spanish, German, and Dutch. It was generally given good reviews in England, but Anthony Trollope did not think highly of it. He disparaged his mother's work: "No observer was certainly less qualified to judge of the prospects or even the happiness of a young nation."

The book was strongly attacked in the United States, which is not surprising. Many reviewers said that Mrs. Trollope had seen very little of America. Mrs. Trollope conceded that she had not traveled widely in America, but her concession seems halfhearted. To those who tell her that she knows "so little about America," she replies: "*It may be so*" (emphasis Trollope's).

In all likelihood Mrs. Trollope overstated her case against American manners deliberately because she knew the English reading public loved being told that Americans were boors and philistines. James Fenimore Cooper wrote to a friend in 1832: "In truth the English reading public would greatly prefer reading abuse of us than anything else. Mrs. Trollope has made three times as much . . . by her travels than I can get for a Novel." Mark Twain, however, said Mrs. Trollope's "snapshots" of American society were accurate. "She did not gild us; and neither did she whitewash us. . . . It was for this sort of photography that poor candid Mrs. Trollope was so handsomely cursed and reviled by this nation."

In *American Notes* (1842) Dickens generally agrees with Mrs. Trollope about the low level of conversation in the United States. He describes a boring dinner on a riverboat. "Nobody says anything, at any meal, to anybody. All the passengers are very dismal, and seem to have tremendous secrets weighing on their minds. There is no conversation, no laughter, no cheerfulness, no sociality, except in spitting." Like Mrs. Trollope, Dickens is disgusted by the habit of spitting. In Washington "several gentlemen called upon me who, in the course of conversation, frequently missed the spittoon at five paces."

Yet Dickens, who also dislikes what he calls "the old Puritan spirit" in America, puts more emphasis on regional differences than Mrs. Trollope does. Boston, which Mrs. Trollope never visited, gets a good rating. "The tone of society in Boston is one of perfect politeness, courtesy, and good-breeding." A Boston social evening is very much like a London one. "I never could find out any difference between a party at Boston and a party in London, saving that at the former places all assemblies are held at more rational hours; [and] that the conversation [in Boston] may possibly be a little louder and more cheerful." He also admires New York society. "The tone of the best society in this city is like that of Boston. . . . [It is] generally polished and refined."

Boston and New York, however, are exceptions. Dickens's general conclusion is that the United States is a place where the pleasures of conversation are rare, mainly because the "love of trade" makes Americans narrowly self-interested. "I was quite oppressed by the prevailing seriousness and melancholy air of business: which was so general and unvarying, that, at every new town I came to, I seemed to meet the very same people whom I had left behind me at the last."

The preoccupation with commerce, Dickens says, makes conversation difficult because American men worry that if they talk too much they will be, in effect, showing their hand. In other words, they approach conversation as a prelude to deal-making. In their minds the conversationalist is never disinterested. Sooner or later he will make a business proposition. Their guiding principle is: Let the conversationalist beware. Dickens notes that Americans boast about their distrust. "The American citizen plumes himself upon this spirit [of "Universal Distrust"], even when he is sufficiently dispassionate to perceive the ruin it works."

What kind of ruin is Dickens talking about? Is he suggesting that this distrust also undermines America's political order? He refers to the "injurious Party Spirit" that sickens and blights everything, but he doesn't suggest that the rage of party will lead to violent civil discord. His main point is: American politicians are vulgar and unprincipled. He speaks of the "despicable trickery at elections [and] . . . cowardly attacks upon opponents, with scurrilous newspapers for shields and hired pens for daggers."

According to Dickens, no self-respecting American would enter politics. "It is the game of these men [the men elected to Congress] . . . to make the strife of politics so fierce and brutal, and so destructive of all self-respect in worthy men, that sensitive and delicate-minded persons shall be kept aloof, and they . . . be left to battle out their selfish views unchecked." But he implies that the political system is stable. Speaking of presidential elections, he says: "Directly the acrimony of the last election is over, the acrimony of the next one begins."

Mrs. Trollope also attacks the party spirit in America—claiming that it ruins conversation. She says that "electioneering madness . . . engrosses every conversation, it irritates every temper, it substitutes party spirit for personal esteem; and, in fact, vitiates the whole system of society." She also asserts—without giving any evidence—that there has been violence against candidates for office, especially in the "warm and mettlesome south-western states." But she does not suggest that the rage of party threatens America's political stability.

Alexis de Tocqueville, whose nine-month stay in America in 1831–32 overlapped with Mrs. Trollope's four-year stay, also had a negative view of American conversation. Good conversation, he says, can be found only in Boston. "Their manners are distinguished, their conversation turns on intellectual matters. One feels one has left behind the commercial habits and financial spirit that make New York society so common." Tocqueville thinks the low level of conversation in America harms its intellectual and cultural life, but he does not think it poses a threat to the country's political stability.

Tocqueville agrees with Hume that commercial expansion promotes political stability because it makes men more moderate in their passions. "In this happy country nothing draws the restless human spirit toward political passions; everything, on the contrary, draws it toward an activity that has nothing dangerous for the state." Americans, Tocqueville says, are driven by self-interest properly understood. This outlook "cannot make a man virtuous, but its discipline shapes a lot of orderly, temperate, moderate, careful, and self-controlled citizens." The inflammatory rhetoric of American political campaigns should not be taken at face value.

Can a country in which commercial men predominate flourish? Tocqueville's answer is: Yes. "America demonstrates invincibly one thing that I had doubted up to now: that the middle classes can govern a State. . . . Despite their small passions, their incomplete education, their vulgar habits, they can obviously provide a practical sort of intelligence that turns out to be enough."

What about enthusiastic religion, which Hume and Johnson thought posed a threat to Britain's political stability? Tocqueville says that Americans are often attracted to enthusiastic brands of Christianity, but America's enthusiastic sects are small and numerous, so they are not likely to be politically dangerous.

Tocqueville, unlike Mrs. Trollope and Dickens, is for the most part favorably impressed by Americans. America's commercial men are remarkable for their intelligence, their industriousness, and their morality. Yet Tocqueville agrees with Mrs. Trollope and Dickens that most American men are, as he puts it, "vulgar and disagreeably uncultivated." In a letter he writes: "I admit the inhabitants of the country are not all the most agreeable company. A great number smoke, chew, [and] spit in your beard."

Tocqueville also complains that Americans are too solemn. "I used to think that the English were the most serious-minded people on earth," he says, "but having seen the Americans, I have changed my mind." He offers a reason. "I think that the gravity of Americans is partly due to pride. In democratic countries even a poor man has a high idea of his personal worth. . . . This disposes them to measure their words and their behavior carefully and not to let themselves go, lest they should reveal their deficiencies. They imagine that to appear dignified they must remain solemn." Raillery, Tocqueville implies, is not in the American grain.

Tocqueville's generalizations about America do not apply to the American South. Owing to slavery, which Tocqueville says "brutalizes the black population and debilitates the white," the South lacks the commercial spirit. But the Southerner's lack of interest in commerce is likely to make him a better conversationalist. The Southerner "is more spontaneous, witty, open, generous, intellectual, and brilliant." The calculating and grave Northerner is boring because he has only one thing on his mind: making money. He has no time for the pleasures of conversation—or the pleasures of the imagination.

Gustave de Beaumont, Tocqueville's traveling partner, agreed. "The fact is that, with the exception of a small circle of literary men whose civilized ways and European manners quite recall our most agreeable *salons,* it can be said that at Philadelphia, as in all the other cities of the United States, American men are occupied with but one single thing, their business."

Tocqueville worries about the narrowness of commercial man's interests; he thinks the passion for commercial gain is at odds with the passion for intellectual achievement. Yet many eighteenth-century British writers and scientists hoped to make money from their writings and inventions. Moreover, conversation flourished in England at the time when England became a great commercial power.

Though Tocqueville dislikes certain aspects of democratic culture, he does not think commercial man's lack of interest in conversation will affect America's political stability. His main worry is that Southerners may become a dangerous political force because they are more likely to be infected with immoderate passions. "The North presents, at least from the outside, the image of a government that is strong, consistent, durable. . . . In the South, there is something feverish, disordered, revolutionary."

Thoreau: Conversation Is a Waste of Time; Melville: The Conversationalist as Con Man

Henry David Thoreau had little interest in conversation, but not because he was preoccupied with commerce. He continually spoke of his disdain for commerce. "This world is a place of business. What an infinite bustle! . . . It is nothing but work,

work, work. . . . I think that there is nothing, not even crime, more opposed to poetry, to philosophy, ay, to life itself, than this incessant business." In a poem he writes:

> In the busy streets, domains of trade,
> Man is a surly porter, or a vain hectoring bully.

Thoreau disliked business, but he didn't dislike conversation. Rather, he thought conversation generally was a waste of time. He preferred to spend his time appreciating the sights and sounds of Nature.

According to Thoreau, you can best appreciate the sights and sounds of Nature in solitude. In *Walden* (1854) he attacks Hume's and Johnson's view that solitude breeds melancholy. "There can be no very black melancholy to him who lives in the midst of Nature and has his senses still. There was never yet such a storm but it was Aeolian music to a healthy and innocent ear." Solitude, he says, enables us to see and hear the natural world. At one time he worried that "to be alone was something unpleasant," but his mood quickly changed. "In the midst of a gentle rain while these thoughts prevailed, I was suddenly sensible of such sweet and beneficent society in Nature, in the very pattering of the drops, and in every sound and sight around my house."

Thoreau does not despise the conversible world. He suggests that solitude may help improve our conversation because it gives us time for serious reading. "Our reading, our conversation and thinking, are all on a very low level, worthy only of pygmies and manikins." But he always argues that society is less satisfactory than solitude. "To be in company, even with the best, is soon wearisome and dissipating. I love to be alone. I never found the companion that was so companionable as solitude."

Sociability, Thoreau says, is a burden. An informal club he belongs to is irksome because of its rules. "We have had to agree on a certain set of rules, called etiquette and politeness, to make this frequent meeting tolerable and that we need not come to open war." Politeness, he implies, is not worth the effort. The cost of pleasing in conversation is greater than the benefit one derives from it.

(According to Emerson, Thoreau's conversation left much to be desired. He "goes to a house to say with little preface what he has just read or observed, delivers it in a lump, is quite inattentive to any comment or thought which any of the company offer on the matter, nay, is merely interrupted by it, & when he has finished his report, departs with precipitation.")

Thoreau has another complaint about the conversible world; it demands intelligibility and common sense. "It is a ridiculous demand which England and America make, that you shall speak so that they can understand you." (Perhaps he singles out England and America because of their predominantly commercial cultures.) Playing on the Latin meaning of extravagant (wandering beyond), he says: "I fear chiefly lest my expression may not be *extra-vagant* enough, may not wander far enough beyond the narrow limits of my daily experience, so as to be adequate to the truth of which I have been convinced. . . . I desire to speak somewhere *without* bounds."

Thoreau does not want to be unintelligible. He wants his language to soar beyond the dull language of ordinary conversation. "There is an incessant influx of novelty into the world, and yet we tolerate incredible dullness." The sounds of Nature are mysterious, unlike the words spoken by people mired "in the dead dry life of society." And the sounds of Nature cannot be measured by the yardsticks of common sense and intelligibility: "For a week I heard the circling groping clangor of some solitary goose in the foggy mornings."

The people who visit Thoreau at Walden are not as interesting as the solitary goose. They are men of business and farmers who "said that they loved a ramble in the woods occasionally, [but] it was obvious that they did not." They are "restless committed men, whose time was all taken up in getting a living or keeping it; ministers who spoke of God as if they enjoyed a monopoly of the subject, who could not bear all kinds of opinions; doctors, lawyers, uneasy housekeepers who pried into my cupboard and bed when I was out." These visitors, Thoreau says, "generally said that it was not possible to do so much good in my position."

Thoreau is not interested in doing good or being useful. He is interested in pleasure, which he associates with Nature. In "Walking" he says: "I wish to speak a word for Nature, for absolute freedom and wildness, as contrasted with a freedom and culture merely civil." A daily walk in the country is necessary for his mental and physical health. "I think that I cannot preserve my health and spirits, unless I spend four hours a day at least . . . sauntering through the woods, and over the hills and fields, absolutely free from all worldly engagements."

Yet in a sense Thoreau wants to do good. He wants his readers to know what they are missing because they are so preoccupied with commerce. In "A Winter Walk" he describes a pickerel fisher as if he were a mysterious god. "Far over the ice, between the hemlock woods and snow-clad hills, stands the pickerel-fisher, his lines set in some retired cove, like a Finlander, with his arms thrust into the pouches of his dreadnaught [heavy overcoat]; with dull, snowy, fishy thoughts, himself a finless fish, separated a few inches from his race; dumb, erect, and made to be enveloped in clouds and snows, like the pines on shore." In this passage dull is an admirable quality. The pickerel fisher's thoughts are dull because he is not only rooted in Nature, he is part of Nature. The pickerel fisher "belongs to the natural family of man, and is planted deeper in nature and has more root than the inhabitants of towns."

Thoreau makes a distinction between men in Nature and men in towns. "In these wild scenes, men stand about in the scenery, or move deliberately and heavily, having sacrificed the sprightliness and vivacity of towns to the dumb sobriety of nature." In the course of two sentences Thoreau uses "dumb" (soundless) twice. One can best appreciate the mystery of Nature when one is silent. "He [the pickerel fisher] does not make the scenery less wild, more than the jays and muskrats, but stands there as a part of it, as the natives are represented in the voyages of early navigators . . . *before they were tempted to loquacity by a scrap of iron*" (emphasis mine).

"Tempted to loquacity" is an extraordinary phrase. Thoreau is implying that progress—the discovery of iron ore?—promotes loquacity, and loquacity undermines the appreciation of Nature. To be loquacious is to lose one's connection with Nature. Thoreau does not say Americans should live in solitude in Nature, yet he implies that the silent pickerel fisher is profound whereas the loquacious town dweller is superficial.

Thoreau, it seems, did not take into account the possibility that the pickerel fisher might be a businessman on a weekend fishing trip. Americans have often sought emotional and spiritual renewal by spending a week or weekend hiking in national parks or fishing in mountain lakes. Most Americans see no contradiction between making money during the week and enjoying the natural world on the weekend. Thoreau would probably dismiss this argument—saying that the man of commerce is still thinking about commerce when he is fishing. In any case, both the American man of commerce and Thoreau agree that conversation is usually a waste of time. They have better things to do.

In 1857 Herman Melville published *The Confidence-Man*, a novel about a day in the life of several passengers on a Mississippi steamer. Melville's view of the conversible world is roughly the same as Fielding's in *Amelia*. The conversible world is a masquerade where polite schemers enjoy deceiving good-natured souls. The confidence man, who assumes eight different disguises, manipulates his fellow conversationalists. There are other con men as well. The subtitle of the novel, which unfolds on April Fool's Day, is: "His Masquerade." The last word of the novel is "Masquerade."

In *The Confidence-Man* Melville deliberately undermines the expectations of the reader with regard to both plot and character. There is no plot development to speak of—only a series of conversations between different passengers. Moreover, the characters are not clearly delineated. Some are given names; others are described only vaguely (the stranger, the merchant, the bachelor, the barber). During the course of the novel some characters—not only the confidence man—change identities.

One passenger offers an accurate description of the novel's atmosphere. He says to a fellow passenger: "What are you? What am I? Nobody knows who anybody is. The data which life furnishes, towards forming a true estimate of any being, are as insufficient to that end as in geometry one side given would be to determine the triangle." Some characters seem trustworthy but as the novel progresses the reader becomes increasingly suspicious of everyone. The novel leaves us bewildered and befuddled. As R. W. B. Lewis says, "The drastic aim of Melville's comedy of thought is to bring into question the sheer possibility of clear thinking itself—of *knowing* anything."

Broadly speaking, *The Confidence-Man* is easy to understand; it is a satire of the American addiction to wheeling and dealing, for it describes men who continually reinvent themselves in order to make sure that they never give a sucker an even break. Some of the schemes to fleece people seem very modern. An "herb doctor" sells "natural" products to improve one's health, including the Omni-Balsamic Reinvigorator and the Samaritan Pain Dissuader. But money is not the only reason why confidence men exist. Melville, like Fielding, says that some people enjoy being deceitful. A character says: "Money, you think, is the sole motive to pains and hazard, deception and deviltry, in this world. How much money did the devil make by gulling Eve?"

The Confidence-Man is a dark satire but not a grim one. The pleasures of conversation are not destroyed because one suspects that one's fellow conversationalist may be a "Mississippi operator: an equivocal character"—to invoke the warning that one passenger makes to another about a person the latter has just conversed with. As if commenting on the novel itself, one passenger speculates: "A man of disposition ungovernably good-natured might still familiarly associate with men, though, at the same time, he believed the greater part of men falsehearted—accounting society so sweet a thing that even the spurious sort was better than none at all." This is an odd defense of sociability, but it is a defense.

Melville admires the energy and invention of confidence men. Describing the passengers on the steamboat, the narrator says: "Here reigned the dashing and all-fusing spirit of the West, whose type is the Mississippi itself, which, uniting the streams of the most distant and opposite zones, pours them along, helter-skelter, in one cosmopolitan and confident tide."

Yet Melville is also delivering an unsettling sermon: America is a nation of strangers because men are so wary of the intentions of others that they reinvent themselves continually. Melville, however, does not suggest that the masquerade we see on the steamboat is a peculiarly American phenomenon. The narrator compares the passengers on the steamboat to Chaucer's pilgrims in the *Canterbury Tales*. He assumes the reader will remember that several pilgrims practiced the art of deception and manipulation. Conversation is often a con game.

Melville's quarrel is less with American commerce than with American ideas of perfectibility. In a letter that refers to *The Confidence-Man,* Melville sarcastically notes that he is looking for "a good, earnest subject" for a lecture, and he offers the following topic: "*Daily Progress of man towards a state of intellectual & moral perfection*" (emphasis Melville's). Melville did not think such progress was possible. *The Confidence-Man* takes aim at the idea of perfectibility. Because humankind will always be driven by the passions of greed and power, conversations will often be encounters where gullible souls are manipulated by confidence men.

In the world described in *The Confidence-Man* the man who wants to strike up a conversation with you probably wants to swindle you. One character says: "A little less politeness and a little more honesty would suit me better." But Melville implies that it is impossible to know if someone is being honest. Moreover, one should be especially wary of a person who says: "I'm going to be perfectly honest with you." Disinterested conversationalists, Melville implies, are very hard to find.

A Conversational Countercurrent:
Oliver Wendell Holmes

Was the conversational landscape in America as bleak as many foreign observers suggested? In *Oliver Wendell Holmes and the Culture of Conversation* (2001), Peter Gibian takes a different view; he speaks of "the dynamic of conversation that came to pervade many areas of mid-nineteenth century American life—in what was known, after all, as America's 'Age of Conversation.'" Gibian notes that Oliver Wendell Holmes's *The Autocrat of the Breakfast-Table* (1858), which purports to be about conversations that took place at a boardinghouse breakfast table, was both a popular and a critical success. Holmes wrote two more books in the same vein: *The Professor at the Breakfast-Table* (1859) and *The Poet at the Breakfast-Table* (1872).

The *Autocrat* is a collection of essays that first appeared in the *Atlantic Monthly*. They are in the familiar style of Addison's essays, but Holmes's essays are less descriptive than Addison's—and they also offer less in the way of conversation. In *The Autocrat* we mostly hear the autocrat genially sounding off on a wide variety of topics and also reciting his own poems. The other boarders have minor roles and are not well defined.

The autocrat, who is a persona created by Holmes, could be called the nineteenth-century American male equivalent of the eighteenth-century French *salonnière*. "I am so well pleased with my boarding-house," he says, "that I intend to remain there, perhaps for years. Of course I have a great many conversations to report." In the opening sentence of the first essay, the autocrat implies that boardinghouse conversation is a disorderly experience. "I was just going to say, when I was interrupted, that one of the many ways of classifying minds is under the heads of arithmetical and algebraical intellects." After three sentences in which the autocrat elaborates upon this point, he says: "They all stared." He means that the other people at the breakfast table didn't understand what he was saying. Yet instead of trying to clarify his point about "arithmetical and algebraical intellects," the autocrat says: "There is a divinity student lately come among us to whom I commonly address remarks like the above, allowing him to take a certain share in the conversation, so far as assent or pertinent questions are involved."

What is going on here? The autocrat is telling the reader that he will be the dominant figure at the breakfast table. He is also saying that he will flit from subject to subject. A breakfast table conversation is not an academic seminar. Though he says that "the business of conversation is a very serious matter," he does not mean that conversation should be grave. By serious he means that the boarders should pay attention to what he says.

In the third essay the autocrat spells out his conversational credo by setting up a straw man: a rigid conversationalist. "Some persons seem to think that absolute truth, in the form of rigidly stated propositions, is all that conversation admits. [The Cambridge Apostles come close to this view.] This is precisely as if a musician should insist on having nothing but perfect chords and simple melodies,—no diminished fifths, no flat sevenths, no flourishes, on any account. Now it is fair to say, that, just as music must have all these, so conversation must have its partial truths, its embellished truths, its exaggerated truths. It is in its higher forms an artistic product, and admits the ideal element as much as pictures or statues. One man who is a little too literal can spoil the talk of a whole tableful of men of *esprit*." The passage, which implies that conversation is a playful performance, is indicative of the autocrat's way of making a point. He often searches for a clever analogy, and he often makes oracular pronouncements. What does he mean when he says that conversation "admits the ideal element"?

Like Mr. Spectator, the autocrat argues that the conversationalist should be good-natured and have a sense of humor. Like Mr. Spectator, he also says that argument is the enemy of conversation. "I will tell you what I have found spoil more good talks than anything else;—long arguments on special points between people who differ on the fundamental principles upon which these points depend." Like Johnson, he says that scholars and teachers often are tedious conversationalists. "All lecturers, all professors, all schoolmasters, have ruts and grooves in their minds into which their conversation is perpetually sliding." And, like Johnson, he dislikes puns. "A pun is *prima facie* an insult to the person you are talking with. It implies utter indifference to or sublime contempt for his remarks, no matter how serious." (Boswell says that Johnson "had a great contempt for that species of wit.")

Holmes's view of conversation is similar to Addison's and Johnson's, but the essays in *The Autocrat* are not as interesting as the essays in the *Spectator*. The autocrat is often verbose and vague. After making a fuzzy remark about the nature of poetry—"Poetry uses the rainbow tints for special effects, but always keeps its essential object in the purest white light of truth"—the autocrat asks his tablemates: "Will you allow me to pursue this subject a little farther?" Then, in brackets, he says: "They didn't allow me at that time, for somebody happened to scrape the floor with his chair just then; which accidental sound, as all must have noticed, has the instantaneous effect that the cutting of the yellow hair by Iris had upon infelix [unhappy] Dido. It broke the charm, and that breakfast was over." The autocrat is saying that the scraping of the chair broke the spell of his discourse, but perhaps the scraping of the chair was a sign that one boarder was not interested in hearing him talk about poetry. (Or maybe the boarder was interested but simply had to leave.) Why the allusion to the *Aeneid* as well as the Latin word *infelix?* Is Holmes satirizing the autocrat for his pompous display of learning? I don't think so.

When Virginia Woolf first read *The Autocrat,* she liked it a lot. "When we take it up at a tender age—for it is one of the first books that one reads for oneself—it tastes like champagne after breakfast cups of weak tea." When she reread it she was not as impressed. "Some of the charm is gone. . . . We are more impressed . . . by the honesty and the common sense of the *Autocrat's* remarks . . . than by the devices with which they are decked out." She dislikes his style. She speaks of "the typical American defect of over-ingenuity and an uneasy love of decoration." I would put it more bluntly: the autocrat's elaborate heartiness is irritating. If I were staying at a boarding house where such an autocrat dominated the breakfast table—making labored attempts to be witty, decorating his comments with learned allusions, and (worst of all) reading his poems—I would breakfast elsewhere.

Is *The Autocrat's* success proof that pre–Civil War America was an age of conversation? Undoubtedly, conversation flourished in Boston, as many foreign observers said. According to the literary critic Van Wyck Brooks, Boston "abounded in good conversation. Experienced outsiders . . . were struck by the quality of this conversation. Sometimes, at two successive dinners, the same men talked for eight hours without a sign of fatigue, and the conversation never fell off in interest."

There were many clubs in Boston, including the Transcendental Club, founded by Ralph Waldo Emerson in 1836, and the Saturday Club. In a footnote to the opening chapter of

The Autocrat, Holmes says: "About the time when these papers were published, the Saturday Club was founded. . . . The club deserves being remembered for having no constitution or by-laws, for making no speeches, reading no papers, [and] observing no ceremonies. . . . There was and is nothing of the Bohemian element about this club, but it has many good times and not a little good talking." Holmes was the "presiding genius" of the Saturday Club, whose members included Emerson, Longfellow, Hawthorne, the scientist Louis Agassiz, and other prominent Americans.

Edward P. Hoyt, Holmes's biographer, claims that Holmes was "the greatest conversationalist in the English language since Dr. Johnson left the scene." But when most nineteenth-century Americans thought of a great conversationalist they had in mind a captivating speaker rather than a person who enjoyed a good-humored interchange of ideas. Holmes was much in demand on the lecture circuit, which had become a major business in pre–Civil War America. According to Gibian, "the Doctor emerged as the most celebrated after-dinner talker in his day, defining a role (later taken up by Mark Twain) as unofficial poet laureate or toastmaster presiding over many of the huge banquets, mass ceremonies, and civic festivities so central to mid-century public life; he was also one of the trailblazers in opening up the Lyceum lecture circuit at mid-century." The *Autocrat* seems more like a compilation of after-dinner informal talks than breakfast-table conversations.

Pre–Civil War America was mainly an age of oratory, not an age of conversation. Gibian quotes Tocqueville, who says: "An American cannot converse, but he certainly can orate; even his intimate talk falls into a formal lecture. He speaks to you as if he were addressing a meeting." Though reading–discussion groups were growing in popularity, most Americans preferred to be uplifted by orators than exhilarated by the pleasures of conversation. "Orations," a contemporary observer said, "constitute our literary staple." Emerson praised the English dinner party for generating brilliant table talk and he praised clubs where "cultivated, genial conversation" flows, but he also said: "I look upon the Lecture room as the true church of today." According to Lawrence Buell, "The nineteenth-century—thanks in good part to star lyceum lecturers like Emerson—was to be the golden age of oratory." The lyceum, Buell writes, was "a loose assemblage of autonomous town-and city-based forums for lectures, debates, and other entertainments of more or less instructive character."

For nineteenth-century Americans a conversation was not like the conversation in French salons or English coffeehouses and clubs. It usually was a public lecture or panel discussion where the audience could ask questions. Bronson Alcott, the father of Louisa May Alcott (and a member of the Transcendental Club), gave "conversations" that mainly were lectures. Emerson admired Alcott's talks: "His discourse soars to a wonderful height, so regular, so lucid, so playful, so new and disdainful of all boundaries of tradition and experience." (Emerson did not think much of Alcott's writing: "I fear he will never write as well as he talks.") Such "conversations" are still found in major American cities. Every year the *New York Times* holds a series of "Candid Conversations" where *Times* staffers interview leading authors and journalists. The 92nd Street Y in New York City offers many "Lectures & Conversations." At these events the audience buys a ticket to watch famous people either be interviewed or participate in a panel discussion. Attending such a "conversation" is similar to watching a television talk show (see Chapter Nine).

Henry James and James Bryce: Washington Is a City of Conversation

Did conversation in America improve after the Civil War? Twain said that Mrs. Trollope's remarks about American manners no longer applied to post–Civil War America. The country had changed. Yet many observers, both foreign and domestic, said that America had not changed very much. American men still were preoccupied with commerce, and American men continued to spit when they talked. When Henry James visited Washington in January 1882, he was dismayed to find the Capitol filled with spittoons.

Despite the spitting, James enjoyed his one-month stay in Washington, which he called "a city of conversation." According to James, conversation flourished in Washington because "it is the only place in America where there is no business." Writing a Scottish friend, he says: "I believe that Washington is the place in the world where money—or the absence of it, matters least. It is very queer and yet extremely pleasant: informal, familiar, heterogeneous, good-natured, essentially social and conversational." Two weeks later he wrote Isabella Gardner (the wealthy Bostonian patron of the arts): "Washington is . . . socially and conversationally bigger and more varied, I think, than anything we have."

James spent most of the time at the salon run by his friends Henry and Clover Adams. "I find here our good little friends the Adamses, whose extremely agreeable house may be said to be one of the features of Washington." He admired Clover Adams's wit, calling her a "Voltaire in petticoats." When she committed suicide in December 1885, he lamented: "What an end to that intensely lively Washington *salon*."

The Adams's salon had been a great success. An invitation was not easy to come by. Political power counted for nothing. Henry Adams said that he extended invitations only to "amusing and interesting" people. He also refused to invite people who were not considered respectable. Matthew Arnold got an invitation; Oscar Wilde did not. In "Pandora," a short story that is a thinly disguised description of the Adams's salon, James says that the salon "left out, on the whole, more people than it took in."

When James returned to Washington twenty-three years later, his view of the city remained the same. He writes Edith Wharton of the "charm, interest, amiability, irresistibility" of Washington. In *The American Scene* (1907), James calls Washington "the City of Conversation pure and simple, and positively of the only specimen, of any such intensity, in the world. That had remained for me, from the other time, the properest name of Washington." He makes the same point that he made two decades earlier: Washington is a city of conversation because there is "a social indifference to the vulgar vociferous Market. . . . Nobody was in 'business'—that was the sum and substance of it; and for the one large human assemblage on the continent of which this was true the difference made was huge."

Washington, James says, is a unique American city. "In our vast commercial democracy, almost any difference—by which I mean almost any exception—promptly acquires prodigious relief." The Washington man, he says, is different from other Americans. "He has discovered that he *can* exist in other connections than that of the Market, and that all he has therefore to settle is the question of whether he may." Going to Washington, he says, makes one "forget for an hour the colossal greed of New York." Yet James may not have been as enamored of Washington as he claimed. Writing to Mrs. William James, he confesses: "to *live* here would be death and madness." Was Washington a city of conversation? Conversation certainly flourished in the salon run by Henry and Clover Adams, but the people James met at the Adams's were not typical Washingtonians. They were independently wealthy men like Adams as well as scientists, foreign correspondents, artists, diplomats, and an occasional politician. They were people like the British historian, Sir James Bryce, who was a friend of James's. (As James lay dying, it was Bryce who came to his bedside on New Year's Day in 1916 to inform him that he had been awarded the Order of Merit, the highest award the Crown could bestow on a civilian.) There may not have been greed in the Washington Adams and James knew, but there was greed in the Washington Twain satirized in his novel *The Gilded Age* (1873).

James was not the only observer to speak of Washington as a city of conversation. In his magisterial study *The American Commonwealth* (1888), Bryce also claims that conversation flourishes in Washington. Washington society is agreeable because it is "small, polished, and composed of people who constantly meet one another." It is also agreeable "because it has a peculiar flavour, is so far from aspiring to political authority as to deem it 'bad form' to talk politics." Yet Bryce, unlike James, thinks conversation flourishes elsewhere in the United States as well. "There are many cities where men of high attainments and keen intellectual interest are found, and associate themselves in literary or scientific clubs."

Bryce—like James—says there is a conversational gender gap. Men mainly read newspapers and usually talk about business and politics. Women mainly read the Bible, fiction, and poetry, and usually talk about religion and art. "In a country where men are incessantly occupied at their business or profession, the function of keeping up the level of culture devolves upon women." James makes a similar point. "It needs little contact with American life to perceive how she [the American woman] *has* pounced, and how, outside business, she has made it over in her image."

Bryce admires the American man of commerce more than James does. "The type of mind which American conditions have evolved is quick, vigorous, practical, versatile." Yet Bryce, like Tocqueville, points out his limitations. "The predominance of material and practical interests has turned men's thoughts and conversation into a channel unfavourable to the growth of the higher and more solid kinds of literature." Bryce hopes that once "the pressure of effort towards material success is relaxed . . . so will the dominance of what may be called the business mind decline." He implies that in the American West this change will not come soon, for Westerners are gripped by a desire for material success. "They are driven to and fro by a fire in the heart." Westerners, he says, "are not a loquacious people."

According to Bryce, most American men remain preoccupied with business, but some things have changed in America. "The sadness of Puritanism seems to have been shaken off." America is "a land of good humor." It is a country where "sociability is the rule, isolation and moroseness the rare exception." As if he were specifically referring to Mrs. Trollope, who said there was no gaiety in America, Bryce says: "And they [Americans] have also, though this is a quality more perceptible in women than in men, a remarkable faculty for enjoyment, a power of drawing . . . happiness from obvious pleasures."

Bryce, unlike Mrs. Trollope, was impressed by American women. American women, he says, often take the lead in con-

versation. "An American lady does not expect to have conversation made to her. It is just as much her duty or pleasure to
lead it as the man's is; and more often than not she takes the
burden from him, darting along with a gay vivacity which puts
to shame his slower wits." He also thinks American men treat
women as intellectual equals. The American man "talks to a
woman just as he would to a man . . . giving her his intellectual
best, addressing her as a person whose opinion is understood
by both to be worth as much as his own." By contrast, "the average European man has usually a slight sense of condescension when he talks to a woman on serious subjects. Even if she
is his superior in intellect, in character, in social rank, he thinks
that as a man he is her superior, and consciously or uncon-
sciously talks down to her."

Whitman and T. S. Eliot: The Tedium
of Polite Conversation

Most foreign observers praised America's polite world but
hoped it would become larger. Whitman disliked the polite
world. "I have myself little or no hope from what is technically
called 'Society' in American cities." Referring to Boston society,
he speaks of "its circles of social mummies, swathed in cere-
ments harder than brass—its bloodless religion, (Unitarian-
ism,) its complacent vanity of scientism and literature." In
Democratic Vistas (1871) Whitman was probably thinking of
Boston's polite world when he says that "conversation [in
America] is a mass of badinage." Conversation is in a sorry
state, he says, because America's elites are arrogant, effete, and
preoccupied with "pecuniary gain."

Whitman's main concern, though, is not bewailing the
state of conversation in America's polite world. It is celebrating

"the rude rank spirit" of American democracy. American literature, he says, "has never recognized the People." In *Song of Myself*, which first appeared in 1855, Whitman tells his readers to listen to the sounds of America—not only the sounds of Nature but also the sounds of a modern industrial nation.

> I hear all sounds running together, combined,
>   fused or
> following,
> Sounds of the city and sounds out of the city,
>   sounds of the
> day and night.

America's polite world might become less anemic—less addicted to badinage—if it read his poetry.

> You will hardly know who I am or what I mean,
> But I shall be good health to you nevertheless,
> And filter and fibre your blood.

Whitman, one might say, celebrates impoliteness. He wears his hat "as I please indoors or out." He is "one of the roughs."

> I too am not a bit tamed; I too am untranslatable,
> I sound my barbaric yawp over the roofs of the
>   world.

Barbaric yawps are not what the eighteenth-century writers on conversation had in mind.

In attacking polite society and preaching the gospel of personal renewal, Whitman sounds like Thoreau. "Democracy most of all affiliates with the open air, is sunny and hardy and sane only with Nature—just as much as Art is." In *Song of My-self* Whitman seems to be referring to Thoreau's pickerel fisher.

> Off on the lakes the pike-fisher watches and waits
>   by the
> hole in the frozen surface.

Yet Whitman, unlike Thoreau, often expresses admiration for men of commerce. Though he speaks of "the depravity of the business classes," he says that America has a "grander future" than Europe in part because of "the complicated business genius" of Americans. In his characteristically grandiloquent manner, he says: "I hail with joy the oceanic, variegated, intense practical energy, the demand for facts, even the business materialism of the current age." If Dickens and Tocqueville were impressed by the conversation in Boston, Whitman is impressed by Boston's "immense material growth—commerce, finance, commission stores, the plethora of goods, the crowded streets and sidewalks."

Whitman's general view of the American future is closer to Franklin's than it is to Thoreau's. He thinks America is animated by the energy of millions of people who are trying to get ahead in life. He writes about New York's "vast amplitude" and its "never-ending currents." A short poem, "Broadway," begins with the following lines:

> What hurrying human tides, or day or night!
> What passions, winnings, losses, ardors, swim thy
>   waters!

Whitman does not ignore the dark side of American life. In many poems he writes about death and suffering, but in *Song*

of Myself he mainly describes Americans who are singing—
usually while they work: the mechanic, the carpenter, the
mason, the boatman, the shoemaker, the woodcutter, "the girl
sewing or washing."

Whitman prefers the Americans who sing to the Americans who converse. He thinks the latter tend to focus on the
negative aspects of American life. "Though I think I fully com-
prehend the absence of moral tone in our current politics and
business . . . I still do not share the depression and despair on
the subject which I find possessing many good people."

T. S. Eliot would seem to have little in common with
Whitman, but he too dislikes the conversation of cultured
Americans. In several poems that he wrote at roughly the same
time James wrote *The American Scene,* Eliot implies that the
conversation of cultured men and cultured women is drearily
earnest. In "Portrait of a Lady," the speaker says:

> And so the conversation slips
> Among velleities and carefully caught regrets
> Through attenuated tones of violins
> Mingled with remote cornets
> And begins.
> 'You do not know much they mean to me, my
> friends,
> And how, how rare and strange it is, to find
> In a life composed so much, so much of odds and
> ends,
> (For indeed I do not love it . . . you knew? you are
> not blind!
> How keen you are!)
> To find a friend who has these qualities,
> Who has, and gives

Those qualities upon which friendship lives.
How much it means that I say this to you—
Without these friendships—life, what *cauchemar!*

The rambling remarks reveal a woman who is pretentious, muddled, and inane. Several decades earlier Margaret Fuller sounded a similar note when she wrote to Emerson: "Let no cold breath paralyze my hope that there will yet be a noble and profound understanding between us." The eighteenth-century writers had a less exalted view of conversation.

The speaker in "Portrait of a Lady" does not find conversation with the overwrought woman enlightening or pleasurable. Listening to her effusions, he (one assumes it is a man) feels ashamed of his servile politeness.

And I must borrow every changing shape
To find expression . . . dance, dance
Like a dancing bear,
Cry like a parrot, chatter like an ape. . . .

The speaker loathes himself for acting like a trained animal. Did Eliot dislike cultured women? When he was the editor of the *Egoist*, he wrote his father: "I struggle to keep the writing as much as possible in Male hands, as I distrust the Feminine in literature." Yet he was a friend of Virginia Woolf's for two decades.

In "The Love Song of J. Alfred Prufrock" Eliot describes a similar salon world—one where effete men are dominated by cultured women who are monotonously high-minded. It is a world where there is no wit or raillery.

In the room the women come and go
Talking of Michelangelo.

J. Alfred Prufrock, the speaker, is a comic and pathetic figure who is afraid of saying anything because he is worried that he might appear ridiculous. "Humiliation," Eliot told Woolf, "is the worst thing in life."

Prufrock is also worried about being misunderstood. He rambles on about how difficult it is for him to say what he means.

> It is impossible to say just what I mean!
> But as if a magic lantern threw the nerves in
>   patterns on a screen
> Would it have been worth while
> If one, settling a pillow or throwing off a shawl,
> And turning toward the window, should say:
> 'That is not it at all,
> That is not what I meant, at all.'

Prufrock feels that his situation in the polite world is hopeless; he will always be misunderstood. He wishes he inhabited a place of utter silence and solitude:

> I should have been a pair of ragged claws
> Scuttling across the floors of silent seas.

In *Mrs. Dalloway* a character who "fish-like inhabits deep seas and plies among obscurities" wants to shoot to the surface. Prufrock wants to go to "silent seas" in order to avoid being humiliated by cultured women. He doesn't hate polite conversation so much as fear it.

In "Portrait of a Lady" and "The Love Song of J. Alfred Prufrock" Eliot implies that polite conversation in America is dominated by women who lord it over weak and excessively self-conscious men. Prufrock, it should be stressed, is not Eliot; he is a character in a poem. Woolf, though, implies that Eliot was a lot like Prufrock. "If anyone asked him whether he meant what he said," Eliot would often say no. When Woolf was trying to help Eliot get a job, she spoke of his "peevish, plaintive, egotistical" indecision. "He elaborates & complicates, makes one feel that he dreads life as a cat dreads water." Eliot, it seems, was not good at the art of pleasing in conversation. According to Woolf, he was "sardonic, guarded, precise, & slightly malevolent." Woolf said that Eliot was a "queer shifty creature," yet she notes that after Eliot obtained a divorce from his mentally ill wife he became more outgoing and his sense of humor blossomed.

Eliot found Bloomsbury's intrigues and gossip distasteful. He wrote his cousin: "Think of this sort of thing as going on continually in a society where everyone is very sensitive, very perceptive and very quick and you will see that a dinner party demands more skill and exercises one's psychological gifts more than the best fencing match or duel." A Bloomsbury dinner party, Eliot implies, is work rather than pleasure.

The Importance of Being Laconic: From Hemingway to John Ford

In sum, though foreign observers often lamented the state of conversation in America, several nineteenth-century American writers did not share their concern. Thoreau was uninterested in conversation, Melville was suspicious of politeness, and Whitman and Eliot thought conversation in the polite world was "a mass of badinage." Ernest Hemingway also took a negative view of conversation. In his novels and stories Hemingway often implies that real men—men who possess courage—are laconic.

In "The Short Happy Life of Francis Macomber," we learn that Macomber likes to talk a lot. We also learn that he is regarded with scorn by both his wife and the hunter-guide Robert Wilson for his lack of courage. When facing a wounded lion, Macomber bolts. Even before Macomber ran away from the lion, the laconic Wilson thought Macomber talked too much. Wilson "had not been thinking about Macomber except to note that he was rather windy." Men of courage are not "windy."

When Macomber probes Wilson about the feelings he has when hunting, Wilson at first tries to answer his questions, but then he says: "Doesn't do to talk too much about all this. Talk the whole thing away. No pleasure in anything if you mouth it up too much." Wilson implies that conversation saps courage.

In *A Farewell to Arms* (1929) Hemingway implies that conversation is a kind of whistling in the dark to overcome the fear of death and the sense of life's meaninglessness. Frederic Henry, the narrator, describes an extended conversation the officers have at the mess. (Henry is an American who serves as an ambulance driver in the Italian army in World War I.) Henry is disgusted with himself for having participated in this conversation. He begins by saying: "They talked too much at the mess and I drank wine because to-night we were not all brothers unless I drank a little and talked with the priest."

Henry does not pay attention to what the priest is saying. He sums up his response to the priest's remarks: "Yes, father. That is true, father. Perhaps, father, No, father. Well, maybe yes, father. You know more about it than I do, father." Henry is bored by the priest's conversation. "The priest," Henry continues, "was good but dull. The officers were not good but dull. The King [of Italy] was good but dull. The wine was bad not dull. It took the enamel off your teeth and left in on the roof of our mouth." The rhythm of Hemingway's sentences reinforces his point: the conversation, like most conversations, was banal and boring.

After quoting snatches of meaningless conversation, Henry describes a round of joke-telling among the officers, but we never learn what the jokes are—the point being that they are not worth repeating. "They poured me more wine and I told the story about the English private solider who was placed under the shower bath. Then the major told the story of the eleven Czecho-slovaks and the Hungarian corporal. After some more wine I told the story of the jockey who found the penny. The major said there was an Italian story something like that about the duchess who could not sleep at night. At this point the priest left and I told the story about the travelling salesman who arrived at five o'clock in the morning at Marseilles when the mistral was blowing. The major said he heard a report that I could drink. I denied this. He said it was true and by the corpse of Bacchus we would test whether it was true or not." The conversation has become a drinking contest. It is like Hogarth's "modern midnight conversation." Henry implies that one can suffer through most conversations if one gets drunk.

Hemingway's "Hills Like White Elephants" is a very short story about the failure of a conversation. An American man and "the girl with him" are sitting in a railroad station café. Their inconsequential conversation about the landscape they see from their table reveals a certain tension in their relationship. Then we learn that the man wants the woman to have an abortion, though he refers to it only obliquely. He says she should do what she wants to do, but it is clear that he is trying to persuade her to get the abortion.

The woman becomes annoyed by the man's unctuous solicitude. "Can't we maybe stop talking?" she asks. A few sentences later she seems on the edge of hysteria. "Would you

please please please please please please please stop talking?"
The woman is sick of the man's pretended concern for her
well-being. After he says something to comfort her, she says:
"I'll scream."

In the two-part story "Big Two-Hearted River," Hemingway sounds like Thoreau. In Part 1 Nick Adams "felt happy"
while walking alone in the woods. "He felt he had left everything behind, the need for thinking, the need to write, other
needs. It was all back of him." In Part 2 a big trout gets away
from Nick but it doesn't bother him. "Nick climbed out onto
the meadow and stood, water running down his trousers and
out of his shoes, his shoes squelchy. He went over and sat on
the logs. He did not want to rush his sensations any." It is scene
out of Thoreau—a "dumb" moment in Nature.

Jay Gatsby in F. Scott Fitzgerald's *The Great Gatsby* (1925)
is a variant of Hemingway's laconic hero—what we might call
the inarticulate hero. Gatsby's conversation is limited to a few
phrases, especially "old sport." Gatsby lies about his past and
consorts with racketeers. Nick Carraway, the narrator, says he
thoroughly disapproves of him, yet he thinks Gatsby is superior to the people who attend Gatsby's lavish parties. He shouts
to Gatsby across the lawn: "They are a rotten crowd. . . . You are
worth the whole damn bunch together."

What is so special about Gatsby? He is a quasi-mythic
figure, a man driven by what Carraway calls "an incorruptible
dream"; he wants Daisy Buchanan to acknowledge that she has
loved him only. Early in the novel there is a Thoreauvian moment when Carraway first sees Gatsby from afar. "A figure had
emerged from the shadow of my neighbor's mansion and was
standing with his hands in his pockets regarding the silver pep-
per of the stars. Something in his leisurely movements and the
secure position of his feet upon the lawn suggested that it was

Mr. Gatsby himself, come out to determine what share was his of our local heavens." Carraway looks at Gatsby in the same way Thoreau looks at the pickerel fisherman; he sees a solitary man who is almost a force of Nature. Carraway implies that Gatsby's inarticulateness is a sign of his intense energy and purpose. He contrasts Gatsby with the people who attend Gatsby's lavish parties. Those people are the equivalent of Whitman's "Society." They may be articulate but they do not burn with intense desire.

The laconic hero (though not the inarticulate hero) is commonplace in hard-boiled detective fiction. In Raymond Chandler's *The Long Goodbye* (1953), Philip Marlowe, the private detective who is the narrator, says to Terry Lennox, a self-pitying alcoholic: "You talk too damn much." Tough guys don't practice the art of pleasing in conversation. Marlowe is not only blunt, he is often insulting.

Marlowe is well read, but he does not think much of cultured people, whom he regards either as phonies or as naïve people who know little about the grim realities of life. There is an odd and implausible literary discussion in *The Long Goodbye*. A "colored driver" who is the chauffeur of a rich woman asks Marlowe about the meaning of two lines from "The Love Song of J. Alfred Prufrock." After Marlowe replies: "Not a bloody thing. It just sounds good," the chauffeur refers to two more lines. "Here's another one. 'In the room the women come and go / Talking of Michael Angelo.' Does that suggest anything to you, sir?" Marlowe replies: "Yeah—it suggests to me that the guy didn't know very much about women." The chauffeur responds: "My sentiments exactly, sir. Nonetheless, I admire T. S. Eliot very much."

Chandler seems to be saying that tough guys know more than cultured men about women and life in general. And you need to be tough to survive in the real world. Referring to a police detective, Marlowe says: "He was a hard tough cop with a grim outlook on life but a very decent guy underneath."

Laconic tough guys are commonplace in film noir movies and in Westerns. In Howard Hawks's *To Have and Have Not* (1944), Humphrey Bogart, the most famous Hollywood tough guy, sounds like Philip Marlowe when he says "You talk too much" to his alcoholic pal, played by Walter Brennan. In the film the cynical Bogart acts courageously in a good cause, though he does so grudgingly. He is a man without illusions. In John Ford's *The Man Who Shot Liberty Valance* (1962) John Wayne, who often played laconic heroes in Westerns, is Tom Doniphon, a tough guy who says "You talk too much" to Ransom Stoddard (played by Jimmy Stewart), a lawyer from the East who wants to become the town's first attorney. Stoddard has second thoughts about staying in the town because he thinks he killed the bad guy, Liberty Valance (played by Lee Marvin). Wayne persuades Stewart to stay in the town by telling him that he was the one who killed Valance. A flashback confirms that Wayne's story is true.

Once law and order is established, Wayne's services are no longer needed. In many Westerns and film noir movies the laconic tough guy is a civilizing force because he kills the bad guys, yet he usually remains an outsider—a solitary figure who is too blunt and tactless to prosper in the civilized world. Henry Fonda, who plays Wyatt Earp in Ford's powerful *My Darling Clementine* (1946), is an exception; he is not a blunt and tactless outsider, but he too is laconic. As Scott Eyman, Ford's biographer, says: the script "stayed close to history in at least one regard, and that was by making Earp fairly laconic."

Ford, who liked to think of himself as a laconic tough guy, deleted several passages in the script in which the charac-

ter explains himself or tells a joke. Ford often cut out dialogue
from scripts. Jimmy Stewart said that if Ford felt a scene was a
little rough, "right in the middle of it he'd say, 'Cut. Everybody's talking too much. You must have different scripts than
I do. I don't have all this stuff.' . . . Lots of times he'd cut eight
or ten lines out of a four or five minute scene."

Like the laconic heroes in the movies he directed, Ford
practiced the art of *not* pleasing in conversation. According to
the director André de Toth, Ford "was not a social person." He
was notorious for humiliating actors. (Fonda once told Charl-
ton Heston that Ford was "a mean son of a bitch.") Ford, like
Hemingway, was preoccupied with the question of courage.
He gave a movie contract to Ben Johnson, a stunt man, because
Johnson stopped a runaway horse on the set of *Fort Apache*
(1948). Ford, like Hemingway, thought "real" men were laconic.
Patrick Ford said that his father "wasn't much of a talker."

Dale Carnegie: Conversation
and Influencing People

In the 1950s many American men (and perhaps American
women as well) admired tough guys who did not practice the
art of pleasing in conversation. Yet many also tried to follow
Dale Carnegie's recipe for success in *How to Win Friends and
Influence People*. First published in 1936, *How to Win Friends*
reads like an updated and expanded version of Franklin's "How
to Please in Conversation." Reprinted many times and translated into many languages, Carnegie's book has sold more than
fifteen million copies. Almost seventy years after its publication, it continues to sell well.

How to Win Friends would not be on Philip Marlowe's
night table. Carnegie's book is not about telling people off; it

is about making people feel good about themselves—or, as Carnegie puts it, nourishing their self-esteem. Twice Carnegie quotes William James's remark: "The deepest principle in human nature is the craving to be appreciated." Carnegie agrees with James's emphasis on the will. In a chapter on the importance of smiling, he quotes James's shrewd remark that "by regulating the action, which is under the more direct control of the will, we can indirectly regulate the feeling, which is not." According to Carnegie, if you "force yourself to smile," you will soon be more well-disposed toward people.

Carnegie admires Socrates for refraining from telling people that they are wrong, and he especially admires Franklin. Calling him "wise old Ben Franklin," he says that Franklin's *Autobiography* is "one of the most fascinating life stories ever written, one of the classics of American literature." Franklin, Carnegie says, transformed himself from an opinionated young man to a statesman who was self-effacing and skilled at the art of pleasing in conversation. "Benjamin Franklin, tactless in his youth, became so diplomatic, so adroit at handling people, that he was made American Ambassador to France. The secret of his success? 'I will speak ill of no man,' he said." Carnegie quotes Franklin's remark that after he made it a rule "to forbear all direct contradiction to the sentiment of others, and all positive assertion of my own . . . the conversations I engag'd in went on more pleasantly."

Though the eighteenth-century writers on conversation would disagree with Carnegie's fatuous remark that "to know all is to forgive all," there is much in *How to Win Friends* that they would agree with. They would agree with Carnegie's warning about "doing the natural thing, the impulsive thing." And they would agree with Carnegie's emphasis on the will— with making a strong effort to be polite. Finally, they would agree with the following point: "So if you aspire to be a good conversationalist, be an attentive listener."

In one major respect Carnegie's book is different from Swift's, Addison's, Hume's, Fielding's, and Johnson's essays on conversation. Carnegie thinks of conversation as instrumental. The title of the book is misleading. The book is not about winning friends, it is about influencing people: impressing superiors, motivating employees, persuading people to do business with you. Carnegie says he wrote *How to Win Friends* because he saw a need for it when he was teaching courses in public speaking for business and professional men and women. He realized that "they needed still more training in the fine art of getting along with people in everyday business and social contacts."

Carnegie's message is clear: remember people's names, let others do most of the talking, and avoid direct criticism. Though Carnegie does not say so, he would probably argue that it is wise to steer clear of raillery, since it could be misconstrued. Above all, try to understand the other person's point of view. Carnegie stresses that "if you get that one thing out of this book, it may easily prove to be one of the building blocks of your career."

Carnegie sends a mixed signal to his readers. On the one hand, he implies it is easy to influence people. All you need do is listen to them and agree with them. On the other hand, he implies that it would be difficult for most people to follow his advice because he says that most people are preoccupied with themselves. "Remember that the people you are talking to are hundred times more interested in themselves and their wants and problems than they are in you and your problems." He also says that "most of us are blighted with preconceived notions, with jealousy, suspicion, fear, envy and pride." The reader is supposed to think that he or she is different from most people. Thus Carnegie flatters his reader: "You are special," he implies. "You can follow my regimen."

Whatever one makes of Carnegie's recommendations, it is clear that the fifteen million buyers of *How to Win Friends* are not mainly interested in becoming conversationalists. They are mainly interested in getting ahead.

Do most Americans take an instrumental view of conversation? It is impossible to answer this question, but according to several foreign observers as well as several American writers most American men have been preoccupied with getting ahead in life. Tocqueville thought the lack of interest in conversation mattered intellectually but did not matter politically because most Americans were political moderates. But with the rise of the counterculture in the 1960s many young Americans were not indifferent to conversation or suspicious of the good conversationalist; many were enemies of the conversible world.

VIII
Modern Enemies of Conversation: From Countercultural Theorists to "White Negroes"

I n the spring of 1968 I attended a lecture at Rutgers University by Norman O. Brown, a professor of classics at Wesleyan who wrote *Life Against Death: The Psychoanalytical Meaning of History* (1959). To say that Brown lectured is a stretch. With eyes closed, he chanted rather than spoke. Toward the end of his talk he suddenly became rigid—grasping the lectern and staring at the ceiling while mumbling something about "the aura in the Laura." He was referring to Petrarch's poems about Laura, but I had no idea what he was saying about them.

A radical Freudian, Brown was a leading guru of the counterculture. His writings were not a direct attack on the conversible world, but he strongly implied that rational discourse was a sickness, a sign of psychic repression. *Love's Body*

(1966), the book that followed *Life Against Death*, is a collection of gnomic paragraphs that celebrate irrationality, even madness. He spoke of "the lunatic state called normalcy or common sense."

Love's Body received mixed reviews, but *Life Against Death* was praised by many members of the intellectual establishment. The distinguished literary critic Lionel Trilling, who was no friend of the counterculture, called Brown's book "one of the most interesting and valuable works of our time." Attempting to clarify Brown's psycho-political agenda, Trilling said Brown "asks for the resurrection of the body, for an end to sublimation, for human relationships that are based on 'erotic exuberance,' and not only on that but on the free expression of narcissism, on these rather than on aggression." What does an "end to sublimation" mean? Several critics, notably Frederick Crews, pointed out that Brown's radical Freudian agenda was unintelligible.

One thing about Brown was clear. Like Herbert Marcuse, the author of *Eros and Civilization* (1956), he was interested in personal liberation, which he thought was the first step toward radical political change. Brown and Marcuse, Morris Dickstein says, were "radical prophets of a new consciousness [who] . . . seemed like a breath of air from another world." The way to achieve a new consciousness, many people thought, was mainly through drugs. In his memoir of the Sixties, *Radical Son* (1997), David Horowitz says that when a friend found out that Horowitz had never taken LSD, he said: "You *have* to take LSD. Until you've dropped acid, you don't know what socialism is."

I make the point about the importance of drugs to the counterculture not to write yet another diatribe about the 1960s but to stress that those who hoped to achieve a new consciousness were not remotely interested in the art of pleasing

in conversation. Their main concern was personal liberation. To become a new person, it was essential to explore one's
psyche—to journey inward. As Leslie Fiedler said: "Poets and
junkies have been suggesting to us that the new world appropriate to the new men of the latter twentieth century is to be
discovered only by the conquest of inner space: by an adventure of the spirit, an extension of psychic possibility." The
counterculture was deeply solipsistic.

Most counterculture theorists were not as enthusiastic
about madness as Brown was, but many viewed rational discourse with distrust. In *The Making of a Counter Culture* (1970)
Theodore Roszak hoped for "a new culture in which the non-
intellectual capacities of the personality . . . become the arbiter
of the good, the true, and the beautiful." Those who questioned what might be called the cult of irrationality often were
dismissed as uptight and repressed.

Some members of the counterculture were not interested
in personal liberation. They did not want to explore their psyche; they wanted to engage in revolutionary violence. They
admired the Algerian writer Frantz Fanon, the author of *The
Wretched of the Earth* (1965), who said: "At the level of individuals, violence is a cleansing force. It frees the native from his
inferiority complex and from his despair and inaction." In an
introduction to Fanon's book, Jean-Paul Sartre argues that "ir-
repressible violence . . . is man-recreating himself."

The violent members of the counterculture were few in
number. Rousseau was a more important influence on the
counterculture than Fanon—the Rousseau who despised the
conversible world because he thought it reeked of hypocrisy.
Like Rousseau, the counterculture yearned for transparency in
human affairs—or what they called authenticity. In *The Politics of Authenticity* (1970), Marshall Berman says that "the search

for authenticity . . . is bound up with a radical rejection of things as they are. It begins with an insistence that the social and political structures men live in are keeping their self stifled, chained down, locked up." The emphasis is on releasing one's passions rather than controlling them.

Countercultural theorists undermined conversation in another way: they dismissed their critics—saying that they suffered from false consciousness. Marcuse, who was for personal liberation but not through drug-taking, said: "It is most striking the extent to which the ruling power structure can manipulate, manage and control not only the consciousness but also the subconscious and unconscious of the individual." The notion of false consciousness undermines the equality that is essential to conversation. Marcuse in effect tells his critics: "Your consciousness is false, so I have no interest in having a conversation with you."

Marcuse's notion of false consciousness was not new. Marxists have always employed this notion. In the 1930s James Thurber described a party he attended that was dominated by leftist intellectuals. "Midnight eventually arrives at our party and everybody begins 'unmasking' everybody else's 'ideology.'" The unmasker, usually a Marxist, always thinks he is superior to the person he is unmasking, who is usually not a Marxist.

In the 1970s, when Marcuse's star waned, the French theorist Michel Foucault became the leading critic of bourgeois society. He advanced an idea that was similar to Marcuse's notion of false consciousness: the vast majority of people are prisoners of a "regime of truth," by which Foucault meant a way of looking at things that is determined by the prevailing norms of a particular society. Thus people who did not agree with him were regarded as unwitting "prisoners" of a regime of truth. They had been brainwashed.

When Foucault spoke of a "regime of truth," he was speaking of bourgeois society. "We must see our rituals for what they are: completely arbitrary things, tied to our bourgeois way of life." It was his mission to "detach the power of truth from the forms of hegemony, social, economic, and cultural, within which it operates at the present time." If one followed his prescriptions, it would be possible "to create a new way of life," yet Foucault changed his political prescriptions frequently. At first he was a communist, then he became a Maoist. Toward the end of his life he spoke of personal liberation through drug-taking and engaging in bizarre sexual practices.

In an interview given shortly before he died Foucault seems to have realized that his notion of a "regime of truth" undermines conversation. Foucault now implies that in order to have a solid conversation one has to assume that no one is a prisoner of a "regime of truth." Or, to put it another way, one must assume that everyone has the same level of consciousness. "In the serious play of questions and answers, in the work of reciprocal elucidation, the rights of each person are in some sense immanent in the discussion."

In several essays Foucault put forth an idea that was at odds with his notion of a "regime of truth." Influenced by Nietzsche, he argued that everyone, including himself, is a prisoner of his own life history. "What I say does not have objective value. . . . Each of my works is a part of my own biography."

If all ideas are personal truths, there can be no solid conversation—no interchange of ideas. Each speaker (or writer) can recite only his or her personal truths. And the audience (or reader) can say only: "Thank you for sharing with me your personal truths." Foucault's ideas, Hitler's ideas, Joe Blow's ideas—they would all have the same value because they would all be personal truths. Yet if all ideas are personal truths, so are Foucault's ideas. Foucault and other thinkers who promoted radical subjectivism are guilty, Ernst Gellner says, of "epistemological hypochondria."

The authors of *Salons: The Joy of Conversation* seem to embrace radical subjectivism insofar as they approve of a "Creativity Salon" where, according to the founder of the salon, "criticism was not allowed." The authors also praise another salon called "Pow-Wows," which were "freestyle gatherings . . . where artists, tech-heads, educational visionaries, painters, and neo-country-western singers ate, sang, danced, talked, and inspired one another." The notion of a salon where criticism is not allowed would have baffled Hume, Diderot, and the intellectuals who attended the Parisian salons of the seventeenth and eighteenth centuries. To their way of thinking a creativity salon would be a mindless form of self-indulgence.

Is postmodernism the same thing as radical subjectivism? The editor of a collection of essays entitled *The Postmodern Reader* (1992) says that anyone attempting to map out postmodernism "will encounter endless contradictions." Some observers have called postmodernism a meaningless term; others have said that postmodernism is a benign paradigm shift in Western thought—benign because it signifies a loss of belief in systems of thought that seek to explain everything. Still others have argued that postmodernism means nihilism. To my mind postmodernism eludes definition but it is a close relative of radical subjectivism.

The 1960s, then, saw the rise of countercultural theorists who undermined conversation by praising irrationality, promoting personal exploration, and championing authenticity. Countercultural theorists generally were not interested in having a conversation about their ideas. They usually dismissed their critics as repressed souls who suffered from false consciousness. A decade or so later radical subjectivists (and postmodernists) opened the door to extreme politeness. The radical subjectivist doesn't "unmask" someone. Rather, he nods attentively. He is listening; he is being supportive. He may even say: "I hear where you are coming from." But it is not easy to be mindlessly polite all the time, so even radical subjectivists at times find themselves raising questions about someone's ideas.

Easy Rider: The Importance of Getting Stoned

One should not make too much of countercultural theorists, since it is unlikely that many members of the counterculture read their books. In a memoir the novelist Robert Stone talks about the time he spent living a countercultural existence. He traveled with Ken Kesey, the leader of the "Merry Pranksters," a group of hippies who roamed around the country in a psychedelic-looking bus. He says they "consumed mind-altering drugs" in great quantity and variety, and they listened to jazz continually. The drugs he names are marijuana, LSD, peyote, methamphetamine, and methedrine.

The Merry Pranksters didn't get much reading or thinking done. Or conversing. As Stone puts it: "There was more hemp than Heidegger at the root of our cerebration, and . . . many of us had trouble distinguishing Being from Nothingness by three in the afternoon." They were "ripped" most of the time. One prankster who took amphetamine "never ate, never slept, and never shut up." He was a manic talker—not a conversationalist.

In my own experience, people who took drugs regularly lost interest in conversation. My graduate school roommate smoked pot during the week and took LSD on weekends. When he smoked pot, he stayed in his room and listened to music. I don't know what he was like when he took LSD because he did it at his parents' apartment in New York. Returning from New York once, he gave me several pages of gibberish that he had written while on acid. I said it made no sense. He said: "You need to be on acid to appreciate it." End of conversation.

The heroes of detective fiction and Westerns are laconic, but when they talk they speak in clear sentences. The heroes of the counterculture are grunters, mumblers, ranters, and cursers. Occasionally they pray, but in unconventional ways; they prefer Native American prayers or Buddhist prayers. In the movie *Easy Rider* the head of a hippie commune in the arid Southwest makes up his own prayer; he prays the grain will grow to provide the commune with "simple food for simple tastes."

Easy Rider, which appeared in 1969, stars Peter Fonda and Dennis Hopper as hippies who travel around the country on their motorcycles—smoking pot continually, snorting cocaine occasionally. They do not worry about time; before the titles come on Peter Fonda throws away his watch. They can live this way because they are drug dealers (the movie begins with their buying cocaine and then reselling it). Their conversation is very limited. Hopper often mumbles about the degree to which he is stoned—punctuating his remarks with a pot smoker's giggle. Fonda, who is supposed to be the more profound of the two, says: "I'm getting my thing together." Sometimes he utters a complete sentence—usually to give an editorial in favor of the counterculture's way of life. He praises a farmer/rancher for living off the land. He lectures Jack Nicholson, who plays a lawyer boozehound, about the art of smoking marijuana. According to Fonda, smoking grass "gives you a whole new way of looking at the day."

The character Nicholson plays—he is a hippie wannabe—talks a lot, but his first extended remarks show him to be a crackpot about UFOs. He earnestly describes how "Venusians" are taking over America—disguising themselves as real Americans. After he learns how to smoke pot, he possesses countercultural wisdom. Speaking of working class people in a small town in the Deep South, he says to Hopper and Fonda: "What you represent to them is freedom." These square people are not free, he continues, because "they are bought and sold in the marketplace."

Nicholson also warns his new friends that ordinary working class people are likely to be violent when they meet up with hippies. That very night, while Nicholson is sleeping in the woods, he is beaten to death by a group of locals. The movie ends with more violence. Riding on their motorcycles, Fonda and Hopper are murdered by two rednecks in a pickup truck.

Is there any implicit criticism in *Easy Rider* of the mindlessness of the counterculture? Toward the end of the movie Fonda says: "We blew it." Is he referring to the bad "trip" he had on cocaine in New Orleans, when he was with a prostitute? Whatever Fonda means by his cryptic remark, he is treated by the director as if he were a quasi-religious figure. The close-ups make him look profound. He is a countercultural sage.

Easy Rider, cultural commentator John McWhorter says, is the first major movie "to celebrate the counterculture in all its variety." *Easy Rider* was a cult movie—an advertisement for the camaraderie of pot smoking. According to film critic Pauline Kael, "the film became a ritual experience." People watched it while smoking a joint. Kael also says that Hopper "became a culture hero." Countless young men wanted to talk the way he did—using "man" all the time and speaking in sentence fragments. Talking this way was a sign of authenticity.

Pot smokers like the characters in *Easy Rider* thought of themselves as radical individualists, but pot smoking promotes conformity because it tends to make one passive and solemn. In the 1960s I had a witty friend who enjoyed verbal wordplay. We used to have lively conversations filled with raillery, but when he began to experiment with drugs his interest in conversation faded; he also lost his sense of humor. When I began to make fun of his solemn drug taking, our friendship withered and eventually came to an end.

The "White Negro": From Norman Mailer to Eminem

If pot smoking was for many members of the counterculture the path to personal liberation, so too was listening to music— especially the music of African-Americans and their white imitators. The blues, jazz, and soul were regarded as authentic music, and the African-American musicians who played this music were celebrated by countercultural theorists. According to Norman Mailer, African-American musicians were not conformists. They were hip, not square.

In "The White Negro," an influential essay that appeared in 1957, Mailer praised "the Negro" in general, not just African-American musicians. The Negro was admirable because he "lived in the enormous present, he subsisted for his Saturday night kicks, relinquishing the pleasures of the mind for the more obligatory pleasures of the body." Mailer was mainly interested in the Negro's music. "In his music he gave voice to the character and quality of his existence, to his rage and the infinite variations of joy, lust, languor, growl, cramp, pinch, scream and despair of his orgasm. For jazz is orgasm."

According to Mailer, if white people listened regularly to

African-American music they would achieve personal liberation—escaping from the repressive world of square culture, a
culture of "slow death by conformity," a culture that stifles
"every creative and rebellious instinct." If whites become what
Mailer calls white Negroes, they would no longer be "trapped
in the totalitarian tissues of American society." Undoubtedly
thinking of himself, Mailer says that some whites have already
become white Negroes. "So there was a new breed of adventurers, urban adventurers who drifted out at night looking for
action with a black man's code to fit their facts. The hipster had
absorbed the existentialist synapses of the Negro, and for practical purposes could be considered a white Negro."

Mailer's essay is an intellectual disaster. First, it is patronizing to view African-Americans as primitives—patronizing
and, I would think, offensive to many African-Americans. And
it is wrong to assume that jazz was solely the creation of African-
Americans—or that jazz is primarily an expression of African-
American rage. It also makes no sense to say that "jazz is orgasm." Jazz is jazz. It is a type of music that at its best has great
subtlety and expressive power. Jazz, Albert Murray says, 'is
essentially an American vernacular or idiomatic modifica-
tion of musical conventions imported from Europe." Murray
speaks of "the rapid rate at which jazz . . . moved from the
level of a popular art around the beginning of the twentieth
century to the precision and the sophistication of a fine art by
the mid-1930s." Finally, it makes no sense to use the word *totalitarian* to characterize American society in the 1950s. During the heyday of Senator McCarthy some people lost their
jobs, but they were not executed in a Moscow prison or sent to
the Gulag.

Though Mailer's notion of jazz is nonsensical, he was
right to argue that music would play an increasingly important

role in the formation of the psyche of young Americans. Nevertheless, he exaggerated the effect of music—implying that listening to jazz would transform Americans. For Mailer music—not drugs—is the path to personal liberation. America, he implies, has a stark choice: either move toward personal liberation by listening to jazz or move toward fascism. He implies that if more whites become white Negroes, the United States is less likely to become a fascist country. (Mailer continues to argue that the United States is in danger of becoming a fascist country. In October 2004 he said "fascism . . . can become our fate if we plunge into a major depression or suffer a set of dirty-bomb catastrophes.")

Mailer was probably not as radical as Norman O. Brown—he didn't call for an end to sublimation—but he too distrusted rational discourse. Referring to "our capacity for mental organization, for mental construction, for logic," he implies these qualities tend to promote fascism. Mailer sees a connection between "civilization" and the concentration camps. "Civilization is so strong itself, so divorced from the senses, that we have come to the point where we can liquidate millions of people in concentration camps by orderly process." Who is the "we" in this sentence? The "we" refers to those who are excessively attached to "civilization." Mailer's prescription for the United States is similar to Brown's: we need to break our connection with civilization. We need to cultivate our emotions. Otherwise we are likely to have more death camps.

Mailer implies that a square American is roughly the same as a Nazi Party member. Like other countercultural gurus, he claims that the most violent Americans are those who are the least hip: fundamentalist Christians, Republicans, southern rednecks—conservatives in general. These people, Mailer implies, have an inordinate hatred of communists, homosexuals, and hippies. They would become more tolerant if they listened to jazz.

Mailer's view of violence is ambivalent. He is against official violence—the violence perpetrated by generals and cops—and he is against the violence of right-wingers, but he regards some forms of violence in a positive light, as expressions of the authentic self. Mailer speaks of a "future [that] we hear raging to be born." Rage, he implies, is good, but only if it is the rage of the hipster.

Mailer, like Fanon, implies that we need violence to ward off violence. He acknowledges that "the removal of all social restraints . . . would open us to an era of incomparable individual violence, [but individual violence] would still spare us the collective violence of rational totalitarian liquidations." Mailer supports individual violence because it will reduce the likelihood of official violence—of impersonal mass murder. In his autobiography *A Margin of Hope* (1982) Irving Howe regrets that he published Mailer's essay in *Dissent*—the magazine he edited. He says it had been "unprincipled" of him to do so because Mailer celebrated violence.

In sum, Mailer endorses a primitivist ethos of feeling and acting. Mailer's real man is not the laconic hunter guide in Hemingway's "The Short Happy Life of Francis Macomber," and he is not the hard-boiled Philip Marlowe in Chandler's *The Long Goodbye*. His real man is part jazz musician, part hoodlum, part boxer, part African-American from the slums. The hipster's "psychic style," he says, "derives from the best Negroes to come up from the bottom."

One of Mailer's favorite words is *energy*. One gains the energy necessary for personal liberation by listening to jazz, which enables one to return to one's senses. The hipster prefers bars and jazz clubs to coffeehouses. Mailer contrasts the hipster with the beatnik. The latter, who is *"more at home with talk, can be found in the coffeehouse"* (emphasis mine). In Mailer's view the beatnik's interest in talk is a bad sign. It means that the beatnik is committed to "civilization." In Mailer's primitivist scheme of things, if you are interested in conversation you are repressed. And you may well be a fascist. Mailer, like Thoreau and Whitman, is a preacher. But his message is different from theirs. He tells his readers: "You need to become a white Negro."

About forty years after Mailer's essay appeared, Marshall Mathers, a young white man from Detroit, in effect became a white Negro; he began his rise to fame as the nation's preeminent white rapper. Appearing under the name of Eminem, he soon became a commercial success. When *The Eminem Show*, his third CD, came out in May 2002, it sold 1.3 million copies in one week; by the end of the year sales reached 8 million. Though many observers—and not just conservatives—said that Eminem's lyrics were obscene, ultraviolent, and misogynistic, critics in the *New York Times Magazine, New York Review of Books,* and *New York Observer* praised his work. Rap music in general is often praised in the mainstream press as authentic music that—to use a contemporary cliché—speaks the truth to power.

Eminem was popular not only with white teenagers and young adults, he was also popular with older whites. Maureen Dowd, a columnist for the *New York Times,* called him "the boomers' crooner." After the film *8 Mile* appeared—a heavily autobiographical film in which Eminem stars—he became the cultural establishment's favorite pop icon.

Did Eminem's success (and the success as well of the foul-mouthed HBO series *The Sopranos)* make it chic for educated people—women as well as men—to use vulgar language not occasionally but regularly, especially the word *fuck?* Fuck, of course, is a very old word. According to the *O.E.D.*, it was first used in the early sixteenth century. Fuck was always used by working class males, but in the 1960s fuck, one might say, came of age. It was now used by middle-class members of the counterculture to advertise their authenticity and their rejection of bourgeois values. Using profanity was a way of identifying oneself with the black underclass—of being hip, not square. The motto of the Filthy Speech Movement that blossomed in Berkeley in the mid-1960s was "Fuck You."

With the rise of rap music in the early 1980s, fuck became part of mainstream pop culture. It was now heard frequently in movies, and it even appeared in some popular magazines. In the last decade the *New Yorker* opened its doors to fuck. In a 29 September 2003 article about the rerelease of *Scarface* (not the original Howard Hawks movie, but the Brian De Palma remake) fuck appears seven times. One person is quoted as saying: "It's a truly fucking great film." Another says: "This movie is so like fuckin' life."

"Eminem loves the word *fuck,*" his biographer Anthony Bozza says. "He uses it like a basketball player uses a dribble, to get from here to there." (In a song Eminem says "*fuck* was the first word I ever learned.") Bozza describes a comment Eminem made to his manager. "Hey, Paul, you're already fired, you fat fuck. . . . You're so fired and rehired, you're tired, you skinny fat fuck! Fuck you, you bald fat fuckin' fuck. Fuck you fuckin' fuck, your life, it's over."

Repeating fuck obsessively, Eminem at times sounds as if he has Tourette's syndrome. Yet he is perfectly capable of avoiding profanity. In a lengthy conversation with Bozza about his young daughter he steers clear of profanity. He also says: "I don't cuss around my daughter." But he says that he is not overly protective of her. "If someone else is around and they say the F-word, she's heard it before; I don't say, 'Hey, watch your mouth around my daughter.' That would be ridiculous. After all, I'm Eminem, Mr. Potty-Mouth King. To me it's different when it's in a song because it's music and it's entertainment."

Being Mr. Potty-Mouth King is a role that Eminem chooses to play, yet he also implies that he needs to be foulmouthed. "I have to tell it like it is," he says. "What I sit around and talk about, you know, I have to go say to the world, otherwise what would I be? If I've got any balls at all, I'll come out and say it, which is what I do." His foulest and most violent language comes from a persona that he created—a dark alter ego called Slim Shady. Slim Shady preaches revenge and destruction. He is misogynistic and homophobic. Venting rage, Eminem says, is therapeutic. "My microphone is my psychiatrist, it listens to me talk. Once I've got it out, I'm not mad any more."

Eminem also likes to think of himself as a jokester—amusing predominantly white middle-class audiences by playing a white trash guy having a tantrum. He is parodying the counterculture's prescription to get in touch with your feelings. "I'm bringing cutting edge humor to hip-hop," he says. "It's been missing that for some time."

If Eminem wants to irritate and amuse by being outrageous, he also wants to irritate and amuse by parading his scorn of everything. There are no sacred cows in his world. "Eminem's attitude," a fellow rapper says, is: "fuck it, I'll say anything, to anyone, anywhere, fuck it, fuck it all. Who's the hottest pop group on MTV right now? Fuck them. What did the president do? Fuck him, too." Roughly half the pictures of Eminem in Bozza's biography have him "flipping the bird," which is a gesture less of anger than of scorn. Eminem's first big hit was: "I Just Don't Give a Fuck." In one album, a critic says, "Nearly every song seems to feature Eminem giving someone the finger."

Eminem says: "If you do something fucked up, you're bound
to be made fun of. If I do something fucked up, I'll make fun
of myself—I'm not excluded from this." For Eminem and
other rappers it seems as if everything is "fucked up."

Whether or not Eminem ever read Mailer's "The White
Negro," he clearly is a child of the counterculture. As one critic
has said: "He is inheriting the whole 'fuck you' culture built
here in the sixties." Yet he is not like the passive hippies in *Easy
Rider* and he is not the kind of white Negro Mailer envisioned.
He is not a hipster. Though his lyrics are often violent, he
doesn't have a theory that celebrates violence. He has been accused of advocating violence against women, but he is not advocating anything. He has no psycho-political project. Moreover, he dislikes those who make too much of his tough
childhood. "I grew up on the East Side of Detroit, but I don't
like to give people a sob story. I had a hard life, blah blah blah.
A lot of people did and a lot of people do."

"I'm not a role model," Eminem says, "and I don't claim
to be. It's what the song 'Role Model' says. I say that I do everything in the song, but it's all fucking sarcasm. How can people
not get it? . . . That's fucking ridiculous. It's obviously saying,
'You wanna grow up just like me? Fuck no, you don't.'"

Many of Eminem's fans see him as an entertainer. They
don't take his lyrics seriously. Describing a song in which Eminem talks about how he kills his ex-wife, Andrew O'Hagan
says: "Fans find the song funny, rather in the way young people
find professional wrestling funny, as if the brutality was a form
of showmanship." Eminem's rapping is so histrionic that it
seems unconnected with reality. It is like a demented Western
takeoff on Japanese ritual drama.

Even if we regard Eminem mainly as a jokester, the concerns of critics about the connection between rap music (es-

pecially so-called gangsta rap) and violence cannot be dismissed. Many rappers have criminal records, and several rappers have been murdered. "There is a fine line," McWhorter says, "between playing the bad boy and becoming one, and in the 'hip-hop community' too often violence jumps out of the quotation marks and becomes a tragic reality." Writing about a new CD issued by a well-known rapper, the reviewer (in the *Washington Post*) says that the singer "lazily rants about his ability to acquire and use semi-automatic firearms." A *New York Times* article about a popular new rapper discusses his violent drug-dealing past.

The idea that rappers are only joking about violence is nonsense. In early March 2005 two well-known rappers and their associates traded gunfire near a recording studio in lower Manhattan. 50 Cent—a well-known rapper—said to a reporter: "You have a higher chance of getting shot because you're talking to me than if you never met me. See, my lifestyle's different from what you'd consider the norm, because I come from an environment where the price of life is cheap." Rappers like to brag about their violent life—and talk about their prison sentences. A *New York Times* article about three rappers in prison has the following headline: "A Rapper's Prison Time as a Résumé Booster."

Whether one finds Eminem (and other rappers) amusing or appalling (or boring), rapping is a form of expression that—to belabor the obvious—is hostile to conversation. Rappers imply that the only way to talk is to vent one's feelings— preferably using profanity. Not all rappers are angry rappers, but rap music is mainly a music that expresses anger. Asked why his lyrics use vulgar language, the rapper Snoop Dog replied: "It's self-expression. I just got a whole lot of feelings that need to get out."

Even if rappers are not a menace to society, the growth of rap music affects the conversational climate. Using profanity is often intimidating. The person who says fuck repeatedly when expressing an opinion is aggressively taking a stand—saying, in effect, "here's what I think. Do you have a problem with that?" The use of profanity makes good-humored disagreement difficult. Eminem says—seemingly in jest—to a disk jockey he knows: "You fuckin' fuck. Fuck you, you fuckin' fuck." One can imagine that if one rapper disagrees with another, the conversation might turn into: "Fuck you." "Well, fuck *you*." "Go fuck yourself." Etc.

Rap also undermines sociability because rappers generally look at other people with distrust. The rapper has a paranoid sense of honor; he is always worried about being dissed. In "Respect Me," the *Washington Post* says, an English rapper issues "plenty of clenched teeth warnings about how 'you people are gonna respect me if it kills you.'" Many rappers also have a very dark view of American society—a view of the United States that is similar to Mailer's in "The White Negro." America, as one rapper puts it, is "Amerikkka." Another popular rapper asks: "Why did Bush knock down the towers?" in a song that was a Top 20 single on the hip-hop charts.

Rapping is not the only contemporary art form in which the performer vents his feelings. On 31 January 2004 the *Washington Post* ran a review of a "performance" by Henry Rollins, a former rock musician who calls himself a "spoken-word artist." Rollins talked for three hours to an audience of eight hundred persons. According to the reviewer, "even at the show's end, Rollins looked as if he could continue his uninterrupted riff for several more hours." What did he talk about? Politics, crime, war, Hollywood, love, and "his own peculiar onanistic habits." Rollins, the reviewer said, is a "diatribist, confessor, provocateur, humorist, even motivational speaker—but he is not a bore."

The success of rap music and the existence of spoken-word artists are symptoms of the extent to which our culture has become a therapeutic culture. In "The White Negro" Mailer says: "To be an existentialist, one must be able to feel oneself—one must know one's desires, one's rages, one's anguish, one must be aware of the character of one's frustration and know what would satisfy it." Mailer and other countercultural theorists, rappers, and spoken-word artists suggest that the frustrated life is an inauthentic life. How does one get rid of frustration? One expresses oneself.

If Thoreau celebrates the "dumb" man who is silent so that he can appreciate the sounds of Nature, and Whitman celebrates the "rough" man who prefers barbaric yawps to polite conversation, and Hemingway celebrates the tough man who thinks men who talk a lot lack courage, Eminem and other rappers celebrate the man with "attitude"—the man who warns people not to dis him and tells everyone that he is fucked up because the world is fucked up. In photos the rapper usually is scowling. He also looks somewhat menacing. A good-humored rapper is an oxymoron.

In 2000 the Brooklyn Museum gave rap music its blessing by putting on an exhibit: *Hip-Hop Nation: Roots, Rhymes, and Rage.* Rap music remains very popular, especially with young people. Reviewing Eminem's fourth album in the fall of 2004, the *New Yorker*'s pop music critic, Sasha Frere-Jones, said that "for people under thirty, Eminem may be the most significant recording artist in the English-speaking world." His new album, she pointed out, "has sold more than a million and a half copies in less than two weeks." By the end of the year, it had sold more than three million copies.

What kind of effect does the popularity of rap music have on American conversation? I suspect that many older Americans dislike rap music. A letter writer to the *Washington Post* complained about "the pervasive influence of television, movies, music and video games that glamorize thuggery, ostentation and antisocial behavior"—what is often called "ghetto behavior." The writer points out that ghetto behavior "extends across income levels and race. Plenty of well-to-do white boys mimic Eminem or his latest incarnation."

Rap's influence is hard to gauge. Many young people I know listen to rap music, yet they are sociable and enjoy the pleasures of conversation. Nevertheless, it is worrisome to think of young people living on a steady diet of rap music, since the rapper is someone who is driven—or at least plays at being driven—by anger, hostility, and paranoia. But it is not only rap music that promotes the notion that it is honorable and healthy to get angry. This notion is widespread in popular culture, and it has affected the way people interact. In January 2005 the *Wall Street Journal* spoke of the "daily bombardments of . . . crudeness—not only on the airwaves but in the streets and most every venue of public life." Four decades ago would a vice-president have told a senator to "go fuck yourself"—not in a bar but on the floor of the Senate?

One can imagine a future where angry narcissists become commonplace—where many people spend hours in virtual reality (see Chapter Nine) and then spend brief periods interacting with others, mainly by talking crudely and in a manic fashion.

Bozza describes a strange conversation that Eminem has—mainly with himself. He and Eminem (and several others) are riding in a taxi. Eminem has taken the drug Ecstasy. "As the E starts to hit him, Eminem becomes a word dervish, a rhyme tornado, a spaz, and a force that can't be reckoned with." Eminem decides he wants to talk to the Sikh cabdriver, but he can't because of the plastic window that separates them. "'S'cuse me, talkin' a me, no?" he says, banging hard on the window. 'S'cuse me fuckin'a talkin' a me? No, I'm a fuckin' a talkin' a you!" The cabdriver, who cannot hear Eminem, doesn't respond, but that doesn't stop Eminem.

Eminem is "soon conducting both sides of the 'conversation' in a wacked-out language known only to him." Bozza says that he and the other passengers were laughing, but there is something pathetic about Eminem's "conversation" with himself. Even when Eminem thinks he is talking to others, he is really talking out loud—talking to himself. Is he really angry or is he playing at being angry? He probably doesn't know himself.

Eminen is an angry narcissist. So are we all on occasion. Driving my car, I mumble to myself—what I call "road rant." Walking in the city, I often find myself talking to myself. Who doesn't have conversations with himself? A New Yorker cartoon captioned "The Muttering Classes" shows sixteen persons talking to themselves on a city street. Montaigne in fact recommended it. "We should set aside a room . . . keeping it entirely free and establishing there our true liberty, our principal solitude and asylum. Within it our normal conversation should be of ourselves, with ourselves, so privy that no commerce or communication with the outside world should find a place there." But for Montaigne conversation with oneself is an occasional thing—a temporary retreat from the conversible world. It is not a way of life.

IX

The Ways We Don't
Converse Now

In Gerald Green's novel *The Last Angry Man* (1983) the main character, an elderly Brooklyn doctor, is angry because he cares deeply about the community, and he thinks too many people, especially young doctors, care only about themselves. His anger signifies that he is a good man; he is not selfish and apathetic. For many Americans anger is a good thing. Why shouldn't they be angry about fundamentalist Republicans or secularist Democrats, about corrupt businessmen or greedy trial lawyers? To paraphrase John Ruskin: Tell me what you are angry about, and I will tell you what your politics are.

According to the comedian Janeane Garofalo, there is more anger on the Right than on the Left. "On the left," she says, "you've got a person who is more willing to engage in conversations that have context and nuance." But angry left-wing books and angry right-wing books sell equally well, so the politically angry are on both ends of the political spectrum.

The ancients said that anger is an enjoyable passion. "A certain pleasure accompanies anger," Aristotle says. In the *Iliad*

Achilles speaks of "that gall of anger that swarms like smoke inside of a man's heart / and becomes a thing sweeter to him by far than the dripping of honey." The ancients argued that in certain circumstances anger is appropriate as an energizing force—a way of promoting action. But they also argued that anger clouds the mind. Renaissance writers on conversation agreed. Bacon offers advice on "how the natural inclination and habit [disposition] to be angry may be attempered and calmed."

Have Americans become angrier about politics since the terrorist attacks of 9/11? Americans have often been angry about politics—as Mrs. Trollope, Dickens, and Tocqueville pointed out. The United States has had two civil wars. We forget that the Revolutionary War was a civil war; many Americans were loyalists—including William Franklin, Benjamin Franklin's son. (He was the royal governor of New Jersey before he was arrested.) Gordon Wood notes that "the two times Franklin met his son . . . in the summer of 1775 [their conversation] ended in shouting matches loud enough to disturb the neighbors." In 1784 William, who was living in London after serving two years in a Connecticut prison and four years as president of the Board of Associated Loyalists, tried to effect a reconciliation with his father, who headed the American delegation to France, but Ben Franklin put off a meeting with him. "I ought not to blame you for differing in Sentiment with me in Public Affairs," the father said. But he did blame him.

Contemporary America is not on the edge of civil war, but it is reasonable to assume that Americans have become angrier since 9/11. "Grief and disappointment," Hume says, "give rise to anger." (There is a lot of anger in the book of Job. Job's wife is angry with God. Job is angry with his friends; the friends are angry with Job.) In late 2003 a report from the Pew Research Center said: "National unity was the initial response to the calamitous events of 11 September 2001, but that spirit has dissolved amid rising political polarization and anger." Bozza, the biographer of Eminem, offers a similar assessment (in the jaunty language of a pop music critic): "In a post 9/11 world, Eminem is less shocking, and understandably so. . . . The violence and hate in Eminem's music . . . is the soundtrack of the times: America is angry, poor, out of work, misunderstood, and gunning for revenge."

Political anger seems to have increased after the U.S. invasion of Iraq in March 2003. Godfrey Hodgson, a British historian, said American politics has become "viciously polarized." *Washington Post* columnist David Ignatius referred to the "vituperative e-mails" he gets from both conservatives and liberals. Senator John McCain told a television reporter: "I've never seen such anger [in Congress]."

Nowadays there is a lot of fuel to keep political anger burning. We can listen to talk radio, view Web sites that provide us with information and commentary on the stupidities of those on the Right (or the Left), and exchange e-mails (and e-mailed articles) with likeminded persons. Political anger is being stoked by publishers who are eager to publish political tirades, which generally sell well. One publisher said recently: "We want people to feel their blood pressure rise when they read our books."

Are Americans increasingly living in what I call anger communities? Anger communities often are preoccupied with their political opponents. To paraphrase a line by Yeats: "More substance in their enmities, than in their loves." Jeanne Marie Laskas, a columnist for the *Washington Post,* says: "We the people never seem to have discussions anymore; we all just rant to our like-minded friends with our like-minded rhetoric."

Anger communities are similar to what Cass Sunstein calls a feuding group. In *Why Societies Need Dissent* (2003), Sunstein says: "One of the characteristic features of feuds is that members of feuding groups tend to talk only to one another, or at least to listen only to one another, fueling and amplifying their outrage." Political anger is a time-saver: one reads only news and opinion that confirm one's views. Almost seventy years ago Paul Valéry said that the vast amount of news that citizens are barraged with every day would have a negative effect on our intelligence. "The daily output of vast quantities of published matter, the flood of printing and broadcasting, wash over our judgments and impressions from morning to night, mangling and mixing them, making of our brains truly a gray matter in which nothing stands out, nothing can last." Valéry was wrong: the vast amount of information does not make us opinionless; it makes it easier for us to have strong opinions, since there is information to confirm almost any thesis.

Because many Americans get angry when discussing politics, it makes sense to avoid conversations about politics. Anne Applebaum, a *Washington Post* columnist, warns against discussing politics at dinner parties. "Anyone who has ever even invited guests of opposing political persuasions over to dinner will know how quickly it can all go wrong. . . . A chilly, polite dinner is more bearable than one that ends with guests stomping out the door."

In Johnson's club politics and religion rarely were discussed, but club members had solid conversations about many other subjects—literature, the nature of the passions, political economy. Nowadays people rarely read the same books or even go to the same movies. Moreover, the fear of getting into an argument about politics and the fear of hurting someone's feelings may be having a chilling effect on solid conversation in general—not only political conversation. At dinner parties I've attended the topics of conversation mainly were restaurants, vacations, and health—all safe subjects.

To engage in small talk is often enjoyable and it certainly is "polite," but a steady diet of conversation about food, vacations, and health is tedious. "Politeness," La Rochefoucauld says, "is essential in social life, but it should have limits; it becomes a kind of slavery when it is excessive." An advertisement in the *New Yorker* for the French liqueur Grand Marnier, which has a Web site that sponsors an Internet chat group, asks: "Isn't there more to talk about than how many carbs you ate today?"

Yet it is hard to avoid saccharine politeness when the alternative is often the angry venting of opinions. Judith Martin says that "she would be only too happy to welcome the return of substantive conversation at dinner parties; goodness knows she is weary of hearing people talk about the food. But conversation requires listening respectfully to others and engaging in polite give-and-take, rather than making speeches and impugning others' motives and judgment."

Is Martin alluding to a new kind of social anxiety: the fear of angry confrontation on social occasions? A woman told Theodore Zeldin that dinner-party conversations are unpleasant because her guests usually are "egos shouting." She said that she prefers to watch conversations on television or listen to conversations on the radio. Since Zeldin is an English historian, the woman he quoted probably is English, but I suspect that many Americans would agree with her, which is why many spend more time watching television talk shows or listening to radio talk shows than having a solid conversation.

Enjoying Ersatz Conversation

Television talk shows offer a variety of ersatz conversations. I call them ersatz conversations because they are semiscripted performances that are concerned with winning and influencing viewers and boosting audience ratings, which are of primary importance to all television stations, including noncommercial ones. Many television talk shows also have a secondary purpose—to promote the products of their celebrity guests, who are invited to plug a new television series, a new movie, a new book, a new CD, even a new line of cookware.

For the politically angry there is also another form of ersatz conversation: talk radio. In the United States there are 1,300 talk radio stations, most of them with right-wing hosts. The leading talk radio host is Rush Limbaugh, who sounds off to roughly 20 million listeners on 580 stations. On the opposite end of the political spectrum is Randi Rhodes, a popular South Florida talk show host whose ratings in her listening area are higher than Limbaugh's. Jason Zengerle writes that Rhodes is proof that "a liberal talk radio host can be just as bombastic, hyperbolic, and plain old nasty as a conservative one." Talk radio, Zengerle says, "is the quintessential 'arena for angry minds.'" (The phrase "arena for angry minds" is from Richard Hofstadter's seminal essay "The Paranoid Style in American Politics.")

There are angry minds on television as well. They appear on political talk shows where pundits with opposing views yell at each other. Michael Kinsley of the *Los Angeles Times* has called them "shoutfests." Are such shows popular? *Crossfire,* the most famous, was cancelled in January 2005 after a twenty-three-year run. CNN president Jonathan Klein said he wanted to move CNN away from what he called "head-butting debate shows." His description of *Crossfire* was accurate. Two men sat across a table—one "from the Left," the other "from the Right." They began a conversation about a political question, but it soon became overheated. A bell then sounded—ending the round. One pundit, now looking at the camera rather than at his "opponent," announced another topic. Another round began.

According to Kinsley, *Crossfire* "didn't cause the ideological divisions in this country. It reflected them. Sometimes it reflected them so well that people got angry, and they shouted. But that anger was usually genuine." To my mind, the anger didn't seem genuine, for the two pundits had no trouble switching from being angry to calmly introducing a commercial break. Alessandra Stanley, the television critic for the *New York Times*, says that "real anger is as rare on television as real discussion."

The cancellation of *Crossfire* does not mean that such political talk shows are unpopular. Similar shows can be found on several stations. Kinsley, who defends such programs, acknowledges that they have a rigid formula. "The conceit that there are exactly 2.0 sides to every question, one 'left' and one 'right,' is a genuine flaw of 'Crossfire'-type shows."

Oprah, a famous daily talk show, has nothing to do with anger and very little to do with political questions. Oprah Winfrey—her last name is rarely used—is a billionaire who has been called "the world's most influential voice" and "one of the most influential women of the 20th century." Her program appears in more than 200 domestic and 130 foreign markets.

When the show comes on the air we see the word Oprah against a swirling yellow and white background. In a voice-over Oprah describes the contents of the day's program. Then we see Oprah walking down an aisle in the studio theater while the predominantly female audience cheers and applauds. There are close-ups of women who look inspired by the sight of her. (Seeing Oprah grab outstretched hands as she walks, I recall the medieval notion of the king's healing touch.) Oprah signals for quiet and begins discussing the first topic of the day. There is a brusque, no-nonsense quality about her. Though she smiles a lot and makes fun of herself, mugging before the camera and occasionally switching into a comic accent, her main purpose is serious: she wants to help women improve their lives.

Oprah's guests usually are people who have an interesting story to tell, especially a story about triumphing over adversity. The stories are fleshed out with video clips. One show was devoted to people who survived a life-threatening ordeal. The first guest was a man who suffered a gunshot at close range. After the audience viewed a videotape of the shooting, the man described what he felt after being shot, and he talked about how the shooting changed his life. He said he now rarely complains about anything. And he appreciates little things much more. He is grateful to be alive. On the same program other survivors—a man who was buried in an avalanche, a woman who was impaled on a fence—talked about their ordeals. A doctor in the audience who wrote a book about these survivors answered several questions about the nature of pain.

Oprah's guests often promote a new book. On one show Hillary Clinton discussed her autobiography. On another show a successful businesswoman talked about the book she wrote: *Powerful Inspirations: 8 Lessons That Will Change Your Life.* Another program was mainly about women who run a successful business while managing a young family. The audience received a gift from each businesswoman—a shrewd way of marketing a new product.

Oprah asks questions and gives answers. One can't imagine a guest saying: "No, Oprah, I don't see it that way." The viewers of *Oprah* want her to give them advice. A blurb for one of her books says she offers "timeless wisdom and savvy advice"—including ten commandments for lifelong success. Oprah believes she has helped people improve their lives. "People have told me their lives have changed because of me. I take away from this the sense that I'm on the right track."

The talk show called *Dr. Phil*—Phil McGraw is Oprah's male counterpart—is also a blend of advice and inspiration. Oprah and Dr. Phil take an instrumental view of conversation. They want to motivate people—to get them to take control of their lives. They are the Dale Carnegies of television—telling viewers how to make the most of their lives.

Ellen DeGeneres, the host of the *Ellen DeGeneres Show,* is not in the advice business. She has only one purpose: to cheer her viewers up. When the show opens, a voice-over says: "Don't get mad, get glad." Then we see the predominantly female audience whistling, clapping, and even dancing in the aisles. DeGeneres once told an interviewer: "There's so much energy in this world that's negative and so much hate; I think I'm actually helping put out good energy."

DeGeneres—who achieved a degree of notoriety a few years ago by declaring on *Ellen,* a television sitcom she starred in, that she was a lesbian—is a good comic, even when her material is weak. Her awkward and hesitant way of speaking is effective. She occasionally looks surprised, as if she doesn't know why she said what she just said, and then she smiles. In effect, she says to her viewers: "I'm a goofy woman who is having a good time. Why not take your mind off things by watching this mindless show?"

Though DeGeneres is amusing, the conversations she has with her celebrity guests usually are insipid—mainly because the guest and the host trade compliments. Interviewing the actor James Caan, DeGeneres says she likes the new NBC show Caan appears in (*Las Vegas*). Caan then says he likes her show.

Caan looked uncomfortable when he made this comment, as if he knew that no one would believe that he watches a morning talk show whose viewers mainly are women.

(Celebrity promotion is not new. In the late 1950s I was a guest on a popular morning radio talk show. I was chosen to be on the show because a friend of my mother's was the show's producer. The other guests included a popular pianist, a movie star, a gossip columnist, and two other celebrities. The pianist performed a lively number, and the other celebrity guests complimented him. Then the host turned to me; he wanted to know what the students at the college I attended thought about the pianist. Without thinking I blurted out: "I've never heard of him." Everyone glared at me and after the show they ignored me. I had broken the iron law of talk shows, which is: never say anything negative about a celebrity guest.)

DeGeneres's show tries to appear informal, as if it were put together at the last minute. DeGeneres's opening monologue conveys a sense of casualness. She flits from one subject to another. Each time I saw the show she was dressed in pants and sneakers—as if she had come to the studio after grocery shopping or working out at a gym. Despite the air of casualness, the show is carefully scripted. DeGeneres does an opening comic monologue that lasts about ten minutes, then she dances for a minute or two, sits down in a chair, takes a sip from a coffee mug, and chats with a young man who is the onstage disc jockey. The chat leads her into the second part of her monologue, which usually has to do with someone who has written to the show or some event from a previous show. After a commercial break the first of three guests appears.

Describing the week's guests, the show's Web site frequently uses the phrase "chats with" or "chats about," but the guests mainly serve as straight men for DeGeneres, who often responds to their remarks with humorous questions. If she makes a remark that is slightly witty (or if she looks at the audience in a funny way), the audience whoops it up, applauding and whistling. Though the show is pure fluff, it is impossible to dislike DeGeneres, who has a great deal of antic charm.

The View, which airs at the same time as DeGeneres's show, is more like a conversation than any other daytime talk show on commercial television. (It was the recipient of the 2003 Daytime Emmy Award for "Outstanding Talk Show.") When the title comes on, we hear the studio audience applauding and yelling while a voice-over describes the highlights of the day's program. Then we see headshots and the names of five women. The women walk onto a set that looks like a dining room, with a living room in the backdrop. On the table there are flowers, coffee mugs, and newspapers—suggesting that the women will be talking about the news of the day.

When I watched the show for two weeks the only woman I was familiar with was Barbara Walters, the show's producer, who appears three days a week. The other regulars are Joy Behar, a stand-up comic, actress, and author; Star Jones Reynolds, an African-American lawyer and former prosecutor who has been a television analyst for many high-profile trials; Meredith Vieira, who is a former television journalist (she is the moderator); and Elisabeth Hasselbeck, the youngest member, who has been a participant on the television show *Survivor.* (She is also married to a professional football player.)

According to the program's Web site, *The View* is an "original forum where real women discuss relevant, everyday issues and share their daily no-holds-barred opinions and lively, colorful conversations." By using the term "real women," the Web site implies that the hosts of the show are accomplished women who are knowledgeable about current affairs.

Yet by saying that the women "share" their opinions, the Web site implies that it is a women's show—one in which the guests are supposed to avoid the blunt disagreement that is de rigueur on male-dominated political talk shows. The Web site is misleading, since only the first segment of the show—"Hot Topics"—attempts to be a conversation. (The rest of the show consists of celebrity interviews or tips for women about buying clothing or preparing a meal.) In three respects the "Hot Topics" segment sounds like conversation. First, there is good-humored disagreement—even what might be called raillery. (DeGeneres occasionally disagrees with her guests, but the disagreement is part of her comic routine.) Secondly, the talk jumps rapidly from one subject to another, though I am certain the women know in advance what topics they are going to discuss. Third, occasionally several people talk at the same time, though not for long. In other words, the show edges toward the disordered world of real conversation, where people are always interrupting people.

The Web site says that the "dynamic" women have conversations about "the most exciting events of the day." On one show someone referred to the 2004 presidential race but the discussion centered on whether the taller candidate usually wins. After a brief conversation about the HBO series *The Sopranos,* the women discussed McDonald's announcement that it would no longer be serving a Double Big Mac, which led to a discussion of whether there should be tax credits for those who get medical treatments to fight obesity. The lengthiest discussion was about the Oscars. On another day the "hot topic" was gay marriage. Four of the five women seemed to be making pitches for recognizing gay marriage. Notwithstanding its claim to be about the "exciting events of the day," *The View* is mainly chitchat about celebrity culture.

Finally, there are the "trash TV" talk shows. The most popular is the *Jerry Springer Show*. The show implies that real conversation is angry confrontation. Springer says in his autobiography: "Our best shows . . . were those where there was real personal conflict, real issues of confrontation." In a veiled criticism of other talk shows, Springer says: we show "real people honestly responding to something they felt deeply about at the moment." The operative word is real.

Springer's show, which has been called "nuts and sluts," is always vulgar and occasionally violent, though the violence is not allowed to get out of hand. The show is as much about the audience as it is about the guests—or about the interaction between the audience and the guests. The mood is set at the opening: we hear the audience screaming "Jerry, Jerry!"—they are told to do so—while we see a disclaimer that the show might not be appropriate for children. The screaming continues while the show's contents are previewed. Then there are shots of the audience, which is composed mostly of young men and women. When the announcer introduces Jerry Springer, the audience, which is still yelling, stands up. The audience stops shouting and for thirty seconds Springer shakes hands with people. Then he announces the theme of the show.

A show I watched, "Hot-headed Hookers," featured four prostitutes who were confronted by people who wanted them to stop hooking: an angry stepmother, two angry boyfriends, an angry husband. Most of the guests acted foolishly, especially the first two prostitutes, who repeatedly bared their breasts and shouted obscenities. The shows are taped in advance, so the obscenities are blipped out and the bare breasts are blurred.

When the first "hot-headed hooker" walked onto the set—a heavyset blonde woman in her late twenties or early thirties dressed in a halter and a skirt—the audience taunted her. She pranced about—defiantly announcing that she was a truck stop hooker who charges forty dollars for ten minutes. While she talked she bared her breasts and butt and yelled at the men in the audience. The audience yelled back, daring her to reveal more. Several women in the audience taunted her, and one bared her breasts, saying: "Here's what good breasts look like." After allowing the antics to go on for a few minutes, Springer asked the guest several questions and then said it was time for a commercial.

The next prostitute was also a proud and defiant exhibitionist. An attractive African-American woman who was a stripper before she became a prostitute, she said she was a high-class whore who charges two hundred dollars. She repeatedly bared her breasts and traded insults with members of the audience. Springer asked her if she would give up prostitution if her boyfriend asked her to do so. She replied that she wouldn't; she needed the money. The woman couldn't focus on Springer's questions because the audience kept shouting crude remarks about her aging body. She answered them as crudely as they addressed her. Finally, the boyfriend came out—seemingly angry because she is a prostitute though she claimed that he was not angry the day before. She traded obscenities with him, and then another man came out—the boyfriend's brother, who apparently was the woman's pimp, and the men started pushing and shoving each other. The audience egged them on.

During the course of his shows, Springer generally keeps a low profile. If the guests become violent, the show's security crew intervenes. Springer doesn't urge the guests to be outrageous. That is the audience's job. In his autobiography Springer says: "The talk show is my job. I love it. It's great fun to do. I meet fascinating people, it pays well." Yet when the guests act up Springer often looks as if he'd rather be somewhere else. At the end of the show Springer sits on a stool and offers what he calls a "Final Thought." He ends with his signature line: "Till next time, take care of yourself and each other." Take care of yourself and each other? The show encourages its guests to trash each other.

In his autobiography Springer offers a number of justifications for his show. He says the unpaid guests volunteer to be on the show, so he is not exploiting them. He also says he does not approve of their conduct. Nevertheless, he brags that when the show stopped editing out the obscenities and the violence "viewership went through the roof. For the first time in ten years, Oprah was surpassed as the number-one talk show in America. Suddenly, everybody was talking *Jerry.*"

Senator Joseph Lieberman and the conservative cultural critic William Bennett have criticized Springer's show as well as other so-called trash TV shows. They argue, among other things, that such shows undermine civility. Many observers agree with their assessment. One critic says of the *Jerry Springer Show:* "America's new No. 1 show gives us butting heads—the perfect visual metaphor for the breakdown of communication, if not civilization." But the show is not very different from the acts of many rappers and performance artists.

What is insidious about Springer's show is that it advertises itself as "real" when it has nothing to do with reality. It is a carefully designed composite of two aspects of America's conversational landscape: the in-your-face side and the non-judgmental side. We see people shouting at each other and we hear Springer trying to be a therapist. The guests on Springer's show are often crude and coarse, yet it is hard not to feel sympathy for some of them when they struggle to express themselves. Watching a boyfriend talking incoherently to a former girlfriend, I thought of a famous sentence in *Madame Bovary:* "None of us can ever express the exact measure of his needs or his thoughts or his sorrows; and human speech is like a cracked kettle on which we tap crude rhythms for bears to dance to, while we long to make music that will melt the stars." What is the appeal of the *Jerry Springer Show?* Some viewers may be moved by the plight of the people on the show, but the antics of the guests provoke laughter in the studio audience. The people in the audience are like the eighteenth-century Londoners who visited Bedlam, an institution for the mentally ill, in order to gape and laugh at the patients. Bedlam—the nickname for Bethlehem Hospital—was a tourist attraction. The novelist Samuel Richardson quotes a young lady who visited the place: "The distemper'd fancies of the miserable patients most unaccountably provoked mirth, and loud laughter" among the visitors.

At the opposite end of the television talk show spectrum from the *Jerry Springer Show* are several programs that feature lengthy interviews with writers, politicians, policymakers, and scientists. In serious interview shows the interviewer plays an active part, and the guests are given enough time to respond cogently. Nevertheless, these shows are mainly interviews.

Dick Cavett, who was a writer for the *Jack Paar Show,* which aired from 1957 to 1962, reports that when he asked Paar what the secret was in doing such a show, Paar replied: "Don't make it an interview, kid. Make it a conversation." According to John J. O'Connor, a former television critic for the *New York Times,* Paar had "an uncanny ability to listen carefully and actually engage in clever and often witty conversation." When Paar died in January 2004, Tom Shales, television critic for the *Washington Post,* said that Paar's "true art was the art of conversation. . . .

To be on Paar's show, your talk had to be witty, amusing, wry, insightful, even educational; guests weren't booked just because they had movies opening or TV series premiering." Paar, he says, "developed his own repertory company of zany conversationalists." Even if Paar was as good a conversationalist as O'Connor and Shales say he was, Paar was mainly concerned with winning viewers. No matter how clever and witty television conversations are, they still are ersatz conversations.

Watching witty and charming people bantering on television talk shows (I am not talking about the people on the *Jerry Springer Show*), viewers may occasionally ask themselves: "Why can't the people I know—family, friends, colleagues— be more like these people?" In the ersatz conversible world one rarely meets irritable or tedious people. (One does meet angry people.) So why not tune in the ersatz world and tune out—as much as possible—the real world?

I have not mentioned television's morning talk–news shows, which regularly attract an audience of roughly eleven million Americans. According to Lee Siegel, the television critic for the *New Republic,* the growing popularity of these shows "might . . . be owed to the heightened American nervousness about 'reality.' The prospect of spending eight to ten hours with real, live, untelevised and uncontrollable humans makes more and more people hasten back as fast as they can into the tube world in which they happily concluded the previous evening." Siegel's point is the same as mine: the ersatz conversible world has many attractions.

No one—except people who suffer from acute social anxiety disorder—wants to live only in the ersatz conversible world. Yet millions of Americans (and millions of people in all advanced industrial nations) spend a great deal of time in that world because it is one they can control. (According to a recent poll, 54 percent of Americans frequently watch television during dinner.) They can choose the kind of ersatz conversation that suits their mood. They can watch people sounding off at political questions, relating inspiring stories, chitchatting about celebrities, telling amusing anecdotes, or cursing their boyfriends. In the ersatz conversible world everything is predictable. Oprah will always be inspirational, Ellen DeGeneres will always be goofy, Jerry Springer will always be nonjudgmental.

There is another reward to watching, or listening to, ersatz conversations. We can insult someone risk-free. Watching a television talk show or listening to a radio talk show, we can comment on the remarks the guests make without worrying about whether we are being rude or boring or misinformed. I often rant at my television set—telling various guests on the *Lehrer News Hour* that they don't know what they are talking about.

Watching ersatz conversation is like talking to one's dog. Dogs do not answer back. (And dogs, unlike most people, give us undivided attention when we say something—unless they see a squirrel.) I read somewhere that talking to a dog or cat on a regular basis is likely to lower one's blood pressure. Watching ersatz conversation may have the same effect, which is perhaps why the Englishwoman said to Zeldin: "I really enjoy other people having conversations for me."

The ersatz conversible world is expanding. In January 2005 I read that new television talk shows are in the works for next year. In April 2005 I saw an ad in the *New Yorker* for a new program called "Dinner for Five." It shows a cartoon of three people in a living room with a television set. One person says: "With 'Dinner for Five'" we don't really need stimulating conversation of our own."

Conversation Avoidance Devices

Near my kitchen window is a bus stop where teenagers wait for the school bus every morning. They are usually wearing headphones and listening to music on a digital music player. The most popular one is Apple's iPod. "An iPodder," the *Washington Post* reports, "has a telltale white cord coming from his coat pocket to his ears and lives in sonic smugness; he walks around in a kind of perpetually happy glaze, with his entire music collection—as many as 10,000 songs—going with him." The iPod, which undoubtedly will soon hold more than ten thousand songs, is what I would call a conversation avoidance device, enabling people to avoid real conversation. So too is the computer because it is the gateway to the world of the Internet.

Neither digital music players nor computers were invented to help people avoid real conversation, but they have that effect. The *Washington Post* describes "a shy 10-year-old girl who has trouble talking face-to-face with other kids," but she has many online friends to whom she sends Instant Messages. Instant Messaging, Deborah Tannen says, is a boon for shy people. With Instant Messages "you can send out a feeler" to a person of the opposite sex "without committing too much. In person, if you don't get a reaction, it's humiliating."

Online conversation is obviously different from real conversation. Raillery, the lifeblood of conversation, is not possible in an e-mail or Instant Message. Raillery is possible when we hear a person's voice on the phone, but it works best when we see a person's gestures and facial expressions. Online conversation has many pitfalls. According to Patricia T. O'Conner and Stewart Kellerman, the authors of *You Send Me: Getting It Right When You Write Online* (2002), "It's too easy to be misunderstood when you're writing modem à modem. Let us count the ways: What's convenient shorthand for you may seem cold and abrupt, even nasty to the reader. Small slights are magnified. . . . The mildest of suggestions may sound like a rebuke. Subtlety, irony, and sarcasm can land with a thud." My experience with e-mails supports their view: slights are imagined when no slight was intended.

Are today's adolescents, who are the first generation to grow up with online conversation, likely to have less interest in real conversation than previous generations? It is impossible to say, but in contemporary Japan young people often spend countless hours on their wireless cell phones (*keitai*), which serve as a laptop computer, personal digital assistant, digital music player, and video game unit rolled into one. Many young Japanese, the *Washington Post* reports, are "*keitai* addicts, oblivious to the world around them." *Keitai* culture, it appears, has had a negative effect on real conversation. A *New York Times* reporter describes a recent prize-winning Japanese novel as one that depicts a world of young Japanese who engage in "unsentimental sex and [have] *a profound inability to communicate verbally*" (emphasis mine).

Interactive video games are also conversation avoidance devices. They enable gamers—the vast majority of whom are males—to spend hours enjoying a fantasy life. Gamers can be courageous warriors, sports stars, or conquerors of women. The *Washington Post* reports that "the game industry is huge, the fastest-growing entertainment sector on the planet." According to the *Post,* a study of "how Americans spend their time found that video games have emerged as the fourth most dominant media among men, firmly displacing print . . . and rivaling the major electronic media for the attention of twenty-somethings and teenage boys." In 2003 the leading producer of interactive video games (Electronic Arts) produced twenty-two titles that each sold more than one million copies. Five sold more than four million.

Which sex is more likely to be affected by conversation avoidance devices? The *New York Times* reports on a study that "found that the amount of Internet use does not differ by gender. But women on average use e-mail, instant messaging and social networking more than men, while men spend more time browsing . . . and participating in chat rooms." The study also reports that Internet use has decreased the amount of time people spend socializing with friends.

The *Washington Post* describes a family that is awash in conversation avoidance devices. The family of six (there are two children from the mother's previous marriage and two from the father's previous marriage) possesses nine television sets, six computers, six VCRs, six cell phones, three stereos, three digital music players, and two DVD players. Family members spend very little time together. They eat dinner quickly and retire to their electronic cocoons. Sometimes a family member exchanges Instant Messages with another family member even though both are at home.

E-mail, Instant Messaging, digital music players, interactive video games—these devices are only the beginning. New conversation avoidance devices are continually entering the marketplace. On 13 October 2004 a new handheld personal computer called the OQO was put on the market. Two weeks later Apple announced that its next generation iPod music player will be able to display digital images as well as play songs, and the *New York Times* reported that developers are working on turning "instant messaging into a multi-pronged medium that goes beyond mere chat to integrate games, e-mail and Web browsing." Jules Urbach, one of the leading developers of hyperfunctional Instant Messaging software, told the

Times: "I love picking a character and going into a [chat] room and leading a virtual life."

Urbach, one assumes, doesn't want to live in the virtual world all the time. No one does except for people who suffer from social anxiety disorder. But there probably is a correlation between the number of electronic devices we possess and the amount of time we spend in the virtual world. Four decades ago most people could view only a dozen television stations. Now, many people have access to more than two hundred stations. One could waste an evening flipping channels. In a witty song called "Clicker," Terri Hendrix, the Texas-based folk singer, complains about being a prisoner of her television remote, and she wails: "I need to get a life." L. Gordon Crovitz, who is in charge of Dow-Jones's electronic-publishing operations, says that "we live in the early days of an Information Revolution that will change our lives just as the Industrial Revolution changed our forefathers."

Will the proliferation of conversation avoidance devices affect our sociability? Will the steady use of such devices affect our ability to converse?

According to Hume, "The propensity to company and society is strong in all rational creatures." If Hume is right, then conversation avoidance devices may not have much of an impact on humankind's sociability. Though many people will spend a great deal of time in the electronic world, most will prefer real conversation. Yet what if "the propensity to company and society" is not as strong as Hume suggests? The eighteenth-century writers on conversation thought sociability was a strong force in human nature, but Thomas Hobbes, the seventeenth-century English philosopher, did not think so. Comparing bees and ants, which "live sociably one with another," to "man-kind," Hobbes says in *Leviathan* (1651) that "men are continually in competition for Honour and Dignity, which these creatures are not; and consequently amongst men there ariseth on that ground, Envy and Hatred, and finally Warre; but amongst these not so."

Sociability exists, Hobbes says, but it is a weak passion. People become sociable, he says, out of fear. We seek out others because we are afraid of a state of nature where anarchy prevails and violent death is commonplace. According to Hobbes, "Men have no pleasure in keeping company, where there is no power able to over-awe them all." But if fear of death makes us sociable, fear of being humiliated and embarrassed may make us avoid face-to-face encounters. It is not surprising that in Japan, where shyness is commonplace, many young people "are walled inside their own little world with their *keitai.*"

There is also the fear of boring others. No one wants to be like the garrulous man in the movie *Airplane!* who causes the man sitting next to him to commit suicide out of boredom. We dislike cocktail parties because it is so easy to feel that one is boring the person one is talking to. We see the eyes of our fellow conversationalist darting elsewhere, as if he or she would rather be talking to someone else. We forget that we are doing the same thing. If we think someone finds us boring, we dislike that person. As La Rochefoucauld says: "We often forgive those who bore us, but we cannot forgive those who find us boring."

Conversation avoidance devices are unlikely to affect the sociability of naturally gregarious people—those who feel little or no social anxiety. But many people suffer from mild forms of social anxiety. "The wise man," La Bruyère says, "sometimes avoids company, for fear of being irritated." The shy and insecure person may prefer online conversation for fear of being slighted, embarrassed, or humiliated.

In *The De-Voicing of Society: Why We Don't Talk to Each Other Anymore* (1998), John L. Locke argues that modern technology has already had a negative effect on sociability. A number of studies, he says, make it clear that many people use e-mail to avoid face-to-face interaction. This trend is disturbing because we learn many things from a person's voice and gestures. "With no access to our species' social feedback and control mechanisms, there will be nothing to keep misunderstanding, incivility, and dishonesty from creeping into our daily life at unprecedented levels." He also argues, as the eighteenth-century writers on conversation did, that simply being with other people improves our sociability—or, as they put it, increases our stock of benevolent passions.

Centuries before the virtual world existed, Montaigne wrote about the "special effects" of face-to-face conversation. "Gestures and movements animate words, especially in the case of those who gesticulate brusquely as I do and who get excited. Our bearing, our facial expressions, our voice, our dress and the way we stand can lend value to things which in themselves are hardly worth more than chatter."

Even when we are having a face-to-face conversation, conversation avoidance devices tend to have a negative effect on our conversational skills. More than a century ago James Bryce complained about "the distractions of American life," but that was long before the existence of portable electronic devices. Our ability to listen to others has been undermined by the ringing, singing, bleeping, buzzing, and chirping of conversation avoidance devices. Some of these devices are even startling. I heard a phone ringing recently that sounded as if it were a woman screaming for help. But even if the sound is not disturbing, it is distracting. I have often had difficulty being a good listener because someone's cell phone began ringing, and I momentarily wondered if it was mine even though my cell phone is usually turned off.

To quote a phrase from Eliot's "Burnt Norton," many Americans are "distracted from distraction by distraction." Steven Pearlstein, who writes a business column for the *Washington Post*, grumbles: "In the past, the conversation at my monthly poker game would turn to politics or sports or real estate or . . . well, you know. But now no longer. These days, my card-playing pals are so busy showing off their new BlackBerrys or boasting about the newest features on the Palm Pilot that we can hardly get in a decent game of Follow the Queen."

In *The New Brain* (2003) Richard Restak, a neurologist and neuropsychiatrist, argues that conversation avoidance devices are actually affecting our brain. "Our brain literally changes its organization and function to accommodate the abundance of stimulation forced on it by the modern world. . . . One consequence of this change is that we face constant challenges to our ability to focus our attention." Attention deficit disorder, he says, is becoming an epidemic among children and adults. Evan Schwarz, a writer for *Wired* magazine, says that America could be on the way to becoming "the first *society* with Attention Deficit Disorder . . . the official brain syndrome for the information age." Treating attention deficit disorder is a big industry. More than thirty million prescriptions were written in the United States between 1999 and 2003. There are also many over-the-counter dietary supplements available. To quote the Web site of one such product: this pill "supports healthy memory, concentration and focus with a unique blend of vitamins, minerals, protective antioxidants, botanical extracts and omega-3 oils."

The eighteenth-century writers on conversation argued that we are egotistical by nature so we have to train ourselves to be good listeners. Those who suffer from attention deficit disorder are likely to have a hard time becoming good listeners, but perhaps many do not care if they are poor listeners, for they prefer to talk rather than listen. They can now do so easily; they can become a blogger and talk without interruption on their own Web site. *Blog,* as most people know, is short for *weblog.* (The word was coined in 1999.) The blogosphere is expanding rapidly. There are currently eight million bloggers, but that number is likely to double by the time this book is published. In November 2004 the *New York Times* reported that in the past five years "the number of people posting blogs . . . has skyrocketed."

In a culture that values self-expression, it is not surprising that people are encouraged to become bloggers. The *Washington Post* titled an article: "How to Start a Winning Blog." In "I Have Seen the Future, and It Blogs," Geoffrey Nunberg lists the new words associated with blogs. Nunberg, who discusses language questions on National Public Radio, speaks of blogrings, blog registries, blog hosting sites, and metablogs. He adds that "there are blog divas, who receive thousands of hits a day, and the wannabes called blog whores, who inveigle other bloggers to link to their pages. There are racy blogs and philosophical blogs and depressive blogs. . . . There are blog groupies and blog stalkers. And there are quarterly blog awards."

John L. Locke says we are moving in the direction of an autistic society. I would say that we are moving in the direction of a solipsistic society. I walk down a street in Washington, D.C., and see numerous men and women talking on their cell phones or listening to music on their digital music players. "Boy With a Headset," a poem by Edward Hirsch, begins with the following lines:

He is wearing baggy shorts and a loud T-shirt
And singing along to his headset on Broadway.

With the advent of the cell phone headset it is not always easy to distinguish between a person who is talking to himself and a person who is talking on the phone. Last year, while in the produce section of a supermarket, I was startled to see a man seemingly talking to the apples—or talking to himself or possibly talking to me. Then I noticed that he was wearing a headset.

Hume may have been wrong when he argued that the expansion of commerce enlarges the conversible world. The rise of commerce at first led to an expansion of the conversible world, but commerce now promotes conversation avoidance devices, so the conversible world is likely to contract.

My wife and I were sitting in an outdoor café a few miles from where we live when a well-dressed woman walked up and started talking to us. She talked first about her abscessed tooth, then about President Reagan's funeral, and finally about Richard Nixon. I nodded but did not respond—mainly because she did not give me time to respond. She did not seem to want to hear what I had to say, for she suddenly said: "Well, nice talking to you," and walked away. Was she mentally ill or was she spending so much time in virtual reality that she had lost the ability to have a conversation?

In "Worriers Anonymous" Charles Simic writes: "It is the season of vague apprehensions / Rambling soliloquies. . . ." Are we heading toward a future where an increasing number of people engage in rambling soliloquies? Are the ways we don't converse likely to increase?

X
The End of Conversation?

In the future will an increasing number of Americans spend most of their day in the virtual world—listening to a talk radio show while driving, watching a television talk show while eating dinner, communicating mainly by cell phone, e-mails, and Instant Messages? A reviewer on Amazon. com (he is reviewing *Oliver Wendell Holmes and the Culture of Conversation*) says: "Conversation is dead now." This is an exaggeration. Walk through the restaurant district—especially on a Friday evening—of any major U.S. city and you will see innumerable people standing at bars or sitting at tables. They are drinking and eating, but they are also having conversations. People go to bars and restaurants for many reasons—to conclude a business deal, to celebrate an occasion, to pick up someone—but for many people the chief reason is the expectation that they will have a pleasurable conversation with friends, spouses, or companions. A correspondent writes Miss Manners about a pub she goes to: "One of the main reasons I frequent this pub is . . . that a variety of interesting people do, too, and we often get into wonderful and interesting conversations." Sir

William Temple, Swift's patron, was probably right when he said that "no man willingly lives without some conversation."

People also go to coffeehouses in order to enjoy the pleasures of conversation. The *Utne Reader* describes the Black Cat Coffeehouse in Ashland, Wisconsin, which has "such a reputation for good conversation that locals call it the Black Hole— once you enter, it may be hours before you come out." Yet many people at the coffeehouses I frequent appear to be discussing business matters with colleagues (except for the occasional mothers with small children). And many are staring at a laptop computer or talking on a cell phone. Sitting in Starbucks while editing this manuscript, I take a quick look around: two men are staring at laptops, a man and a woman seem to be discussing business (they have spreadsheets out), and two men in their late 50s or early 60s seem to be having a conversation. They are chuckling a lot.

The expansion of coffeehouses in the past two decades probably has promoted conversation. So has the growth of large bookstores, which often serve as venues for book discussion groups. Community reading programs, usually sponsored by local libraries, are growing in number. On the Internet one can find them in many U.S. cities. There is even a new profession: a reading group guide. A Web site lists 1,320 such people. Many people I know belong to discussion groups. Two years ago a male friend of mine organized a discussion group composed of retired men. They meet once a month at his house. There is no format. They talk about whatever comes up. My friend also belongs to an interfaith Bible discussion group composed of three men and three women. It also meets once a month. A female friend of mine belongs to two discussion groups. One meets weekly for two hours to read Christian classics—novels, poems, memoirs, theological tomes. The other meets monthly to read classic novels aloud. "We usually talk for at least half an hour before picking up the book, then interrupt our reading to comment as the spirit moves us." The group usually reads nineteenth-century novels.

According to several observers, book discussion clubs have become very popular in recent years. I belong to a discussion group but we don't discuss books. We meet once a month for two hours to discuss a question chosen by one of the members—usually a public policy question. It is a small group—composed of eight to ten persons. We have different political views, and occasionally the conversation gets mildly heated, but no one has ever left the group because of political differences. I also enjoy conversation with fellow tennis players at a sports club I belong to. After we finish playing we often sit around for thirty to sixty minutes—discussing a wide range of topics, from politics to books and movies. (By "we" I mean anywhere from three to seven persons.) Finally, once a year I get together for a long weekend with five old friends. We have extended conversations about a wide range of subjects, including politics and religion—always conducted in a spirit of raillery.

In the summer of 2004 I attended a meeting of the Socrates Café, which is the trademark name for informal discussion groups that meet once a month for two hours. There are 150 such groups worldwide that meet in coffeehouses, bookstores, libraries, churches, and community centers. Socrates Café was launched a few years ago by Christopher Phillips, a former teacher and journalist. He came up with the idea when he was in college and he and other students would meet with a favorite professor at a local bar. He thought: "Wouldn't it be wonderful just to have these great conversations all the time." In *Socrates Café: A Fresh Taste of Philosophy* (2001), Phillips says there was another reason for starting a conversation group. In his journeys across the United States in the 1980s "I had become increasingly disturbed by what I perceived as an extreme and pervasive self-absorption and intolerance among people. . . . We hadn't just become the 'what's in it for me' society; we'd become the 'to hell with you' society." Like the eighteenth-century writers on conversation, Phillips hopes that if people participate in a Socrates Café they will become more sociable.

What questions are discussed at a Socrates Café? According to Phillips, "Just about any question can be grist for a meaningful dialogue." His main concern is not the topic, which he says should be chosen by the participants. It is that the conversation does not become a vehicle for advice-giving or for winning friends and influencing people. To those who may want to start a Socrates Café, he says: "Please never affiliate with us . . . if you aspire to promote coaching or counseling or guidance services." Phillips also says the facilitator, who should be "a very engaged listener," should not strive for a consensus. "It doesn't matter if everyone begins and ends a dialogue with disparate perspectives. There's never any need to try to force any sort of agreement." Though Phillips speaks of a facilitator, he does not want anyone to lead the discussion. "There is no teacher or guide or guru."

"Socrates Café," Phillips says, "is meant to cultivate new habits of discourse in which the primary purpose is to inspire each person within the community of inquiry further to cultivate and discover his/her unique point of view, nothing more and certainly nothing less." Socrates would have been puzzled by the notion that the purpose of a Socratic conversation is to discover one's "unique point of view." He wanted his fellow conversationalists to rigorously examine the assumptions they live by, so that they think more clearly. Whether or not they arrive at a unique point of view is irrelevant.

There were nine people at the Socrates Café I attended—six women of various ages and three men (also of various ages). We discussed two questions, which were chosen by a vote of the attendees: "What is Faith?" and "What is Justice?" (We devoted an hour to each question.) Phillips does not want to a discussion to be based on a text. "A directed or suggested reading beforehand is much too controlling, and too much like other types of groups that are claiming to bring philosophy out of the classroom, but end up bringing the classroom model along with them."

Two things were especially impressive about the conversation. First, no one mentioned his or her profession. Secondly, everyone seemed to listen carefully and respond to what others said. Was the conversation like the conversations in Plato's dialogues? Not at all. It was too polite. There was no raillery. And there was no one who dominated the conversation, as Socrates does in the dialogues.

There is another national organization dedicated to promoting conversation. Conversation Café, founded in July 2001 in Seattle by Vicki Robin, is similar to Socrates Café. It bills itself as a one-and-a-half-hour hosted conversation, held in a public setting. (There are now approximately one hundred Conversation Cafés in the United States and Canada. Most are on the West Coast, in Washington, Oregon, and California.) Conversation Cafés, its Web site says, "aren't group therapy . . . aren't church . . . aren't lectures, but you'll learn a lot from the people who come. Conversation Cafés aren't going out and getting drunk with your buddies—thank heavens." Conversation Café differs from Socrates Café in minor ways. It has a more structured conversational format, and it seems to have a

mildly activist purpose, though Robin says that its main purpose is conversation. "What makes people return each week
is the energy that emanates from thoughtful dialogue." She en-
visions creating "a culture of conversation" in communities
throughout the country.

If bars and restaurants are crowded, local discussion
groups are flourishing, and national groups such as Socrates
Café and Conversation Café are expanding, am I being overly
pessimistic when I speak of the end of conversation? Perhaps,
but the forces sapping conversation seem stronger than the
forces nourishing it.

First, Americans are not particularly interested in the art
of conversation. Articles and books on conversation are mainly
in the Dale Carnegie vein: how to develop conversational skills
that will help you get ahead. Roxanne Roberts, the social reporter for the *Washington Post*, writes about the importance of
being good at small talk. "The ability to connect in short, casual conversations can make or break careers, friendships and
romances. . . . If you don't believe me, there are thousands of
consultants, authors and communication coaches who will
(for a fee) share their wisdom and tips for breaking the ice."
Moreover, many Americans prefer to spend their leisure time
taking courses or attending lectures. In search of advice and
inspiration, they listen to motivational speakers, pundits, gurus,
financial analysts, preachers, writers, and assorted experts. In
search of psychological health, they talk regularly to psychologists, clinical social workers, and psychiatrists.

Secondly, popular culture is generally hostile to conversation. It encourages excessive politeness—"Don't be judgmental!"—and it also encourages excessive impoliteness: "Express yourself!" It also implicitly endorses anger, which is
regarded as manly and honorable. In popular culture angry

expression, which is usually laced with profanity, is often called "real" talk. A late-night talk show where profanity is commonplace is called *Real Time*. After a guest made an obscene remark, Bill Maher, the host of the show, said: "That's keeping it real." The *Washington Post* reports that, according to many teachers, "young people are using inappropriate language more frequently than ever. . . . Not only is it coarsening the school climate and social discourse . . . it is evidence of a decline in language skills. Popular culture has made ugly language acceptable and hip."

Finally, the ersatz conversible world is expanding and conversation avoidance mechanisms are becoming increasingly popular. Not only can we listen to or watch talk shows all day long, but we can watch videos or play video games anywhere using mobile phones or portable play stations. In the fall of 2004 Apple reported that it sold more than two million iPods in the last quarter of its fiscal year—a 500 percent increase over the comparable period in 2003. In February 2005 the *New York Times* noted that soon one can have a virtual girlfriend on one's cell phone—that is, a computer-generated woman who can converse on thirty-five thousand topics. The girlfriend will have a large database "for processing those difficult conversations about romance and intimacy." In March 2005 the *Washington Post* ran an article titled "How to Maximize Your iPod." It begins: "Your iPod is already your new best friend."

One way of thinking about the state of conversation in the United States is to imagine that the members of Samuel Johnson's club have been transformed into contemporary Americans—especially young Americans. The club members are poor listeners because they find it hard to resist multitasking. While Joshua Reynolds is talking about the sublime in art, Edmund Burke is secretly checking his e-mail on his Black-

Berry. While Adam Smith is talking about the benefits of economic growth, Edward Gibbon is reading a text message on his
cell phone.

The virtual world is hard to resist. It calls to us: "Come on
in. There is so much to do here." Last year I found myself checking my e-mail six times a day, reading the *New York Times* online morning and afternoon, and frequently Googling people I
met or read about—simply out of idle curiosity. A friend tells
me she knows people who take out their cell phones every
hour or so to check on sports scores, business news, e-mail, Instant Messages, whatever. Once one gets on the Instant Messaging train—something I've avoided—it's hard to get off. My
daughter says that students IM each other while attending a
class in law school. She admits that at times it is annoying and
distracting to get an IM during class, yet she keeps her IM on.
"Sometimes the prof is boring, so . . ."

In April 2005 the Kaiser Family Foundation published a
study that claimed children are increasingly living in the virtual
world—packing roughly eight and a half hours of media expo-
sure into six and a half hours each day, seven days a week. (They
often have several media going at the same time.) Since 1999,
when the first study of young people's media habits was made,
the time they devote to video games and computers has more
than doubled. "Without question," the report concludes, "this
generation truly is the media generation, devoting more than a
quarter of each day to media. As media devices become increasingly portable, and as they spread even further through young
people's environments . . . media messages will become an
even more ubiquitous presence in an already media-saturated
world." (A friend told me of a birthday party his grandson
went to where nine-year-olds were asked to bring a computer
so that they could play video games.)

It would be wrong, though, to take a uniformly negative view of these developments. Many observers have pointed out that the Internet enables people to make connections with other people, and many of these virtual connections lead to real meetings. Many people have told me how they have renewed old friendships—especially high school and college classmates whom they had lost touch with—through the Internet.

Many observers have also argued that the Internet promotes freedom because it undermines government control of information. The Internet has grown explosively in China. According to Perry Link, it has become "the biggest obstacle to the government's control of information. ... E-mail—flexible, fast, and unorganized—is the most frustrating medium the Party has every confronted." Nicholas Kristof says that until recently "the [Chinese] government and the people have been equally afraid of each other. But increasingly, people are losing their fear." And they are not afraid to meet in person after they have "met" in the virtual world.

Wall Street Journal columnist Daniel Henninger says that cell phones played a major role in creating a mass democratic movement in Ukraine in late 2004. "Using the phones' SMS messaging technology, demonstrators sent messages to meet 10 or so more friends, who'd each send the message to 10 more friends, and so on." Dictators, Henninger adds, "now face the possibility of having their information monopoly hammered by ... smart cell phones, communication satellites, e-mail, Web logs ... and a seemingly endless stream of information sharing programs."

Does the Internet promote sociability or undermine it? It does both. In China and other dictatorial regimes it undermines the social isolation that comes from fearing the government. In the United States and other democratic regimes, it probably increases social isolation, for the proliferation of conversation avoidance devices makes it easy for people to cocoon themselves in the virtual world. The mother of a ten-year-old boy who is addicted to Instant Messaging worries that her son is not developing the "interpersonal skills" he needs. In the *Wall Street Journal,* Cameron Stracher asks: "What are television, e-mail, chat rooms and blogs if not our lonely selves reaching out for comfort, approval, feedback and distracting noise? The lie of each is that we can somehow feel connected by engaging in activities that are, at their heart, isolating."

The virtual world is like alcohol: a modest amount may be good for you (or harmless) but an excessive amount is bad for you. What constitutes an excessive amount? It is hard to say, but in the *Washington Post* Catie Getches, a twenty-something freelance writer, describes her eleven-year-old niece, who has a computer, a cell phone, and an iPod. "At any given time, late at night, far or near, messages filled with such eloquence as 'RUOK,' 'CUL8R' and 'DEGT' ('Don't Even Go There'), are zapped back and forth and then lost forever." Getches says that "it's so common now to correspond by e-mail alone; it's easy to go for days without actually interacting with a real live human being."

Zealots: The Enemies of Conversation

Not only is conversation being undermined in various ways, it is also being attacked by zealots. In the eighteenth century zealots were called enthusiasts. Enthusiasm, Hume says, "produces the most cruel disorders in human society." Hume was mostly concerned about religious enthusiasts, but he also worried about secular enthusiasts. Enthusiasts see disagreement as a sign of treason or corruption or evil. The nineteenth-century Swiss historian Jacob Burckhardt called such people "terrible simplifiers."

In the twentieth century the worst enthusiasts were secular, not religious. In the countries where secular enthusiasts gained power—Nazi Germany and the Soviet Union—it was risky to have a solid conversation. Writing about life under Stalin, Rachel Polonsky speaks of "the terrible strain to which friendships and family relationships were subjected at a time when people found themselves in mortal fear."

In Stalin's Soviet Union, Mao's China, and Pol Pot's Cambodia a grotesque version of a conversation was commonplace. Jamey Gambrell points out that the KGB called their regimen of intensive grilling—aided by sleep- and food-deprivation, physical humiliation, beatings, and mock executions—a conversation. "Soviet investigators," he says, "scrupulously recorded the time their 'conversations' began and ended, and they had their prisoners sign their confessions and each page of the transcripts." China and Cambodia perfected the so-called self-reproach conversation, where men and women were pressured to confess that they had been deficient in enthusiasm. In *The Gate* (2003), a memoir of his life as a prisoner of the Khmer Rouge, François Bizot describes a self-abasement "conversation" that begins with a Khmer Rouge leader who says: "Comrades, let us appraise the day that has passed, in order to correct our faults. We must cleanse ourselves of the repeated sins that accumulate, slowing down our beloved revolution." After confessing their failures, the revolutionaries were urged to denounce the failings of their comrades.

In the twenty-first century the most dangerous enthusiasts mainly are religious. The members of radical Islam, like the followers of Mao and Pol Pot, hate modern urban culture, which they think is rootless, materialistic, and corrupt. When Sayyid Qutb, the Egyptian writer who is regarded as the founding father of radical Islam, visited New York in the late 1940s he complained that Americans liked to have conversations only about money, popular music, cars, and movie stars.

In the movie *Osama*, which is about life in Afghanistan under the radical Islamic regime of the Taliban, the conversible world is nonexistent. The citizenry are supposed to unthinkingly accept the dictates of the religious authorities. Solid conversation is out of the question and light conversation is risky. Women are supposed to talk only to males who are members of their family, and they are not supposed to go anywhere if they do not have a male family member as an escort. Of course there is no joking about the Taliban's version of orthodoxy. The regime's grim police look as if they are determined to eradicate pleasure in general.

It is impossible to have a conversation with those who think God is on their side. As Azar Nafisi says in *Reading Lolita in Tehran* (2003), her memoir about life in the Islamic Republic of Iran: "I realized how futile it was to 'discuss' my views with Mr. Bahri [a former student of Nafisi's who had become a leading supporter of the new Islamic Republic]. How could one argue against the representative of God on earth?"

Fundamentalist Christians have some traits in common with those who subscribe to radical Islam, but there is a major difference. Fundamentalist Christians do not want to destroy the conversible world; they show no sign of wanting to persecute those who disagree with them. Yet fundamentalist Christians are enemies of conversation insofar as they continually refer to the Bible and they often say that there are only two sides to a question—God's and Satan's. This view is especially common among Christians who believe in the "Rapture"—the sudden accession of Christian believers to heaven. On a four-hour plane trip a few years ago I sat next to a young engineer who began talking about the Rapture. I listened to him for a few minutes as he gave his minisermon, and then I took out a notebook and said I had to finish an essay I was working on. The believers in Rapture are preoccupied with obscure prophetic passages in the book of Revelation. They want to know what God thinks—not what their fellow men and women think. For a fee the Left Behind Prophecy Club discusses such questions as whether God is for regime change in Iraq (he is) or whether God wants Israel to withdraw from Gaza (he does not). Those preoccupied with divining the future—whether they pore over the book of Revelation or consult the oracle at Delphi or look at the entrails of chickens—are not interested in the pleasures of conversation.

Rescuing Conversation: A Quixotic Enterprise?

Oakeshott spoke of rescuing conversation, but he said that he no idea of how to go about it. Cameron Stracher has one suggestion: use a device called TV-B-Gone, which turns off television sets by emitting an infrared stream of the most popular television remote codes for "Off." He had the temerity to shut down two television sets in a crowded bar. "A remarkable thing happened. People turned to each other and resumed their conversation. . . . A bar, after all, is a place to meet people and converse, with the assistance of a social lubricant—alcohol."

Stracher knows that he is engaged in a quixotic enterprise, for someone will soon turn the television set back on again. Moreover, if the owner or other patrons find out that he did the zapping, they will probably throw him out. But that night he had a victory of sorts. "When they turned a television back on, I switched it off again. Eventually, they shook their heads and gave up."

Rescuing conversation may be a quixotic enterprise for other reasons. Many people have become addicted to conversation avoidance devices, and many people do not think conversation is important. "The image of human activity and intercourse as a conversation," Oakeshott says, "will, perhaps, appear both frivolous and unduly skeptical." In the view of many people the world needs more activists, not more good conversationalists. A recent advertisement (for a bank) says: "Chatter less. Matter more." And then it says in small print: "Actions speak louder than words."

George Orwell was a political activist, but he worried as much as Oakeshott did about the decline of conversation in England. "The whole trend of the age," Orwell said in 1943, "is away from creative communal amusements and toward solitary mechanical ones. The pub, with its elaborate social ritual, its animated conversations . . . is gradually [being] replaced by the passive, drug-like pleasures of the cinema and the radio." People go to pubs, he says, "for conversation as much as for the beer."

In 1946 Orwell argued that the radio was undermining conversation in the home. "In very many English homes the radio is literally never turned off, though it is manipulated from time to time so as to make sure that only light music will come out of it. I know people who will keep the radio playing all through a meal and at the same time continue talking just loudly enough for the voices and the music to cancel out. This is done with a definite purpose. The music prevents the conversation from becoming serious or even coherent."

Orwell thought a decline in pub-going would make the English people less able to resist totalitarianism. A constant diet of radio music, Orwell suggests, may lead to the atomization of society. His point is similar to Hume's: sociability is an important aspect of political stability, since sociability promotes moderate passions. Orwell also thought that swearing undermined conversation. "The habit of swearing," he says, is "degrading to our thoughts and weakening to our language."

Zeldin wants to do more than rescue conversation; he wants to reform it. Referring to the darkness caused by "the conflicts which surround us," he says: "I should like some of us to start conversations to dispel that darkness, using them to create equality, to give ourselves courage, to open ourselves to strangers, and most practically, to remake our working world, so that we are no longer isolated by our jargon or our professional boredom." The writers on conversation—from Hume and Johnson to Orwell and Oakeshott—would question Zeldin's notion that conversation should "create equality." In their view equality is a prerequisite for conversation. And they would probably say that it is unrealistic to assume that conversation can create courage and remake our working world.

Hume, Johnson, Oakeshott, and Orwell would agree with Zeldin that there is a political dimension to conversation. Hume saw a connection between politeness and freedom. If politeness becomes a weak force, the conversible world will probably contract. And in free societies the smaller the conversible world, the greater the likelihood of violent civil discord. Hume would agree with Oakeshott, who says: "Political education is learning how to participate in a conversation."

Though Hume implied that it is our civic duty to learn the art of conversation, he knew that pleas to be civic-minded always fall upon deaf ears. One is not likely to get many people interested in the art of conversation by stressing that being a good conversationalist makes one a better citizen. The main point Hume makes is: it is in our self-interest to be polite. Politeness is essential for conversation, and conversation is one of the great pleasures of life.

Politeness, Hume says, is not a natural passion. What is "natural to the human mind," he says, are "presumption and arrogance." We have to work hard to control our antisocial passions. "The eternal contrarieties, in *company*, of men's pride and self-conceit have introduced the rules of Good Manners or Politeness, in order to facilitate the intercourse of minds, and an undisturbed commerce and conversation." La Rochefoucauld would agree with Hume. He said that "most young people think they are being natural when they are really just [being] ill-mannered and crude."

Hume argues that if one cannot curb one's natural presumption and arrogance, one should at least conceal them. "Wherever nature has given mind a propensity to any vice, or to any passion disagreeable to others, refined breeding has taught men to throw the biass [*sic*] on the opposite side, and to preserve . . . the appearance of sentiments different from those to which they *naturally* incline" (emphasis mine). Lady Mary Wortley Montagu also argues that politeness means concealment. "In this Moral state of Imperfection Fig leaves are as necessary for our Minds as our Bodies, and tis as indecent to shew all we think as all we have."

Politeness, Hume says, is necessary for conversation, but to be a good conversationalist one should also possess wit. "We approve of another [person]," Hume says, "because of his wit, politeness, modesty, decency, or any agreeable quality which he possesses." (Henry Adams makes roughly the same point when he says that he invites only "amusing" people to his Washington salon.) According to Hume, "in order to render a man perfect *good company*, he must have Wit and Ingenuity as well as good manners [i.e., politeness]." Hume adds that wit "may not be easy to define; but it is easy surely to determine that it is a quality immediately *agreeable* to others." Hume argues that in France "the first questions with regard to a stranger are: *'Is he polite? Has he wit?'*" Hume realizes that not everyone can have wit, but he thinks that most people can learn to be polite.

Hume creates a character, Cleanthes, who is his conversational ideal. The speaker says of Cleanthes: "I met him lately in the circle of the gayest company, and he was the very life and soul of our conversation: so much wit with good manners; so much gallantry without affectation; so much ingenious knowledge so genteelly delivered. . . . That cheerfulness, which you might remark in him, is not a sudden flash struck out by company: it runs through the whole tenor of his life, and preserves a perpetual serenity on his countenance, and tranquillity in his soul."

Hume was probably thinking of his native Edinburgh when he says that in polished societies "particular clubs and societies are every where formed." In such clubs and societies people become more refined from "conversing together, and contributing to each other's pleasure and entertainment." And their conversations promote "*knowledge, and humanity.*"

A study by Aron Seigmen, professor of psychology at the University of Maryland, argues that it is good for one's health to control one's antisocial passions. He says that "people who are chronically irritable are as prone to cardiovascular disease as those who are always angry and ready to explode." According to Seigmen, "The outward expression of anger seems to be the most toxic. People who respond in this way need to relearn their responses and to change their view of situations to defuse the toxic effect of their emotions on their cardiovascular health." The counterculture's exhortation to "let it all hang out" turns out to be poor advice.

Unfortunately, in the last four decades the angry unclubbable Rousseau—the champion of authenticity—has had a greater influence on American culture than the genial clubbable Hume. Rousseau despised politeness and disliked raillery. The railleur, a word that has been obsolete since the eighteenth century, is an attentive listener who offers good-humored disagreement. "To railly well," Fielding says, "it is absolutely necessary that Kindness must run thro' all you say." The railleur is a person who enjoys ribbing others and takes no offense at being ribbed. The railleur can move from light conversation to solid conversation and then back again.

Raillery is a great solvent of cultural and social differences. My wife and I are irreligious Northerners, yet many years ago we were invited to dinner by neighbors who are deeply religious Southerners (they say a prayer before every meal). Moreover, the husband was at the time an army colonel, whereas I had gone to graduate school to avoid being drafted. Soon after we arrived, the ramrod-straight colonel looked at my wife— he knew she had emigrated from Hungary—and said: "So you're Hungarian. I hear that Hungarians are the scum of the earth." We instantly knew from his expression that he was joking. And the fact that he could ridicule someone's ethnicity made us realize that he enjoyed raillery. The evening and its conversation were pleasurable, and we remained friends with this couple even after they moved to another state.

Perhaps we need to rate the level of raillery in a country. A raillery index would suggest how politically stable a country is— how much its citizens can engage in good-humored disagreement. Twentieth-century totalitarian states had a raillery index

of near zero. Raillery was far too dangerous for the citizenry.
Even people at the highest level of power had to be very careful
about what they said. "It is good manners to joke and be witty,"
Della Casa says, but it would have been foolhardy to joke and
be witty in the presence of Stalin or Hitler or Mao or Pol Pot.
Ian Buruma speaks of the dinners at "Stalin's many country houses, where the extreme boredom of the Leader's rambling monologues could instantly turn to panic at the smallest
hint of his displeasure." Hitler, like Stalin, was mainly a monologist who would rarely entertain a question. In his introduction to *Hitler's Table Talk,* H. R. Trevor Roper quotes one of
Hitler's secretaries about Hitler's monologues (these took place
after the defeat at Stalingrad). "Every evening we had to listen to
his monologues. . . . It was always the same. . . . On every subject we all knew in advance what he would say. In course of time
these monologues bored us. But world affairs and events at the
front were never mentioned; everything to do with the war was
taboo." According to the secretary, a monologue sometimes
lasted all night. "In 1944 I sometimes found myself still sitting
up with Hitler at 8:00 a.m., listening with feigned attention to
his words." Trevor-Roper adds: "There was no subject, however ignorant, [that] Hitler was not prepared to dogmatise."

   In the United States raillery seems to be in decline, owing
to excessive politeness and insufficient politeness. It is difficult
to engage in raillery with someone who "shares" his or her
thoughts, and it is impossible to engage in raillery with someone who offers opinions in an abrasive and vulgar manner.
Geoffrey Nunberg says we live in "confrontational times." The
adjectives *confrontational* and *confrontationist,* which came into
use in the late 1960s, are a legacy of the counterculture.

   Finally, one cannot engage in raillery with a person who
doesn't, broadly speaking, share one's own view of the world.

"The delight of social relations," La Bruyère says, "between friends is fostered by a shared attitude to life, together with certain differences of opinion on intellectual matters, through which either one is confirmed in one's own views, or else one gains practice and instruction through argument."

In the past year twice I've heard what I would call conversation stoppers—remarks that reveal a gulf between my views and a friend's (or acquaintance's) views. When one hears a remark that one regards as beyond the pale—a remark that shows there is not a wide gap but an abyss between my view of the world and the other person's view—one can ignore it and change the subject. Or one can break off the conversation. I approve of what a friend of mine did at a dinner party. When the hostess said that wars are always wrong and that we should have negotiated with Hitler, my friend turned to his wife and calmly said: "I think it's time for us to leave."

Some people would say that maintaining a friendship is so important that if there is a difference of opinion on a particular subject why not avoid that subject. But it is difficult to be friends with someone who makes what one considers to be an outrageous or irrational remark. I would have no trouble continuing a conversation with someone who is deeply religious so long as he or she was not a zealot who believed in Biblical inerrancy, but I would find it hard to continue a conversation with someone who believed in astrology or thought Stalin was basically a good guy.

I agree with Swift, who says we should not try to please unreasonable people, but in this country many people have set the bar for unreasonableness very low. Angry Democrats regard those who vote Republican as unreasonable and irrational— or even immoral. Angry Republicans have the same view of Democrats. Many people seem to cultivate anger. Being angry makes them feel good about themselves: their anger is a sign that they are conscientious citizens—that they "care." Swift enjoyed being angry, and he ended up isolated, but now we can join anger communities, which flourish on the Internet.

Conversation is difficult even in the best of circumstances. La Bruyère says that "in conversation we all talk impetuously, often moved by vanity or ill-humor, seldom paying enough attention" to what others are saying. Conversation is not going to flourish when people have no interest in controlling their anger. Plutarch warns: "If anger becomes constant and resentment frequent, the mind acquires the negative condition known as irascibility, which results in prickliness, bitterness and a sour temper."

Sitting in the National Cathedral and listening to the Cathedral Choral Society sing Verdi's *Requiem,* I ask myself: Am I overrating the pleasures of conversation? Great music possesses clarity, elegance, and order. And it is often sublime, which conversation can never be. Moreover, conversation is often disorderly, confusing, and occasionally tedious. (Hume rightly complains of "the teller of long stories" and "the pompous declaimer.") Moreover, an evening of conversation occasionally leaves me with regrets: Did I talk too much? Did I interrupt frequently? Did I repeat an anecdote that I had told a few months earlier? "In conversation," Della Casa says, "one can err in many various ways."

Morose, a character in Ben Jonson's *Epicene,* hates conversation. "All discourses but mine own afflict me; they seem harsh, impertinent and irksome." Who doesn't at times feel the way Morose feels? Yet if I sometimes agree with Morose, I usually agree with Montaigne, who said: "If there is any man or any good fellowship of men in town or country, in France or abroad, sedentary or gadabout, whom my humours please and whose humours please me, they have but to whistle through their fingers and I'll come to them, furnishing them with 'essays' in flesh and blood." Notwithstanding his praise for Sparta, his complaints about poor conversationalists, and his occasional wish for solitude, Montaigne greatly enjoyed the pleasures of conversation.

When the *Requiem* at National Cathedral ends I remember that in an hour my wife and I are going to meet two couples for dinner at a restaurant in Georgetown. The six of us are of varied backgrounds. Two are native-born Americans. The others emigrated from Canada, Ecuador, Hungary, and Thailand. Three are of Jewish descent, one is Catholic, one is Protestant, and one is Buddhist. Our political views vary—from liberal democratic to moderate Republican. We have one thing in common: we enjoy light and solid conversation laced with raillery. We would all agree with Johnson, who told a friend: "I dogmatise and am contradicted, and in this conflict of opinions and sentiments I find delight."

Is it possible that the dinner will turn out to be a disaster—that we will become "egos shouting"? The chances for an unpleasant evening are exceedingly slim, for all of us are polite. Though I am not polite as often as I would like to be, I am always polite with them. The essence of friendship is good-humored conversation, which cannot take place without politeness, so politeness is the path to friendship. As Della Casa says: "Men who are affable and polite will . . . have friends and acquaintances wherever they may be."

To rescue conversation, people need to be persuaded that the benefits of politeness exceed the costs. But I am not confident that many people will agree with my view of politeness, since the leading figures of popular culture and high culture admire authenticity and have a therapeutic view of self-expression. Conversation avoidance devices also are enemies of politeness insofar as they make it difficult for people to be attentive listeners.

According to Hume, "among well-bred [polite] people, a mutual deference is affected; contempt of others disguised; authority concealed; attention given to each in his turn; and an easy stream of conversation maintained, without vehemence, without interruption, without eagerness for victory, and without any airs of superiority."

In the United States, where people are admired for being natural, sincere, authentic, and nonjudgmental—for being more like Rousseau than like Hume—the prospects for conversation are not good.

Bibliographical Essay

The three writers who have most strongly influenced my thinking on conversation are David Hume, Samuel Johnson, and Michael Oakeshott. Hume, as every person who has taken an introduction to philosophy course knows, is one of the leading British philosophers. In the eighteenth century he was mainly known as a political essayist and historian. Most of the essays I discuss are available in *Political Essays,* ed. Knud Haakonssen (Cambridge, 1994). A key essay, "Of Essay Writing," is available only in *Essays Moral, Political, and Literary,* ed. Eugene F. Miller (Indianapolis, 1985). I also rely heavily on Hume's *Enquiry Concerning the Principles of Morals,* which, Hume said, "is of all my writings, historical, philosophical, or literary, incomparably the best." It is available in *Enquiries Concerning Human Understanding and Concerning the Principles of Morals,* ed. L. A. Selby-Bigge and P. H. Nidditch (Oxford, 1975). Hume's six-volume *History of England* (Indianapolis, 1983), which was a best-seller when it was published, is well worth reading. The scholarly literature on Hume—and all the principal figures I discuss—is vast. In *Philosophical Melancholy and Delirium: Hume's Pathology of Philosophy* (Chicago, 1998), Donald L. Livingston discusses the importance of conversation to Hume.

E. C. Mossner's *Life of David Hume* (Oxford, 1954) is readable and informative. A good general introduction to Hume is *The Cambridge Companion to Hume,* ed. David Fate Norton (Cambridge, 1993).

The best one-volume paperback edition of Johnson's work is *Samuel Johnson: A Critical Edition of the Major Works,* ed. Donald Greene (Oxford, 1984). Greene, though, offers a very limited selection of Johnson's essays. Another good collection is *Samuel Johnson: Selected Poetry and Prose,* ed. Frank Brady and W. K. Wimsatt (New York, 1977). Two collections of Johnson's essays are *Samuel Johnson: Essays from the Rambler, Adventurer, and Idler,* ed. W. J. Bate (New Haven, 1968), and *Samuel Johnson: Selected Essays,* ed. David Womersley (London, 2003). I cite several essays that do not appear in these volumes. The complete essays are found in vols. 2–5 of *The Yale Edition of the Works of Samuel Johnson* (New Haven, 1958–). I also quote from Johnson's *Lives of the Poets,* 2 vols. (Oxford, 1972). There are many editions of Boswell's *Life of Johnson.* I used the *Life of Johnson,* ed. G. B. Hill, rev. L. F. Powell, 6 vols. (Oxford, 1934–64). Johnson's *Journey to the Western Islands of Scotland,* together with Boswell's *Journal of a Tour to the Hebrides with Samuel Johnson, LL.D.,* is available in a number of paperback editions.

There are many biographies of Johnson. I recommend Robert DeMaria Jr., *The Life of Samuel Johnson* (Cambridge, MA, 1993) and also James Clifford, *Dictionary Johnson: Samuel Johnson's Middle Years* (New York, 1979). *The Cambridge Companion to Samuel Johnson,* ed. Greg Clingham (Cambridge, 1997), is a good general introduction to Johnson. It includes Catherine Parke's "Johnson and the Arts of Conversation," and Eithne Henson's "Johnson and the Condition of Women." In *The Passion for Happiness: Samuel Johnson & David Hume*

(Ithaca, 2000), Adam Potkay argues that Hume and Johnson have much in common. An essay I wrote on Johnson, "Why Read Samuel Johnson?" appeared in the *Sewanee Review* (Winter, 1999): 44–60. An amusing and informative book that discusses Johnson's conversation is *Samuel Johnson's Insults: A Compendium of Snubs, Sneers, Slights, and Effronteries from the Eighteenth-Century Master,* ed. Jack Lynch (New York, 2004). In the "Introduction" Lynch talks about how much Johnson loved "the sport of conversation." Lynch is also the editor of *Samuel Johnson's Dictionary: Selections from the 1755 Work That Defined the English Language* (New York, 2002). A very useful guide to Johnson is Pat Rogers, *The Samuel Johnson Encyclopedia* (Westport, CT, 1996).

The citations from Michael Oakeshott are from the essays that appear in *Rationalism in Politics and Other Essays* (Indianapolis, 1991), which includes a bibliography of works by Oakeshott and studies of his work. There are also important essays by Oakeshott in *The Voice of Liberal Learning* (Indianapolis, 2001). I found helpful an essay on Oakeshott by Kenneth Minogue, *Times Literary Supplement,* 27 June 2003, 14–15, and a review-essay of books on Oakeshott by George Feaver, *Times Literary Supplement,* 7 May 2004, 8–9. See also Paul Franco, *Michael Oakeshott: An Introduction* (New Haven, 2004).

For the history of conversation, see Peter Burke, *The Art of Conversation* (Ithaca, 1993). Burke has a twenty-eight-page bibliography of books on conversation. Three key texts in the history of conversation are: Cicero, *On Duties,* ed. M. T. Griffin and E. M. Atkins (Cambridge, 1991); Baldesar Castiglione, *The Book of the Courtier,* trans. George Bull (London, 1976); Giovanni Della Casa, *Galateo: A Renaissance Treatise on Manners,* trans. Konrad Eisenbichler and Kenneth R. Bartlett (Toronto, 2001). An influential scholarly work on the history of manners in Europe is Norbert Elias's *The Civilizing Process,* trans. Edmund Jephcott, 2 vols. (New York, 1978). I did not find it especially useful for my purposes. For an introduction to conversation analysis, see David Silverman, *Harvey Sacks: Social Science & Conversation Analysis* (New York, 1998). For a view of conversation that is somewhat different from mine, see Diane McWhorter, "Talk," *The American Scholar* (Winter, 2004): 47–53.

The leading contemporary scholar of politeness is Lawrence E. Klein. A concise discussion of politeness can be found in his introduction to the Earl of Shaftesbury's *Characteristics of Men, Manners, Opinions, Times* (Cambridge, 1999). See also Klein's "Coffeehouse Civility, 1660–1714: An Aspect of Post-Courtly Culture in England," *Huntington Library Quarterly* 59 (1997): 31–51. I also recommend Klein's "Sociability, Solitude, and Enthusiasm," *Huntington Library Quarterly* 60 (1998): 153–77, and "Liberty, Manners, and Politeness in Early Eighteenth-Century England," *Historical Journal* 32.3 (1989): 583–605. Klein's major work on politeness is *Shaftesbury and the Culture of Politeness: Moral Discourse and Cultural Politics in Early Eighteenth-Century England* (Cambridge, 1994). A good introduction to politeness is Philip Carter, *Men and the Emergence of Polite Society, Britain 1660–1800* (Harlow, 2001). It includes a lengthy bibliographical essay on books about politeness. Two other books were helpful: Peter France, *Politeness and Its Discontents: Problems in French Classical Culture* (Cambridge, 1992), and Anna Bryson, *From Courtesy to Civility: Changing Codes of Conduct in Early Modern England* (Oxford, 1998).

I quote frequently from the great French essayists and aphorists of the sixteenth and seventeenth centuries—Montaigne, La Bruyère, and La Rochefoucauld. Their writings are available in paperback: *Montaigne: The Complete Essays,* trans.

M. A. Screech (London, 1991); *La Bruyère: Characters,* trans. Jean Stewart (London, 1970); La Rochefoucauld, *Maxims,* trans. Leonard Tancock (London, 1959). Another translation I used is: *The Maxims of La Rochefoucauld,* trans. Louis Kronenberger (New York, 1959). I also used *La Rochefoucauld: maximes et réflexions diverses* (Paris, 1976). To learn more about La Rochefoucauld, who was greatly admired by Swift and Johnson, I recommend W. G. Moore, *La Rochefoucauld: His Mind and Art* (Oxford, 1969). I also cite Madame de Sévigné. A selection of her letters is available in English, *Madame de Sévigné: Selected Letters,* trans. Leonard Tancock (London, 1982).

For speculation about the beginning of conversation, see Richard G. Klein (with Blake Edgar), *The Dawn of Human Culture* (New York, 2002). For Sumerian society I found the following books useful: Samuel Noah Kramer, *History Begins at Sumer: Thirty-Nine 'Firsts' in Recorded History* (Philadelphia, 1981); Karen Rhea Nemet-Nejat, *Daily Life in Ancient Mesopotamia* (Westport, CT, 1998); Gwendolyn Leick, *Mesopotamia: The Invention of the City* (London, 2001). (The two Mesopotamian conversation poems I cite are from *Daily Life.*) There are many translations of the book of Job. I found the translation by Stephen Mitchell the most powerful: *The Book of Job* (San Francisco, 1987). The commentary by Raymond P. Scheindlin in his translation is illuminating: *The Book of Job* (New York, 1998). I also recommend Moshe Greenberg's essay "Job," in *The Literary Guide to the Bible,* ed. Robert Alter and Frank Kermode (Cambridge, MA, 1990).

For *The Symposium* I used the Penguin edition: *Plato, "The Symposium,"* trans. Christopher Gill (London, 1999). For an understanding of Socrates see Gregory Vlastos, *Socrates: Ironist and Moral Philosopher* (Ithaca, 1991). I also benefited from R. M. Hare, *Plato* (Oxford, 1982). I refer to *Four Texts on*

Socrates, trans. Thomas G. West and Grace Starry West (Ithaca, 1984). For Xenophon's view of Socrates, see *Xenophon: Conversations of Socrates,* trans. Hugh Tredennick and Robin Waterfield (London, 1990). J. K. Anderson's *Xenophon* (New York, 1974) is a readable biography, but much about Xenophon's life is speculative. The leading contemporary scholar of Sparta is Paul Cartledge. Two of his works are available in paperback: *Spartan Reflections* (Berkeley, 2001), and *The Spartans: The World of the Warrior-Heroes of Ancient Greece, from Utopia to Crisis and Collapse* (New York, 2002). I also found the following books helpful: Anton Powell, *Athens and Sparta: Constructing Greek Political and Social History from 478 B.C.* (London, 1991); Robert Garland, *Daily Life of the Ancient Greeks* (Westport, CT, 1998), and Robert Flacelière, *Daily Life in Greece at the Time of Pericles* (New York, 2002). I benefited from two reviews of books on ancient Greece: Jasper Griffin, "It's All Greek!" *New York Review of Books,* 18 December 2003, 62–65; Alan Griffiths, "I, the oracle," *Times Literary Supplement,* 26 March 2004, 28. The citations from Plutarch are from *Plutarch: Essays,* trans. Robin Waterfield (London, 1992). I also benefited from William V. Harris, *Restraining Rage: The Ideology of Anger Control in Classical Antiquity* (Cambridge, MA, 2001).

Lucian is worth reading, since his dialogues influenced the Renaissance writers on conversation and also influenced Hume: *Selected Satires of Lucian,* trans. Lionel Casson (New York, 1962). Adam Ferguson's major work is available in paperback: *An Essay on the History of Civil Society,* ed. Fania Oz-Salzberger (Cambridge, 1995). For a critical study of Ferguson, see David Ketler, *The Social and Political Thought of Adam Ferguson* (Ohio, 1965). For a study of the rebirth of the dialogue form in the Renaissance, see Perez Zagorin, *How the Idea of Religious Toleration Came to the West* (Princeton, 2003). The quotations from

Erasmus are from *The Praise of Folly*, trans. Clarence H. Miller (New Haven, 1979).

An excellent general introduction to eighteenth-century British culture is John Brewer, *The Pleasures of the Imagination: English Culture in the Eighteenth Century* (New York, 1997). The most thorough study of coffeehouses in Britain is Markman Ellis, *The Coffee House: A Cultural History* (London, 2004). Ellis is especially good on the period from 1650 to 1700. There are many scholarly articles on coffeehouse culture. I recommend Steven Pincus, "'Coffee Politicians Does Create': Coffeehouses and Restoration Political Culture," *Journal of Modern History* 67 (1995): 807–34. See also Brian Cowan, "Mr. Spectator and the Coffeehouse Public Sphere," *Eighteenth-Century Studies* 37 (2004): 345–66. In *A Land of Liberty? England 1689– 1727* (Oxford, 2000), Julian Hoppit discusses the fragility of Britain's political order in the second decade of the eighteenth century. The next volume in this series—the New Oxford History of England—is also readable and informative: Paul Langford, *A Polite and Commercial People, England 1727–1783* (Oxford, 1992). Langford discusses politeness and he also looks at the rise of the culture of sensibility after mid-century. For a study of eighteenth-century British clubs, see Peter Clark, *British Clubs and Societies: 1580–1800* (Oxford, 2000). Two works that discuss the clubs that promoted scientific progress are Jenny Uglow, *The Lunar Men: Five Friends Whose Curiosity Changed the World* (New York, 2002), and Roy Porter, *The Creation of the Modern World: The Untold Story of the British Enlightenment* (New York, 2000). I also recommend Porter's *London: A Social History* (London, 1994).

For information about coffeehouse culture in the Dutch Republic, see Simon Schama, *The Embarrassment of Riches: An Interpretation of Dutch Culture in the Golden Age* (New York,

1987). For coffeehouse culture elsewhere in Europe, see Thomas Munck, *The Enlightenment: A Comparative Social History 1721–1794* (London, 2000). See also T. C. W. Blanning, *The Culture of Power and the Power of Culture: Old Regime Europe 1660–1789* (Oxford, 2002), and James Van Horn Melton, *The Rise of the Public in Enlightenment Europe* (Cambridge, 2001). For anecdotes about Goethe's conversation, see *Goethe: Conversations and Encounters,* trans. David Luke and Robert Pick (London, 1966). I also benefited from James Gleick, *Isaac Newton* (New York, 2003).

For a popular study of the Scottish Enlightenment (to my mind it should be called the Anglo-Scottish Enlightenment), see Arthur Herman, *How the Scots Invented the Modern World* (New York, 2001). For an introduction to the Scottish Enlightenment, see the *Cambridge Companion to the Scottish Enlightenment,* ed. Alexander Broadie (Cambridge, 2003). For the world of the French *salonnières,* see Benedetta Craveri, *The Age of Conversation* (New York, 2005), and Dena Goodman: *The Republic of Letters: A Cultural History of the French Enlightenment* (Ithaca, 1994). See also Daniel Gordon, *Citizens Without Sovereignty: Equality and Sociability in French Thought, 1670–1789* (Princeton, 1994). For a somewhat different view of politeness than mine, see Jenny Davidson, *Hypocrisy and the Politics of Politeness: Manners and Morals from Locke to Austen* (Cambridge, 2005).

Rousseau's works are widely available in paperback. For an understanding of Rousseau, Maurice Cranston's three-volume biography is essential, especially the second and third volumes: *The Noble Savage: Jean-Jacques Rousseau, 1754–1762* (Chicago, 1991), and *The Solitary Self: Jean-Jacques Rousseau in Exile and Adversity* (Chicago, 1997). An excellent critical study of Rousseau is Jean Starobinski, *Jean-Jacques Rousseau: Trans-*

parency and Obstruction, trans. Arthur Goldhammer (Chicago, 1988). I also recommend *The Cambridge Companion to Rousseau,* ed. Patrick Riley (Cambridge, 2001). For Priestley's negative view of Sparta, see *Joseph Priestley: Political Writings,* ed. Peter Miller (Cambridge, 1993).

The major eighteenth-century British writers on conversation are, in addition to Hume and Johnson, Joseph Addison, Jonathan Swift, Henry Fielding, and James Boswell. Two other important writers are Richard Steele—Addison's collaborator on the *Spectator* as well as the chief author of the *Tatler*—and Daniel Defoe. Defoe's major writings are available in paperback, including *A Tour Through the Whole Island of Great Britain,* ed. Pat Rogers (London, 1971). For a biography of Defoe, see Maximillian E. Novak, *Daniel Defoe: Master of Fictions* (New York, 2001). Many of my citations from Addison and Steele are from the standard edition of the *Spectator,* ed. Donald F. Bond, 5 vols. (Oxford, 1965). There are three paperback editions of selections from the *Tatler* and the *Spectator: Addison and Steele: Selections from "The Tatler" and "The Spectator,"* ed. Robert J. Allen (New York, 1970); *Richard Steele and Joseph Addison: Selections from "The Tatler" and "The Spectator,"* ed. Angus Ross (London, 1982); and *The Commerce of Everyday Life: Selections from "The Tatler" and "The Spectator,"* ed. Erin Mackie (Boston, 1998). For information about coffeehouse culture, see Mackie's edition, since she includes additional material about coffeehouses and other aspects of London life. Allen's and Ross's editions are more comprehensive; Ross's includes the essays Addison wrote on "The Pleasures of the Imagination." Addison is not read much nowadays, but both Hume and Johnson praised him highly. To understand why Addison launched the *Spectator,* see Peter Smith, *The Life of Joseph Addison* (Oxford, 1968).

The best one-volume paperback edition of Jonathan Swift is *Jonathan Swift: A Critical Edition of the Major Works*, ed. Angus Ross and David Woolley (Oxford, 1984). It includes Swift's essay on Esther Johnson. It also includes the very funny introduction to *Swift's Polite Conversation* as well as one dialogue from the work. *Swift's Polite Conversation*, ed. Eric Partridge (London, 1963), is out of print but readily available. Swift's other essays on conversation are available in *The Prose Works of Jonathan Swift*, ed. H. J. Davis, VOL. 4 (Oxford, 1968). Several essays are also available online. The standard biography is Irvin Ehrenpreis, *Swift: The Man, His Works, and The Age*, 3 vols. (Cambridge, MA, 1962–83). A good one-volume biography is David Nokes, *Jonathan Swift, A Hypocrite Reversed: A Critical Biography* (Oxford, 1985). There is also Victoria Glendinning, *Jonathan Swift* (London, 1998). I found the following books helpful: F. P. Lock, *Swift's Tory Politics* (London, 1983), and *The Character of Swift's Satire: A Revised Focus*, ed. Claude Rawson (London, 1983).

Fielding's novels and *Journal of a Voyage to Lisbon* are available in paperback. "Essay on Conversation" and "Essay on the Characters of Men" are found in *Henry Fielding, Miscellanies: Volume One*, ed. H. K. Miller (Middletown, CT, 1972). The most informative biography is Martin Battestin (with Ruth Battestin), *Henry Fielding: A Life* (New York, 1989). I also recommend Ronald Paulson, *The Life of Henry Fielding* (Oxford, 2000).

The section on Boswell in Chapter Four is based mainly on Boswell's *London Journal 1762–1763*, ed. Frederick A. Pottle (New York, 1950). There are nine other volumes of Boswell's journal. I quote from the last two volumes: *Boswell: The English Experiment 1785–1789*, eds. Irma S. Lustig and Frederick A. Pottle (New York, 1986), and *Boswell: The Great Biographer 1789–1795*, ed. Marlies K. Danziger and Frank Brady (New

York, 1989). A good biography is Peter Martin, *A Life of James Boswell* (New Haven, 2000). I also recommend Frederick A. Pottle, *James Boswell: The Earlier Years, 1740–1769* (New York, 1966), and Frank Brady, *James Boswell: The Later Years, 1769–1795* (New York, 1984). To understand the importance of politeness to Joshua Reynolds, see Richard Wendorf, *Sir Joshua Reynolds: The Painter in Society* (Cambridge, MA, 1996). See also *The Letters of Sir Joshua Reynolds,* ed. John Ingamells and John Edgcumbe (New Haven, 2000).

A good paperback selection of Lady Mary Wortley Montagu's letters is: *Lady Mary Wortley Montagu: Selected Letters,* ed. Isobel Grundy (London, 1997). Grundy is the author of an excellent biography: *Lady Mary Wortley Montagu* (Oxford, 1999). For a somewhat different view of the Pope-Montagu quarrel, see Maynard Mack, *Alexander Pope: A Life* (New York, 1985). I found two other biographies of eighteenth-century women helpful: James L. Clifford, *Hester Lynch Piozzi (Mrs. Thrale),* second edition with a new introduction by Margaret Anne Doody (New York, 1987); Claire Harman, *Fanny Burney: A Biography* (New York, 2000).

The second half of the eighteenth century is often called the Age of Johnson, but it may be more appropriate to call it the Age of Gray, since Gray was more in accord with the spirit of the age. Moreover, Gray's poetry was widely admired—even by such clubbable people as Boswell and Smith. For Gray's life see Robert L. Mack, *Thomas Gray: A Life* (New Haven, 2000). For the idea of the sublime see Edmund Burke, *A Philosophical Enquiry into the Origin of Our Ideas of the Sublime and Beautiful,* ed. James T. Boulton (Notre Dame, 1968). For the poetry of sensibility see Patricia Spacks, "The Poetry of Sensibility," in *The Cambridge Companion to Eighteenth Century Poetry,* ed. John Sitter (Cambridge, 2001). The anthology also includes an interesting essay on "Couplets and conversation" by J. Paul Hunter.

The literature on Wordsworth is vast. I recommend the biography by Stephen Gill: *William Wordsworth: A Life* (Oxford, 1990). De Quincey's and Hazlitt's essays on conversation are available online. For the state of conversation in Britain at the turn of the nineteenth century, see Paul Langford, *English-ness Identified: Manners and Character 1650–1850* (Oxford, 2000). Virginia Woolf's novels and essays are available in paperback. I rely heavily on the autobiographical essays in *Moments of Being* (New York, 1985). A biography of Woolf that I found perceptive and informative is Hermione Lee, *Virginia Woolf* (New York, 1996). Noel Annan's biography of Woolf's father is informative: *Leslie Stephen: The Godless Victorian* (Chicago, 1984).

The works by Mrs. Trollope, Dickens, Thoreau, Melville, Holmes, James, Whitman, Eliot, Hemingway, Fitzgerald, and Chandler are all available in paperback. Benjamin Franklin's "How to Please in Conversation" is in *A Benjamin Franklin Reader,* ed. Walter Isaacson (New York, 2003). The anthology also includes two letters Franklin wrote to Hume. I recommend three biographies of Franklin: Edmund S. Morgan, *Benjamin Franklin* (New Haven, 2002); Esmond Wright, *Franklin of Philadelphia* (Cambridge, MA, 1986); and Gordon S. Wood, *The Americanization of Benjamin Franklin* (New York, 2004). For a biography of Tocqueville, see André Jardin, *Tocqueville: A Biography,* trans. Lydia Davis with Robert Hemenway (New York, 1988). The quotations from *Democracy in America* are from *Democracy in America,* ed. J. P. Mayer, trans. George Lawrence (New York, 1969). For a view of conversation in prewar nineteenth-century America that is different from mine, see Peter Gibian, *Oliver Wendell Holmes and the Culture of Conversation* (Cambridge, 2001). For Bronson Alcott, see Geraldine Brooks, "Orpheus at the Plough," *New Yorker* (10 January 2005): 58–65. James Bryce's *The American Commonwealth* is available in paperback from Liberty Press (Indianapolis, 1995). For John Ford I relied on the biography by Scott Eyman, *Print the Legend: The Life and Times of John Ford* (New York, 1999). For a somewhat different approach to American conversation, see Judith Martin, *Star-Spangled Manners: In Which Miss Manners Defends American Manners (For a Change)* (New York, 2002). I also found Lawrence Buell's study of Emerson illuminating: *Emerson* (Cambridge, MA, 2003).

Most of the critical studies I refer to in the chapter on modern enemies of conversation are available in paperback. For a biography of Michel Foucault, see James Miller, *The Passion of Michel Foucault* (Cambridge, MA, 2000). I have written about Foucault in "The Future of Disinterest," *Partisan Review* 1 (1997): 28–36. For a discussion of the effect of rap music on American politeness, see John McWhorter, *Doing Our Own Thing: The Degradation of Language and Music and Why We Should, Like, Care* (New York, 2003). For Eminem, see Anthony Bozza, *Whatever You Say I Am: The Life and Times of Eminem* (New York, 2003). For a definition of jazz, see Albert Murray, "Jazz: Notes Toward a Definition," *The New Republic* (18 October 2004): 25–28.

The literature on conversation in contemporary America (and Britain) is growing. I refer to Theodore Zeldin, *Conversation: How Talk Can Change Our Lives* (London, 1998); Deborah Tannen, *The Argument Culture: Moving from Debate to Dialogue* (New York, 1998); Cass R. Sunstein, *Republic.com* (Princeton, 2001) and *Why Societies Need Dissent* (Cambridge, MA, 2003); John L. Locke, *The De-Voicing of Society: Why We Don't Talk to Each Other Anymore* (New York, 1998); and Jaida N'Ha Sandra and Jon Spayde, *Salons: The Joy of Conversation* (Minneapolis, 2001). A number of contemporary writers discuss what is called "public discourse." My idea of conversation is different from theirs, but our broad concerns are roughly the same. Two recent books on public discourse are: *Public Discourse in America: Conversation and Community in the Twenty-first Century*, ed. Judith Rodin and Stephen P. Steinberg (Philadelphia, 2003), and *The Changing Conversation in America: Lectures from the Smithsonian*, eds. William F. Eadie and Paul E. Nelson (Thousand Oaks, CA, 2002). In her books and biweekly columns, Judith Martin (Miss Manners) often discusses the art of conversation. See especially *Miss Manners' Guide to Excruciatingly Correct Behavior* (New York, 1983). I also found the following book useful: Geoffrey Nunberg, *Going Nucular: Language, Politics, and Culture in Confrontational Times* (New York, 2004). For many online articles on the Internet and American life, see the Pew Internet & American Life Project (www.pewinternet.org).

Three powerful memoirs describe the lack of a conversible world in the Soviet Union, Nazi Germany, and Cambodia under the Khmer Rouge. They are: Nadezhda Mandelstam, *Hope Against Hope: A Memoir*, trans. Max Hayward (New York, 1976); Victor Klemperer, *I Will Bear Witness*, trans. Martin Chalmers, 2 vols. (New York, 1999–2001); François Guizot, *The Gate*, trans. Euan Cameron (New York, 2004). The citation from Flaubert in Chapter Nine is from *Madame Bovary*, trans. Francis Steegmuller (New York, 1957); the citation from Valéry in Chapter Nine is from *History and Politics*, trans. Denise Folliot and Jackson Mathews (New York, 1962). For a study of the effect of conversation avoidance mechanisms on the brain, see Richard Restak, *The New Brain: How the Modern Age Is Rewiring Your Mind* (Rodale, 2004).

Index